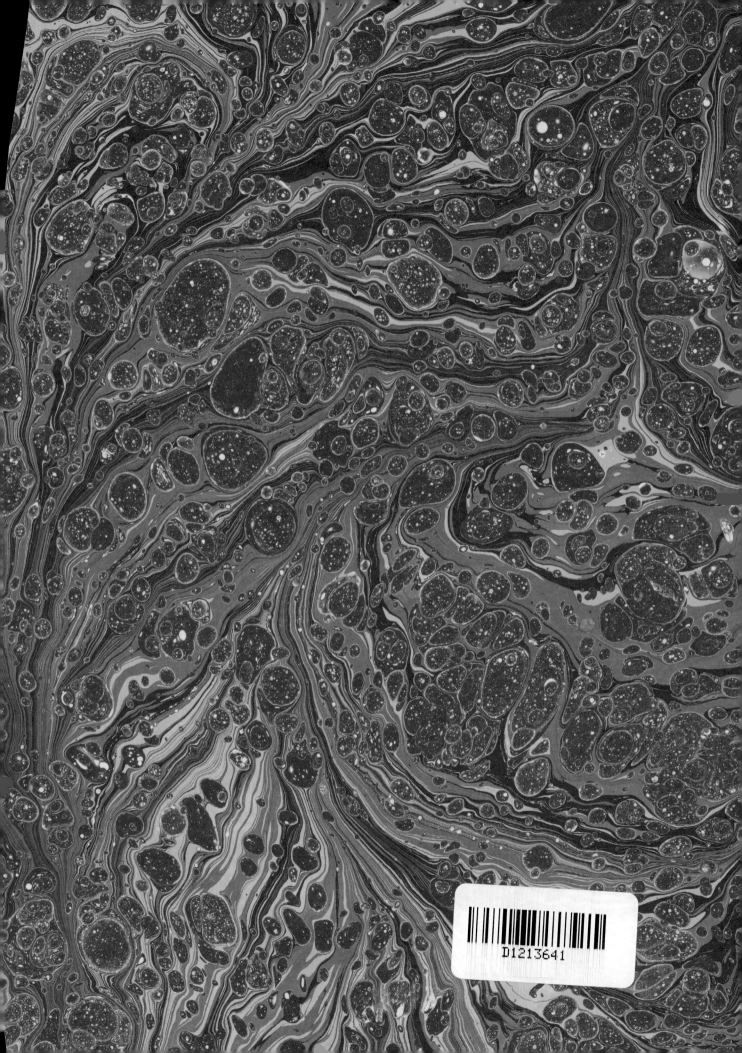

White Sands Proving Ground

The Rockets and Missiles of

White Sands Proving Ground

1945-1958

Gregory P. Kennedy

Schiffer Military History
Atglen, PA

Dedication
for my lovely bride Marta

Book Design by Ian Robertson.

Copyright © 2009 by Gregory P. Kennedy.
Library of Congress Control Number: 2008943511

Printed in China.
ISBN: 978-0-7643-3251-7

We are interested in hearing from authors with book ideas on related topics.

Published by Schiffer Publishing Ltd.
4880 Lower Valley Road
Atglen, PA 19310
Phone: (610) 593-1777
FAX: (610) 593-2002
E-mail: Info@schifferbooks.com.
Visit our web site at: www.schifferbooks.com
Please write for a free catalog.
This book may be purchased from the publisher.
Please include $3.95 postage.
Try your bookstore first.

In Europe, Schiffer books are distributed by:
Bushwood Books
6 Marksbury Avenue
Kew Gardens
Surrey TW9 4JF
England
Phone: 44 (0) 20 8392-8585
FAX: 44 (0) 20 8392-9876
E-mail: Info@bushwoodbooks.co.uk.

Contents

Acknowledgments and Preface

Acknowledgements

While writing this book, I have received help and support from many people. First and foremost, I have to thank my new bride Marta for her patience and loving support while I spent all those hours sitting in front of the computer. Once again, I am indebted to my friends and professional colleagues at the New Mexico Museum of Space History: George House, Michael Smith, and Jim Mayberry, who patiently reviewed and commented upon my manuscript. Fellow authors Walt Trizna and John Errigo reviewed select chapters and provided valuable feedback. I would be remiss if I didn't mention my fellow writers at the Wordwrights group: Sherrie, Walt, Nicole, Tom, Stephen, Bob, Joyce, Chris, Gloria, Allan, and Nancy at the Barnes and Noble in Exton, PA. Throughout the creative process for this manuscript, your camaraderie and moral support was always appreciated.

One of the most enjoyable aspects of this and other writing projects I have been involved in has been that they brought me into contact with individuals who share my interests and passions for a particular topic. While working on this book I became friends with Bill Beggs, a fellow V-2 enthusiast and White Sands history aficionado. Bill not only reviewed the manuscript and made many valuable suggestions, but also provided many of the photos in this book from his personal collection.

Finally, I would like to acknowledge the help, advice, and patience of Bob Biondi and Ian Robertson at Schiffer Publishing.

Thank you, one and all.

Preface

White Sands Proving Ground (WSPG) was activated in 1945 as a testing center for United States Army missiles. In 1958, the Army reorganized its missile programs to better respond to threats posed by the Soviet Union, and WSPG became the White Sands Missile Range (WSMR). This book focuses on the period between 1945 and 1958; the WSPG years. Most of the weapons tested at WSPG during that era grew out of American experience during the Second World War.

During this era, American rocketry in general, and WSPG in particular, evolved. When it was first created, WSPG was a testing center for basic rocket technology. Many of the rockets launched at WSG during its first few years were research vehicles that laid the foundation for subsequent applications. When they created a guided missile program, Army planners realized that before the rocket could be harnessed as a weapon system, basic technologies had to be developed. As rocket technology matured, the emphasis of firings at WSPG shifted to testing specific weapon systems. During the early years at WSPG, the *WAC Corporal*, *Hermes*, and *Viking* rockets established many of the techniques that would be applied to *Nike*, *Corporal*, and *Sergeant*.

World War II saw the introduction of such weapons as radar, guided missiles, and the atomic bomb. During the last year of World War II Germany unveiled the V-2, a long-range ballistic missile. At that time, Germany led the world in missile development. Fortunately for the Allies, they did not seriously pursue the development of an atomic bomb, so the V-2 was limited to a one-ton high explosive warhead. While this could have devastating results for those on the receiving end of the missile, it was not the decisive weapon the Nazis hoped it would be. Because the V-2 was a very complex weapon that consumed highly volatile liquid oxygen, the German field batteries could only launch about a dozen missiles per day. This hardly compared to the destructive potential of the hundreds of American and British bombers that struck German targets each day and night. While its warhead was too small to seriously affect the outcome of the war, military leaders knew the V-2 was a harbinger of things to come, especially if a missile could be tipped with an atomic warhead.

Senior commanders also saw the destructive potential of aerial bombardment, particularly with the use of atomic bombs over Hiroshima and Nagasaki. Advances in aircraft design showed a need for improved antiaircraft systems—conventional antiaircraft guns were not effective against high speed jet powered aircraft. Rockets offered the greatest potential for countering this threat, so in the years after the war, antiaircraft guided missiles were another major focus of Army research.

Before either surface-to-surface or surface-to-air missiles became a reality, larger and more capable rockets had to be developed. In the United States, much of this development took place in southern New Mexico, at WSPG. Established while the war was still going on, in the late 1940s and 1950s WSPG became the premiere center for missile testing in the Western hemisphere.

For this book a topical, rather than a day-by-day chronological approach has been taken. Throughout the late 1940s and 1950s, there were a number of major programs undergoing simultaneous development at WSPG. A chronological narrative that describes these programs simultaneously would be difficult to follow, so for the sake of simplicity, programs and projects are treated individually, or at least (in the case of some tactical missiles) grouped together by function. While this will not produce a strictly chronological work where the first chapter begins in 1945 and the final chapter ends in 1958, hopefully the finished product will be both informative and easy to read. Similarly, in the interests of providing a context, some chapters chronicle missiles for the duration of their service careers, beyond the date when WSPG became WSMR.

At the same time, it is important to keep in mind that many of these programs used the same facilities. For example, the first *Viking* rockets blasted off from the same launch area used for the *V-2* and *WAC Corporals*. This would, of course, present scheduling challenges for WSPG managers, because a delay in preparing one rocket could impact another project. This became more acute as the pace of activities increased. For example, in 1945 there were 20 launches from WSPG, 14 of which were for the *WAC Corporal* program. The following year there were 44 launches, as flights with *V-2* and *Nike* missiles began. The pace continued to increase in subsequent years with the growth of military and scientific research programs. By the mid-1950s, thousands of rockets were being launched each year. In 1953 there were 1,125 firings of the *Loki* antiaircraft rocket alone.

Approaching the history of WSPG on a project by project basis has resulted in some overlap between individual chapters, but efforts have been made to keep this to a minimum. A certain amount of overlap cannot be avoided with this approach, as techniques developed and tested with one rocket were often employed on another. An example of this would be the use of a burst diaphragm to control fuel flow in pressure-fed rockets. The first American vehicle to use this was the *WAC Corporal* meteorological rocket; this technique was adopted for the second stage of the *Nike Ajax*

antiaircraft missile. Other evolutionary lines of development may be found in the propulsion area, most notably the use of an aniline mixture as a fuel and nitric acid as an oxidizer.

Researchers at the California Institute of Technology (CALTECH) developed a rocket engine that burned nitric acid and aniline in the early 1940s. These compounds ignite spontaneously on contact, thus simplifying the ignition system. They can also be stored at room temperature. The V-2 used liquid oxygen as an oxidizer, which rapidly boils away. If you want to create a ballistic missile that will be fired when it is ready, this is a drawback that can be overcome. On the other hand, for an antiaircraft rocket that must remain ready to launch for an indefinite time, storable propellants have a clear and decisive advantage.

In 1944, the research group at CALTECH formed the Jet Propulsion Laboratory and used an acid-aniline engine in the *WAC Corporal*. This same type of engine was used for the *Nike Ajax* surface to air missile, *Aerobee* research rocket, and *Corporal* tactical ballistic missile. The engines for these missiles were built by the Aerojet Corporation, which was also created by members of the CALTECH group to market their rockets. In a similar vein, Douglas Aircraft Company was the contractor for the *WAC Corporal*, Bumper *WAC*, *Corporal E*, and *Nike Ajax* liquid-fuel vehicles and the *Honest John* solid fuel rocket. Understanding the shared heritage of these rockets is important to understanding how they evolved. Therefore, it is sometimes necessary to refer back to an earlier project when describing a particular missile.

Historical information on the region is also furnished to put WSPG in its proper context. For example, the first atomic bomb was detonated within the boundaries of WSPG but had no connection to the Army's missile program. In a similar vein, events that occurred during the early history of the area resulted in such colorful names as the *Jornada del Muerto*, the "Journey of the Dead Man," and Las Cruces, "The Crosses."

For the sake of completeness, limited coverage is given to the post-WSPG era for individual missiles, but the emphasis of this work remains rocket activities prior to May 1, 1958, which is when WSPG became WSMR. The reason for imposing such a structure may seem arbitrary, but by that time intercontinental ballistic missiles were a reality, satellites were orbiting overhead, and the world was very different than it was when World War II ended.

1

Early American Rockets

The logo for White Sands Missile Range (WSMR) proclaims it is the "birthplace of America's missile and space activity." Established in 1945 as the White Sands Proving Ground, WSMR was the place where Americans gained their first experience assembling, handling, and launching large liquid fuel rockets. Situated in southern New Mexico, the first American-built rocket to reach space lifted off from White Sands. America's first battlefield ballistic missile, the *Corporal*, was tested there during the early years of the Cold War. White Sands has a rich and storied history, and the list of "firsts" made there can fill pages. That is mainly due to the fact that whenever someone did *anything* at White Sands, they were frequently doing it for the first time. This

book chronicles the early years of WSMR, when it was known as White Sands Proving Ground (WSPG) and many of those "firsts" occurred.

However, it should be pointed out that the first rockets launched in New Mexico did not lift off from WSPG. A decade earlier, rockets were blasting off from the Eden Valley, near Roswell. During the 1930s, Dr. Robert Hutchings Goddard moved from his native Massachusetts to New Mexico, where he pioneered the development of liquid fuel rockets. Goddard was born on October 5, 1882, in Worcester, Massachusetts. He suffered from chronic respiratory problems while growing up and was frequently bed ridden, a situation that gave him a lot of time to read.

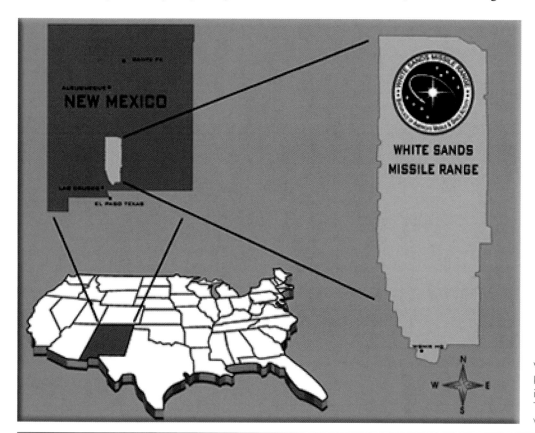

White Sands Missile Range, previously known as White Sands Proving Ground, is located in south-central New Mexico. The range is approximately 40 miles wide and 110 miles long.

Dr. Robert Hutchings Goddard, father of American rocketry.

One of the books he read as a youth was H. G. Wells' *The War of the Worlds*. After finishing the book, Goddard climbed a cherry tree on his family's farm and imagined the Martian war machines below him. This sparked a lifelong passion for rocketry, for he knew rockets would be the only way to travel between planets. For the rest of his life he would mark that day, 19 October, in his diary as his "anniversary day."

Initially, Goddard set a more modest goal than travel between planets; namely, to use rockets as a means to convey meteorological instruments into the upper atmosphere. In 1908, he began a series of experiments with small solid fuel rockets at Worcester Polytechnic Institute, where he'd earned his undergraduate degree and was a physics instructor. These experiments frequently filled the laboratory with dense, acrid smoke, so he was asked to stop all indoor testing. Goddard subsequently earned Masters and Ph.D. degrees in Physics from Clark University in Worcester, where he later became a Professor. Wanting to continue his rocket research, Goddard approached the Smithsonian Institution for support. The $5,000 grant he received from the Smithsonian in 1917 allowed him to begin another series of experiments with solid fuel rockets.

With the United States' entry into the First World War, Dr. Goddard offered his services to the War Department. At the time, the only project American military officials could think of for the Professor from Massachusetts was to build a small tube-launched projectile powered by smokeless powder. He conducted firing tests of these rockets on the grounds of the Mount Wilson Observatory in California, but they never progressed beyond the experimental stage.

In 1919, the Smithsonian published Dr. Goddard's monograph "A Method of Reaching Extreme Altitudes." While most of this slim volume comprised mathematical formulae and discussions of technical problems of rocket design, it contained a section stating it was possible to build a rocket capable of reaching the Moon. Goddard further speculated that upon striking the Moon, a charge of flash powder in the vehicle's nose would signal its arrival to observers on Earth. Professor Goddard even conducted experiments to gauge how much powder would be necessary.

Sadly, Goddard's suggestion earned him considerable ridicule. Focusing on the sensational aspect of this section of the report, the press labeled him "the loony moon man," and *The New York Times* chided him for failing to realize a rocket could not work in space because there was nothing for the exhaust to push against!

Of course, Goddard knew the *New York Times'* editors were wrong. He understood Newton's Third Law of Motion, which English scientist Sir Isaac Newton explained in the 17th century, and knew that a rocket's exhaust did not need anything "to react against" to produce thrust. In fact, Goddard performed experiments in 1915 that proved a rocket would generate thrust in a vacuum.

Despite such uninformed criticism, Goddard continued his research. He realized the key to getting the best performance from a rocket required the use of liquid propellants, something no one had ever done. After three years of experimental trials on the ground, he launched the world's first liquid fuel rocket on March 16, 1926, from a cabbage patch on his Aunt Effie's farm. Goddard's rocket burned liquid oxygen and gasoline, and reached an altitude of 41 feet. In a report to Smithsonian Undersecretary Charles Abbot on May 5, 1926, Goddard wrote:

In a test made on March 16, out of doors, with a model of this lighter type, weighing 5 ¾ lb empty and 10 ¼ lb loaded with liquids, the lower part of the nozzle burned through and dropped off, leaving, however, the upper part intact. After about 20 sec. the rocket rose without perceptible jar, with no smoke and with no apparent increase in the rather small flame, increased rapidly in speed, and after describing a semicircle, landed 184 feet from the starting point – the curved path being due to the fact that the nozzle had burned through unevenly, and one side was longer than the other. The average speed, from the time of the flight measured by a stopwatch was 60 miles per hour. This test was very significant, as it was the first time that a rocket operated by liquid propellants traveled under its own power.

Professor Goddard in front of his chalk board. He considered the problem of flight to the moon as early as 1919.

Encouraged by this success, Dr. Goddard continued building rockets which grew larger and noisier until 1929, when several people called the fire department, thinking one was a crashing airplane. This resulted in a request that he visit the State Fire Marshal, who asked Dr. Goddard to move his experiments out of the Commonwealth of Massachusetts. Through the intervention of the Smithsonian, arrangements were made for Goddard to conduct his experiments on the artillery range at Camp Devens, Massachusetts, but with strict limitations. He was only allowed to launch rockets immediately after a rainfall or when there was snow on the ground.

Goddard needed a sparsely populated, wide open area with few neighbors who would be bothered by his noisy, spectacular experiments. He asked Dr. Charles F. Brooks, a meteorologist at Clark University, to help him find such a place. Goddard's requirements included clear skies with a minimum of precipitation for most of the year; a place without extremes of temperatures;

and an area where he could count on considerable periods without wind. In other words, Goddard sought a place that had good conditions for working outdoors throughout the year.

They decided the high plains of east central New Mexico best met the requirements. Goddard found a suitable site in the Eden Valley about twelve miles northwest of Roswell. By this time, Doctor Goddard was working with support from the Daniel and Florence Guggenheim Foundation. Besides attracting the attention of the Fire Marshall, Goddard's 1929 flight caught the attention of famed aviator Charles Lindbergh. After meeting Goddard on November 29, 1929, Lindbergh approached philanthropist Harry Guggenheim to arrange a $50,000 grant so the rocket experiments could continue.

In 1930, Professor Goddard moved to the Mescalero Ranch, near Roswell. In addition to setting up a complete machine shop where he could fabricate rockets, he created a rocket launch range. Always very frugal, he brought the 60-foot tall launch tower that

On March 16, 1926, Goddard launched the world's first liquid fuel rocket.

(l. to r.) Harry Guggenheim, Robert Goddard, and Charles Lindbergh in front of the launch tower. Goddard's work at Roswell, New Mexico, was supported by the Guggenheim Foundation.

he'd been using in Massachusetts with him and set it up in the desert. On December 30, 1930, the first Goddard rocket lifted off from New Mexico. This rocket was 11 feet long and attained an altitude of 2,000 feet.

Working in a systematic way on such problems as gyroscopic guidance systems and propellant pumps, Goddard began his research in the New Mexico desert. He made great strides during his first year and a half in Roswell and launched the first gyroscopically-controlled rocket on April 30, 1932.

Unfortunately, the Great Depression interrupted Goddard's work the following month when the Guggenheims could not renew his grant. Professor Goddard returned to Clark University. After a two-year hiatus the Guggenheim Foundation was once again able to fund his research, so Goddard returned to the Mescalero Ranch. Doctor Goddard worked with a staff of just four people.

Dr. Goddard and his staff are shown working on one of his P-series rockets. The P-series were the most advanced rockets built by Goddard.

(Five, counting his wife Esther, who sewed parachutes and was the group's photographer.) He eventually received 214 patents, including one for multi-stage rockets. (131 of these patents were filed by his wife after his death.)

His A-series of rockets, which he constructed between 1934 and 1935, tested gyroscopic guidance systems. A gyroscope in the nose of the rocket sensed the vehicle's motion. If it veered more than 10 degrees off course, the gyroscope sent a signal to a set of movable vanes in the rocket's exhaust. The vanes deflected the exhaust to return the rocket to vertical flight. There were seven A-series flights, the most successful of which reached an altitude of 7,600 feet and a speed of 700 miles per hour on May 31, 1935.

The next batch, which he designated the L-series, were even more successful. On March 26, 1937, rocket L-13 reached an altitude of 9,000 feet, the highest attained by any of his rockets. The L-series comprised 30 tests. Goddard's most advanced rockets, and the last ones he flew in Roswell, were the P-series, which tested propellant pumps. Built between 1938 and 1941, the P-series rockets stood more than twenty feet tall. While they never flew as high as the L-series, these rockets incorporated all of Professor Goddard's innovations and results.

Just as he'd done in World War I, Dr. Goddard offered his services to the government when America entered World War II. This time, the only response he received was from the Navy, which asked him to build a liquid-fuel rocket to help heavy seaplanes take off. In 1943, Professor Goddard left Roswell for the last time and headed to Annapolis, Maryland, to work on the project. During his time in New Mexico Goddard had attempted to launch 48 rockets, 31 of which actually flew.

Although many people in the Navy regarded liquid propellants as too temperamental to place aboard operational aircraft, Goddard was given the task of building a variable thrust engine, which he did. While working in Annapolis, he also served as a consulting engineer for the Curtiss-Wright Corporation, a company that later built rocket engines. The Navy had another rocket development program underway at Annapolis, this one being run by (then) Lieutenant Robert C. Truax. Like Goddard, the Truax group

The smoke trail left by this A-series rocket clearly shows the effectiveness of the steering mechanism Goddard devised.

worked on liquid fuel rocket motors. By the summer of 1945 Dr. Goddard's health was failing—he had throat cancer. On August 10, 1945, Robert Hutchings Goddard died at Johns Hopkins University Hospital in Baltimore.

Sadly, the United States military failed to realize the full potential of the rocket as a weapon, and only asked Goddard to work on very small-scale projects. This was not the case in Germany, where the world's first large ballistic missile, known as the V-2, was built. The V-2 dwarfed anything Goddard built. Standing 46 feet tall, the V-2 delivered a one-ton warhead to targets 150 miles away. In the closing months of the War Germany launched thousands of these missiles against Allied targets. Shortly before his death, Dr. Goddard had an opportunity to examine some captured V-2 components.

Although American military leaders virtually ignored Goddard, who had been first to establish many of the technologies necessary for liquid-fuel rockets, this did not indicate a lack of interest in the area. The Army Air Corps supported another rocket group during World War II. This group was at the California Institute of Technology (CALTECH). Like Goddard, the CALTECH group benefitted from the generosity of the Daniel and Florence Guggenheim fund during the 1930s. Interestingly, Nobel Laureate Robert Millikan, who chaired the CALTECH Executive Committee, also sat on a committee that advised the Guggenheims regarding their support of Goddard.

Theodore von Kármán, the brilliant Hungarian-born aerodynamicist, headed the Guggenheim Aeronautical Laboratory at CALTECH, which was known by the acronym GALCIT. By the time Frank J. Malina arrived at GALCIT in 1934 as a graduate student, the laboratory was one of the leading centers for aeronautical research in the United States. For his Masters thesis, Malina performed research on the performance of airplane propellers. Realizing the limitations of propellers for high speed flight, he became interested in rockets and the possibilities they offered to improve aircraft performance.

Early in 1936, graduate assistant William Bollay delivered a lecture on the possibilities of rocket powered aircraft at CALTECH. As a result of this lecture and the newspaper article it generated, John W. Parsons and Edward S. Forman contacted GALCIT. Parsons was a self-trained chemist; Forman was a skilled mechanic who had been helping him build small black powder rockets. After meeting with Bollay, Parsons, and Forman, Malina mapped out a program to develop a high-altitude sounding rocket. He submitted a proposal to von Kármán that his doctoral thesis be on rocket propulsion, along with a request that Parsons and Forman assist him. This was somewhat unusual, because neither was a student nor member of the CALTECH staff. Despite the unusual circumstances, von Kármán approved Malina's plan. With von Kármán's approval, the GALCIT Rocket Research Program was born.

The initial GALCIT program comprised two parts: theoretical studies and experimental work, which included both solid and liquid fuel rocket motors. Funding was a problem in this early period, so the group pooled what money they had in order to buy enough materials to start testing. They began conducting static tests

in the Arroyo Seco, on the western edge of Pasadena, California. In the spring, another GALCIT graduate student, Apollo M. O. Smith, joined the rocketeers.

Seeing the value in combining the efforts of the two rocket efforts being supported by his family's foundation, Daniel Guggenheim believed Goddard and von Kármán should collaborate. In August 1936, Goddard visited Caltech at Guggenheim's request. Malina and von Kármán were eager to have him share his data and experimental results, but Goddard held back. Doctor Goddard was very secretive by nature, and wanted to file patents on all his developments before releasing them to anyone. He invited Malina (who was preparing to visit his parents in Texas) to stop by Roswell. Malina eagerly accepted. The results of Malina's visit proved disappointing. Rather than share any information, Goddard spent most of the visit showing Malina his machine shop, static test stand, launch tower, and watercolors of the New Mexico landscape. When he did point out one of his rockets, it was hidden under a canvas tarpaulin. Goddard suggested that Malina join him in Roswell once he finished his graduate studies, but remained unwilling to share his results with the GALCIT group. Malina left Roswell without learning anything new about rockets.

Upon his return to California, Malina undertook a series of static tests of a gaseous oxygen-methyl alcohol motor. The results were so promising that von Kármán gave his continued support to the project, albeit without any funding. Malina gave a presentation on his work at a GALCIT seminar, which attracted the attention of Weld Arnold, who worked in the university's astrophysical laboratory. Arnold was so enthused by the presentation that he donated $1,000 for further experimental work as long as he could participate. At around this same time, another one of von Kármán's graduate students, Hsue Shen Tsien, joined the group.

The rocket research group—Malina, Bollay, Parsons, Forman, Smith, Arnold, and Tsien—embarked on a series of tests in the GALCIT laboratory basement involving a motor that burned methyl alcohol and nitrogen dioxide. When one of the early tests misfired, nitrogen dioxide and alcohol fumes spread throughout the laboratory. This left a fine layer of rust on most of the laboratory equipment and earned the group the nickname "the suicide squad." It also got them evicted from the laboratory building. All future tests would have to be conducted outdoors.

By 1938, enough progress had been made that von Kármán and Millikan sent Malina to Washington, D. C., to address the National Academy of Sciences Committee on Air Corps Research. General Henry "Hap" Arnold, Commanding General of the Army Air Corps, had previously consulted the Academy regarding the use of rockets to help heavy aircraft take off. Malina's testimony resulted in GALCIT Project No. 1, a $10,000 contract for "jet propulsion research" for the Air Corps. (Rockets were not yet regarded as a respectable endeavor, and were considered to be "Buck Rogers stuff," hence the description as jet propulsion.)

Under the contract, GALCIT looked at three applications for rocket power: to shorten the time and distance required for takeoff; to boost an airplane's rate of climb; and to provide a temporary increase of speed while in level flight. At that time, the literature that had been published on rockets only indicated it was possible to build a liquid-fuel rocket, not how to build one. (In 1936, Goddard published his second Smithsonian report, titled *Liquid Propellant Rocket Development*. While it described the tests that he'd conducted through 1935, Goddard did not include any data on motor design.) Therefore, the GALCIT group had to conduct their own basic research. They decided to pursue both solid and liquid fuel rockets for aircraft application. By the spring of 1941, the Army Air Corps removed the National Academy of Sciences from the project and negotiated directly with GALCIT.

In the United States, the use of rockets for take-off was termed "Jet Assisted Take Off," or JATO. (The British prefer the term "Rocket Assisted Take Off," or RATO.) The solid fuel line of research bore results first. On August 12, 1941, an Airco *Ercoupe* became the first airplane to take off with rocket assistance in the United States. (Then) Captain Homer A. Boushey, Jr., took off from March Field, California, with the assistance of rockets to supplement the power of its propeller. The performance advantages were obvious: an *Aeronca* that began its takeoff roll at the same time was still on the ground, while the *Ercoupe* was several hundred feet in the air. The rockets used a solid propellant designated GALCIT 27 and delivered a thrust of 28 pounds for 12 seconds. Eleven days later, the CALTECH engineers used 12 JATO units to fly the *Ercoupe* on rocket power alone. This was the first rocket-powered airplane flight in the United States. Unfortunately, everyone's enthusiasm over the successful tests proved short lived. Nearly every GALCIT 27 filled JATO rocket exploded after accelerated storage tests.

Working in parallel with the solid fuel development effort, Malina's group created and tested an engine that consumed nitric acid (HNO_3) and gasoline. This propellant combination could be stored at ambient temperature, an obvious advantage for field use. They soon discovered that by dissolving nitrogen dioxide in the nitric acid the performance of the rocket motor could be improved. This mixture became known as Red Fuming Nitric Acid, or RFNA. While the oxidizer worked well, the same could not be said for the fuel. Gasoline would not burn evenly, and induced "throbbing" in the combustion chambers that frequently led to explosions.

Take-off of an ERCO *Ercoupe* assisted by solid-fuel rocket motors developed by the Jet Propulsion Laboratory. This was the first rocket-assisted aircraft take-off in America.

Malina visited Truax in Annapolis in early 1942 and learned he was considering using aniline as a gasoline additive in their rockets because it ignited spontaneously on contact with nitric acid. On his way back from Annapolis, it occurred to Malina to try replacing the gasoline altogether with aniline. The results were immediate—the combustion problems encountered with gasoline disappeared and the RFNA/aniline motors ran smoothly. On April 15, 1942, the first American takeoff of an airplane assisted by a liquid fuel JATO took place at the Army Air Force Bombing and Gunnery Range at Muroc, California, using an RFNA/aniline rocket. Situated in the Rogers Dry Lake, the Army Air Force had a base there. What's more, a short time later Mark Mills and Fred Miller developed an asphalt-potassium perchlorate solid fuel they named GALCIT 53 that proved very stable. Therefore, the GALCIT group had achieved successes with solid and liquid fuel rockets. (Muroc Army Air Field was the site where America's first jet aircraft, the Bell XP-59A *Airacomet*, was tested. In 1949, Muroc became Edwards Air Force Base.)

Even before these successes, Malina talked to von Kármán about rocket engine production. He was sure the War Department would order large numbers of JATO units, and realized that CALTECH was not organized for such large-scale production. An independent, private company would be needed. With the assistance of von Kármán's attorney, Andrew Haley, a new company, the Aerojet Engineering Corporation, was incorporated on March 19, 1942. Von Kármán was President and Director; Malina was Treasurer and Director; Haley was Secretary and Director; and Parsons, Summerfield, and Forman were Vice Presidents.

Army leaders saw the potential for rockets, and created the Rocket Branch within the Technical Division of the Office, Chief of Ordnance, in September 1943. Officers in this new organization realized that in the past, too much effort had been expended to create slight improvements in existing weapons. Since they were dealing with an entirely new class of weapons—guided missiles—Army policy planners decided to begin a long-term program of basic research in the field. They simply didn't have the knowledge or expertise needed to begin immediate development of a guided missile or rocket as a tactical weapon system.

Colonel W. H. Joiner, the Army Air Corps Materiel Liaison Officer at CALTECH, suggested that von Kármán prepare a theoretical study of a long-range missile. Malina and Tsien assisted with the preparation of this report. They also attempted, based largely on British intelligence reports regarding German rocket programs, to reconstruct the V-2 on the drawing board. With such reports showing German progress in the field, work on GALCIT Project No. 1 gained greater importance. An analysis of these reports, along with a memorandum that discussed the possibilities for long-range missiles, was submitted in November. This report carried yet another organizational designation, that of the *Jet Propulsion Laboratory* (JPL).

Based on this report and recommendations of other officers, Major General Gladeon M. Barnes, the chief of the Research and Development Service, Office of the Chief of Ordnance, requested that JPL undertake an expanded missile development program. This became known as the ORDCIT, for Ordnance and California

Institute of Technology, Project. Army Ordnance awarded a contract to the JPL on June 22, 1944. The objectives of the ORDCIT Project were to develop a missile and launching equipment that could deliver a 1,000-pound high explosive warhead over a range of 75-100 miles. Dispersion was not to exceed 2%, and the missile was to travel fast enough that it could not be intercepted by a fighter aircraft. Recognizing the state of missile development at that time, the contract also called for basic research on rocket and ramjet powered vehicles, guidance equipment, and aerodynamics. On 1 July, Army Ordnance established the Research and Development Services Sub-Office (Rocket) at CALTECH. The Jet Propulsion Laboratory set up operations in the nearby Arroyo Seco, portions of which CALTECH leased from the City of Pasadena.

The first solid fuel missile developed by the JPL under the ORDCIT project was the XF10S1000-A, more popularly known as the *Private A*. The designation meant X for experimental; F for fin stabilized; S indicated it used solid propellant; the number 10 meant it was ten inches in diameter; 1000 was the thrust; and A meant it was the first model of the type. It was built around the Aerojet 30AS1000 JATO motor, which produced an average thrust of 1,000 pounds for 30 seconds. The motor contained 192 pounds of GALCIT 61-C propellant, which consisted of 76% potassium chlorate and 24% of an asphalt-oil mixture that served as both fuel and binder. *Private A* had a booster of four Army 4.5-inch T-22 artillery rocket motors. These motors delivered a thrust of 22,000 pounds for 0.18 second. A hollow cone attached to the top of the assembly transmitted the thrust of the booster to the large external nut threaded on the nozzle of the missile. It should be pointed out that there was no solid connection between the booster and the *Private*. When launched from its 36-foot long, four-rail launcher, *Private A* and its loosely mated booster constituted a crude step rocket, likely the first one built in the United States. The booster imparted a 33-g acceleration on the missile, which left the launcher at 190 feet per second.

JPL considered a *Private B*, which had a different fin configuration, but it never progressed beyond the drawing board. It had a different tail fin configuration, a ring encircling four blades. The diameter of the ring would have been less than that of the missile body, giving it an appearance resembling an aircraft bomb.

The *Private A* was 92 inches long and 10 inches in diameter; 132.75 inches long with its booster. The missile comprised a cylindrical body topped by a conical nose cone, and had four fins at its base. Gross weight of the *Private A* was 500 pounds, including a 60-pound payload of lead ballast. Maximum range of the missile was about 11 miles. JPL personnel launched 24 of the missiles at Leach Springs, which was located in Camp Irwin, California, during the first half of December 1944. From these flights, JPL personnel gained experience in the operation and instrumentation of missile tests.

Frank Malina was not present during the *Private A* tests—he was in Europe, finishing up an Ordnance Department mission to study V-2 installations that had been captured in the Pas-de-Calais area of France. On his way back from Europe he stopped in Washington, D.C., to visit (then) Colonel Gervais W. Trichel in the Rocket Research and Development Division of the Ordnance Department. Malina pitched the idea of building a high-altitude sounding rocket, a vehicle that could carry 25 pounds of meteorological instruments to an altitude of 100,000 feet. The Army Signal Corps wanted such a rocket, and it would serve as another step towards the development of a land combat missile.

JPL's next missile, the *Private F*, also burned solid fuel. The missile body was essentially the same as the *Private A*, but instead of four fins, it had one fin and two lifting surfaces that spanned approximately five feet. Two forward horizontal fins were added near the base of the nose cone to control fore and aft trim of the rocket. These forward fins had a three-foot span. The JPL Outside Fabrication Department contracted with the Consolidated Steel Corporation in Maywood, California, to fabricate the wings. The lifting surfaces were expected to double the range of the *Private F* over its predecessor. Between April 1 and 13, 1945, JPL fired 17 of these rockets at the Hueco Range at Fort Bliss, Texas. Every one of the *Private Fs* began to roll about ten seconds after launch. After the first few firings changes were made to the fins, but the rolling motion was never eliminated. From these tests, Malina realized that production tolerances for missiles would have to be extremely precise, or that a missile would need an active guidance system for control.

Recognizing that the long-range missile developed under the ORDCIT project would likely use liquid-fuel, the JPL staff

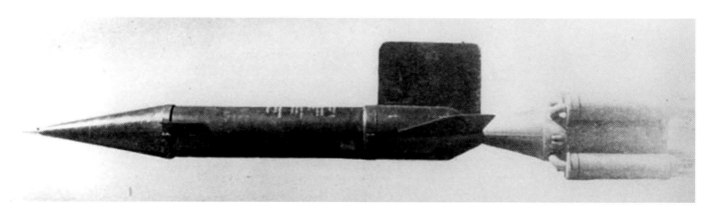

The *Private F*. This was essentially a *Private A* with wings. *Source: U.S. Army photograph.*

began work on a 20,000-pound thrust rocket motor. Calculations indicated such a motor would be needed to achieve a range of 75 miles with a 1,000-pound warhead. At the time, this was the largest rocket motor yet built in the United States. Before the motor could go into a flying missile it would need to be thoroughly tested on the ground. On January 2, 1945, JPL secured approval to build the first large-thrust rocket motor test station in the United States at Muroc.

Work on the long-range missile had reached a point by mid-January 1945 where it had been named *Corporal*, which was the next progression after *Private*. By this time work was underway on the sounding rocket that Malina suggested. This rocket, which was 16 feet tall, 12.2 inches in diameter, and weighed about 2,000 pounds, would also serve as a test vehicle for the combat missile. Because of its ties to the large missile it was named the *WAC Corporal*. Many people assumed the name of the rocket (*WAC*) was a tribute to the Women's Army Corps, as stated by Frank Malina in a memoir paper he prepared in 1964. However, the more

generally accepted source of the name is that it was an acronym for the manner in which the rocket flew—Without Attitude Control. The *WAC Corporal* was a two-stage rocket with a solid-fuel booster and a liquid-fuel sustainer that burned RFNA and aniline. Compressed air forced the propellants from their tanks into the combustion chamber. The rocket was fin stabilized and did not have an active guidance system.

To check the operation of the propulsion system, ORDCIT personnel built a prototype model with the same tanks, plumbing, and electrical circuits planned for the final rocket. This prototype underwent static testing at the ORDCIT Test Station at Muroc. When they designed the *WAC Corporal*, JPL's planners considered using a monopropellant like nitromethane, but didn't have a lot of experience with this type of rocket. Rather than embark on a totally new line of engine development, they decided to stick with the nitric acid/aniline propellants they were familiar with. The engineers opted for compressed air to pressurize the propellant tanks, rather than nitrogen or another inert gas, because of the relative ease of providing the former in a field environment.

Private F on its launcher. Test launches of the Private F were conducted at Fort Bliss, Texas. Source: U.S. Army photograph.

Building the *WAC Corporal* presented a number of challenges. When ORDCIT was founded, it included a machine shop that could produce specialized apparatus and equipment not commercially available on a limited scale. Initially, the machine shop turned out small experimental devices. Theoretically, the prototype for any new design could be fabricated in the shop, but the ORDCIT machine shop actually did very little fabrication work because it did not have the extensive facilities or manpower required. Rather than go to the expense of expanding the shop, the JPL created the Outside Fabrication Department to locate vendors who could fabricate hardware based on laboratory designs and specifications. In general, the Outside Fabrication Department sought small, independent vendors who could respond quickly to the Laboratory's requests. All the large aviation companies were fully committed to large defense contracts and weren't interested in small fabrication projects.

When it came time to build the *WAC Corporal* rockets, the Outside Fabrication Department sought a series of contractors who could build individual components and subassemblies rather than the entire vehicle. The nose cone, for example, presented several problems. The specified material was JIA magnesium, which had to be formed around a mandrel and welded. The Research Welding Company received the contract for this component. A Mr. Bennett of the company designed a wooden cone with a stainless steel longitudinal inlay for welding the long seam. When formed around the cone the magnesium sheet hardened, but this condition was overcome by annealing the material twice during the process. Once the magnesium was wrapped around the wooden cone, the sheet was held in place by several mild-steel rings. After several experiments, company personnel found the best weld method was to use a heliarc with argon gas and JIA magnesium rod. The rings held the edges parallel during the tacking and welding process so that a continuous bead could be started at the base of the cone. Next, a skin of the same material was formed around a cylindrical mandrel, welded together, and then attached to the base of the cone by a circumferential seam. The nose assembly was then finished by welding caps, clips, and a solid magnesium tip to the cone, followed by weld grinding and the application of a protective coat of wax.

The tail section of the *WAC Corporal* comprised the aft shell, thrust ring, tail ring, fin mounts, and fins. Presidential Silver

Company fabricated these parts. The limited number of units being produced made regular production tooling too expensive, so temporary tooling had to be improvised. Tolerances on these sections were critical, because the entire rocket was assembled by orientation from the faced diameter of the tail casting. After delivery to the project, three units were pulled at random and subjected to precise dimensional inspection and static load testing.

Southwest Welding Company produced the propellant tanks. Because the material specified (4-6 chrome steel) had never been used in the fabrication of light-gauge, high-pressure vessels, a great deal of testing was necessary throughout the manufacture process. Approximately twenty different welding techniques were tested before the one capable of withstanding 3,000 psi operating pressures could be found. Electric arc welding with 4-6 chrome rod proved to be the best technique.

Before the full sized rocket flew, its design was tested using a series of ten 1/5th scale models launched from July 3–5, 1945, at Goldstone Lake, California. The Outside Fabrication Department was given just 20 days to come up with the test rockets. Department personnel contacted a number of smaller fabricators and machine shops because larger concerns were already busy with War Department contracts. Fortunately, the test rockets did not represent any difficult machining problems; the main challenge was one of meeting the tight schedule without violating the close tolerances required. One of the most noteworthy contractors was the Western Drilling Company, which completed the 20-foot tall launch tower in just 5 days by putting three shifts on the job.

Model tests were necessary because there were concerns about the behavior of the full size rockets. Calculations showed the booster would still be firing when the *WAC Corporal* left the launch tower, which raised questions regarding the stability of the booster/sustainer combination. Another unknown was how the booster might affect the second stage at separation. Therefore, it was decided to perform tests using dynamically similar scale models. Dubbed the *Baby WAC* by its designers, this rocket was solid fueled. Among other things, these flights validated the use of three fins instead of the traditional four, and external placement of propellant lines with a cover that protruded from the missile body. As the full size rocket took form, it was clear that a new launch area would be required. Anticipating such a facility might be needed, the Army began looking for a suitable site in 1944. Rocketry was about to return to New Mexico.

2

Crosses, Cottonwoods, and Mushroom Clouds

New Mexico, the Land of Enchantment, is a remarkable study of contrasts, especially in the southern portion of the state. It can be both a place of great scenic beauty and a place of danger. The desert has a beauty of its own, especially when the cacti are in bloom. Plants that are usually muted shades of green and tan produce vibrant blossoms. Whole sections of desert fill with delicate white flowers of the yucca. Throughout the year, the sky is usually a rich blue with few clouds. Sunsets are frequently breathtaking. Standing on a mountain peak, one can see for hundreds of miles. At night, thousands of stars light up the sky, and the Milky Way is clearly visible, like a veil across the heavens.

Yet, at the same time, the New Mexico desert can be a dangerous, inhospitable place for the careless, uninitiated, or unprepared. Water is scarce, and the local fauna includes rattlesnakes, scorpions, and tarantulas. Even the plant life can be dangerous. Cacti and other plants with spines or sharp, pointed leaves can cause painful encounters. Dried riverbeds, called *arroyos*, cut across the terrain. When rain occurs, water drains into the *arroyos*, particularly out of the mountains, and fills the ordinarily dry channels with torrents of water.

One of the early bands of European explorers to venture into the southern portions of present-day New Mexico, a group of Spaniards led by Don Juan de Oñate, found the region particularly inhospitable. In 1598, Oñate and his group ventured through the Great Pass of the North (today's El Paso, Texas) in search of gold. They followed the Rio Grande River northward so they would have a supply of water as they trekked across the desolate landscape towards Santa Fe. The trail they blazed became known as the *Camino Real*. At first, the journey wasn't too difficult.

Unfortunately, the explorers soon encountered problems, and not all of Oñate's men made it to Santa Fe. As they followed the Rio Grande, a series of natural barriers forced them to turn away from the river and their water supply. Some of the men died of thirst as they traveled across the blistering, arid desert. This deadly portion of the *Camino Real* became known as the *Jornada del Muerto*. Often erroneously translated as the Journey of Death, it is properly known as the Journey of the Dead Man.

The *Jornada del Muerto* was named for Bernardo Gruber, a German Protestant trader. In 1670, Gruber tried to reach Santa Fe after being imprisoned for two years by agents of the Inquisition in Mexico. He died at a point along the trail now known as *Aleman* (which is German in Spanish.)

The desert was not the only hazard faced by early travelers through the region. Apache raids were an all too frequent occurrence. According to one legend, in 1830 a bishop, a priest, a Mexican Army colonel, a captain, four trappers, and four choirboys were attacked near the *Jornada del Muerto*. Only one member of the party—one of the boys—survived. Crosses were erected to honor the casualties, giving a stark reminder to others of the hazards of crossing the desert. The area around the crosses became known as *El Pueblo del Jardin de Las Cruces* (the City of the Garden of Crosses). Another legend claims multiple crosses were erected in the area to mark the graves of a group of 40 travelers from Taos, New Mexico, who were killed by Apaches just as they reached the area.

Sovereignty over the region was often contested during the early 1800s because of its proximity to Mexico. The issue was finally settled in 1848 with the Treaty of Guadalupe Hidalgo, which ended the Mexican War and ceded territory east of the Rio Grande to the United States. Settlers soon flocked to the area to claim land. In an effort to protect the emerging communities, the United States Army dispatched Lieutenant Delos Bennett Sackett and a contingent of 87 troopers from Fort Gibson, Oklahoma, to the area. These communities included El Paso (or Paso del Norte) and Doña Ana, a small village headed by Don Pablo Melendres.

Because of the chaos that ensued when many settlers tried to claim land just acquired by the Treaty of Guadalupe Hidalgo, Melendres asked Sackett to survey and plot a new town in the area. Sackett and the troopers mapped out a new town comprising 84 square blocks. Taking its name from the nearby *El Pueblo del Jardin de Las Cruces,* this town became known as *Las Cruces*.

Each block comprised four lots, and the town included areas designated for a plaza and a church. Once construction started, it became clear that Sackett, who had only the most rudimentary surveying equipment, plotted a town with crooked streets. Even with designated building lots, houses crowded against each other in some areas. Adding to the troubles of the new community, people dug holes in the streets to make adobe blocks for their houses. It became such a problem that Judge Richard Campbell ordered the townspeople to stop making adobes on Main Street and fill in the holes.

Not everyone who lived in the area was happy to become an American citizen. While the creation of Las Cruces may have eased the pressure caused by the rapid influx of settlers, it didn't ease the anti-United States sentiments harbored by some residents who preferred Mexican rule to that of the United States. These sentiments eventually led to the formation of another village. In 1850, some 60 families moved west of the Rio Grande, into what was still Mexican territory. They founded the village of *Mesilla*. The settlers soon became United States residents again when the Gadsden Purchase, finalized in 1854, turned over a 30,000 square mile strip of land from Mexico for $10 million. The area west of Las Cruces that surrounded the Rio Grande became known as the Mesilla Valley.

Las Cruces and the Mesilla Valley are situated on the west side of the San Andres and Organ Mountains. The two mountain ranges form part of the boundary of the Tularosa Basin. The Tularosa Basin was once a vast volcanic dome. About ten million years ago, the center of the dome collapsed and created a basin that was some 60 miles across, bordered by the San Andres and Organ Mountains to the west and the Sacramento Mountains to the east. A divide between the San Andres and Organs provided access through the ranges into the Tularosa Basin. This was named the San Augustin Pass.

The most prominent geological feature in the Tularosa Basin is the area known as White Sands. An area of 275 square miles, White Sands comprises gleaming white dunes of gypsum powder. There are massive underground deposits of gypsum beneath the Tularosa Basin. The waters of Lake Lucero dissolve the gypsum and bring it to the surface. The term "lake" is somewhat of an overstatement—Lake Lucero is better described as a *playa* (a seasonal lake), with water that is only a few inches deep. Still, it is enough to dissolve the gypsum. As water evaporates from the shores of the lake, the gypsum is left behind. Desert winds then wear down the deposited gypsum and blow it into the dune fields north and east of the lake.

The first European settlements in the Tularosa Basin were the Hispanic farming villages of Tularosa and La Luz, both founded in the early 1860s. With the end of the Apache Wars in 1861, more settlers came to the area. During the decades after the Civil War various industries came to the Tularosa Basin. A few cattle ranchers managed to eke out an existence, but the grazing was poor due to the sparse vegetation. The most successful rancher was Olliver Lee. Those who settled in the Sacramento Mountains had better luck. The mountains supported a profitable logging industry. To the north, gold strikes in the Sierra Blanca gave rise to several boomtowns.

In the 1880s two brothers from New York, Charles and John Eddy, came by stagecoach to the Pecos River valley in eastern New Mexico, where they built a cattle ranch. Seeing an economic opportunity in the Tularosa Basin, Charles Eddy approached a group of investors in El Paso, Texas, to propose a rail line between that border town and the mines to the north. By 1897 he garnered enough support for construction of the El Paso and Northeastern Railroad (EPNE), which by 1901 connected with the Rock Island and Pacific Railroad line at Santa Rosa, New Mexico. Eddy established a township along the EPNE, about 15 miles from the White Sands dune fields.

The town was named *Alamogordo*, which means "fat cottonwood." Eddy saw the location as well suited to take advantage of the ranching and logging industries in the area. It was also at a convenient point along the line where the locomotives could take on water. He formed the Alamogordo Improvement Company as a subsidiary of the EPNE to oversee development of the community. Water was vital to the life of the community, and the EPNE purchased Olliver Lee's Alamo Ranch and its water rights for $5,000. To maintain a stable work force, Eddy limited the production and distribution of alcohol to a single site in the township, across from the railroad station. (There are those who contend the real reason for the limitation was so the conductors knew where to find everyone when the trains were ready to continue up the line.) Within twelve months of its founding, Alamogordo grew to 1,000 inhabitants.

When New Mexico became a state in 1912, Alamogordo became the county seat of Otero County. Las Cruces was in Doña Ana County. There was a plaster of Paris production plant in the White Sands, and the community of Alamogordo stabilized at around 3,000 residents. Even the establishment of the "White Sands National Monument" under the National Park Service did little to affect the population. The National Monument was established at the southern end of the dune field in 1933 and opened to the public on April 19, 1934.

World War II brought major changes to the Tularosa Basin. In 1941, the British looked to establish a training base adjacent to Alamogordo for bomber training. The British eyed southern New Mexico because it contained large expanses of land for a bombing range and good weather that allowed year-round flying. Although the United States had not yet entered the war, Washington allowed England to train Royal Air Force pilots in America under the British Overseas Training Program.

Technically, the British pilots who trained in America at that early stage of the war were civilians learning to fly under contract with civilian flight schools. To maintain the official stance of American neutrality, Royal Air Force pilot cadets first traveled to Canada, where they resigned from the British military. They were then allowed to enter the United States on six-month tourist visas to attend flight school. Upon completion of their training, the students returned to Canada, where they rejoined the Royal Air Force.

The first of these schools, the No. 1 British Flying Training School, was created under the aegis of the Dallas Aviation School. British students began training at Dallas Love Field in June 1941. By the end of the summer, they moved to a training field built in Terrell, Texas, that was paid for by the British government.

Eventually, the British signed contracts for six flight schools in the United States, where thousands of RAF pilots received their flight instruction. (A seventh school was built in Sweetwater, Texas, but no British pilots ever graduated from there. As the school was being finished and the first class of students began training, the American War Department took over the base for the Women Airforce Service Pilots, or WASPs, who delivered aircraft from factories to the military.) In addition to the British Flying Training Schools, the British government sought another site for training bomber crews and looked to the Tularosa Basin.

The British surveyed a site near Alamogordo for a bomber training base, and were prepared to start construction when the Japanese attacked Pearl Harbor. With the entry of the United States into World War II, the War Department took over the project and decided to use it for American aircrew training. Construction began at the base on February 6, 1942, and units began arriving in May. During the war, the Alamogordo Army Air Field served as a training center for B-17, B-24, and B-29 bomber crews. A bombing and gunnery range was established north of the base, extending into Socorro County.

New Mexico was also home to the Manhattan Project, America's effort to develop the atomic bomb. In 1938, a pair of physicists working at the Kaiser Wilhelm Institute in Berlin, Otto Hahn and Fritz Strassmann, discovered when uranium atoms were bombarded with neutrons, the atoms split into two lighter elements with atomic numbers equal to that of the original element. This process of atom splitting is known as fission. During fission an atom releases great quantities of energy.

Leo Szilard, a Hungarian-born physicist who first fled to England, then to America when the Nazis came into power, had already theorized fission was possible. The idea came to him while standing on a street corner in London. He rushed back to his hotel room, where he further refined the concept while soaking in the bathtub. Szilard had numerous idiosyncrasies. For example, he preferred to live in hotels, with two packed suitcases next to the door in case he had to leave quickly. He maintained this lifestyle until only a few years before his death. He would also spend hours at a time in the bathtub, contemplating some physics problem.

Danish physicist Neils Bohr told colleagues of Hahn's and Strassmann's work while visiting Princeton University. The news from Germany troubled Szilard, because he feared where it might lead. Then, working at Columbia University where he had guest privileges, Szilard made an even more startling discovery. He found that during the fission process, a uranium atom released two or three neutrons that could strike other atoms and release still more neutrons. Szilard realized this meant it was possible to create an expanding chain reaction that would produce an explosion, the likes of which had never been seen.

Fearing the outcome of further research in Nazi Germany, Szilard convinced his friend Albert Einstein to write President Roosevelt in 1939 warning that the power of the atom might be unleashed as an explosive device. Such a device would have enormous destructive power and could very well make a nation invincible. Szilard was particularly worried that Hitler might develop an atomic bomb and use it to dominate the world. He urged Roosevelt to begin a program immediately to ensure America had such a weapon first.

Due in large part to Einstein's influence, Roosevelt formed a special committee to investigate the feasibility of creating an atomic bomb. The committee reported it would be possible to develop a nuclear reactor within a year and a half, and a bomb within four years. With the feasibility established by the committee, President Roosevelt approved a project to develop the atom bomb. What followed was one of the largest mobilizations of scientific talent in history—the Manhattan Project. The project was assigned to the Manhattan District of the Army Corps of Engineers, hence its name.

Major General Leslie Groves was appointed to lead the Manhattan Project. Groves previously made a name for himself as the manager of the Pentagon construction project. General Groves selected Dr. J. Robert Oppenheimer as Manhattan's scientific director. Oppenheimer began recruiting the best scientific minds he could find, and soon such giants of modern physics as Enrico Fermi, Neils Bohr, and Hans Bethe were working on Manhattan. While some scientists continued working at their universities, Oppenheimer assembled most of his team in the mountains of northern New Mexico.

As a youth, Oppenheimer camped in the region and came to love its scenic beauty. He continued visiting the area as an adult, and eventually purchased a small ranch in the Sangre de Cristo Mountains north of Santa Fe. When he and Groves sought a locale for the Manhattan Project's main laboratory, he steered the General to the site of a former boy's school about twenty miles northwest of Santa Fe that was near his ranch. Although water was scarce and electrical power was inadequate, the mesa in the Jemez Mountains was ideal from a security perspective, which was one of Groves' main concerns. Whatever logistical shortcomings the site presented could be overcome. Groves and Oppenheimer selected the school site as the locale for *Site Y*, the main laboratory where the scientists would design and build the bomb. The laboratory was named Los Alamos.

The Manhattan scientists threw themselves into their work, but still hadn't built a bomb by the time the German Reich collapsed. As intelligence teams would discover, it turned out Germany had not really pursued the atom bomb. Instead, the Germans focused their resources on weapons like the V-2 ballistic missile which carried a conventional warhead.

Germany's surrender did not slow work on the atomic bomb. Japan continued its fierce resistance in the Pacific and showed no signs of capitulation. Even though conventional bombing by B-29 bombers and the sinking of merchant ships had virtually destroyed their economy, the Japanese continued to fight. Suicide attacks by *kamikaze* pilots became an accepted military tactic, and Japan's military leaders even resorted to suspending bombs from balloons that were released to follow the jet stream across the Pacific Ocean. The Japanese hoped the balloons would start massive forest fires in the Pacific Northwest and induce panic to force the Americans into a truce. None of these tactics halted America's advances, but the Japanese fought on. It looked as though the only way to end the war would be to invade Japan.

Plans for the invasion, codenamed *Operation Downfall*, called for two amphibious landings. The first, codenamed *Coronet*, would be on Kyushu, the southernmost of the main Japanese home islands, and was scheduled to commence on November 1, 1945. Once the southern third of the island was secured and turned into a logistical base, the invasion of Japan's main island would take place. Codenamed *Olympic*, this phase of *Downfall* was planned for the spring of 1946. Japanese military leaders did not know the details of *Operation Downfall*, but they were sure an invasion was coming. Preparing for the inevitable invasion, the Japanese stockpiled *kamikaze* planes, weapons, and ammunition in caves and underground bunkers along the coast. Naval personnel would attack landing craft with explosive-carrying boats and undersea divers while pilots crashed their airplanes into surface ships.

Although American military planners did not know of the stockpiled aircraft and suicide tactics planned for the landing craft, everyone agreed the invasion would be brutal. *Operation Downfall* would surely result in a bloodbath on both sides. Japan's military was prepared to fight to the death, and civilians were being trained to fight the Americans with bamboo spears and farm tools. The atomic bomb offered an alternative to a full-scale invasion. If Japan's leaders could be shown the United States had a weapon that could annihilate them, surely they would surrender.

The Manhattan scientists developed two types of bomb. The simplest was a so-called "gun type," where two subcritical masses of uranium were brought together to create a supercritical mass and the desired explosion. Uranium for this device was processed in a gigantic plant built in Oak Ridge, Tennessee. The second device contained a mass of plutonium surrounded by lens-shaped explosive charges. When detonated, the explosives would compress the plutonium so that neutrons would collide with other atoms fast enough to trigger an atomic explosion. Everyone was reasonably sure the uranium-type bomb would work, but not the plutonium implosion device.

The explosives had to be detonated with great precision at points surrounding the core to ensure symmetrical compression of the plutonium, or else the chain reaction would not occur. Achieving simultaneous detonation of the charges that surrounded the core was a problem. Before it could be used in combat, the plutonium implosion device had to be tested. The uranium bomb, nicknamed "Little Boy" because it was smaller than the "Fat Man" plutonium device, would be committed to combat without a test. It was just as well the scientists were sure the Little Boy would work, because they only had enough uranium to build one bomb.

The plutonium processing plant was in Hanford, Washington. Manufacturing plutonium was difficult, but there was enough to build two bombs. That meant one bomb could be detonated in a test, which in turn meant Oppenheimer needed a place to test the plutonium bomb. Obviously, the site had to be well away from populated areas, rail lines, air lanes, and highways. He looked at eight potential sites in California, New Mexico, Texas, and Colorado. After weighing the advantages and disadvantages of each site, Oppenheimer finally settled on the northern end of the Alamogordo Bombing and Gunnery Range, about 90 miles north of the town. (Although the detonation has been linked to

Alamogordo, the town of Socorro is much closer, and the site isn't even in the Tularosa Basin or Otero county.) Situated in the *Jornada del Muerto*, the site was close enough to Los Alamos so traveling there would not be too inconvenient, but not too close in case something went wrong.

Inspired by a poem by John Donne that contained a stanza about a three-person God that could "break, blow (and) burn," Oppenheimer named the site "Trinity." Personnel and equipment began arriving at Trinity in the fall of 1944. On December 30, 1944, a contingent of Military Police arrived and set up checkpoints around the area.

A 100-foot tall steel tower was erected at ground zero. The bomb, which was often referred to as "the gadget," would be detonated on top of the tower so the explosion could be observed and recorded with high speed instruments. The Army built a "base camp" for the scientists about ten miles southwest of the tower. In the area around ground zero there were three observation points, each one 10,000 yards from the tower. The south bunker contained the control center. A nearby ranch house (about two miles from ground zero) that had belonged to the George McDonald family became the assembly building for the gadget's core. The McDonald family had vacated the ranch in 1942 with the creation of the Alamogordo Bombing and Gunnery Range.

The test was set for 14 July, but Oppenheimer begged to have it delayed for 48 hours. Groves reluctantly agreed. President Truman was in Potsdam, Germany, meeting with British Prime Minister Winston Churchill and Soviet Premier Joseph Stalin. Knowing the United States had a working atomic bomb would certainly bolster Truman's confidence and his ability to be firm with Stalin regarding the post-war world. Forty-eight hours, but no more, Oppenheimer was told.

On 12 July, a courier left Los Alamos for the Trinity Site, carrying two hemispheres of plutonium. At the McDonald ranch

Trinity site—the hundred-foot tall steel tower that held the world's first atomic bomb is visible on the right.

The Trinity Device in the top of the tower. The wiring harnesses for the detonators can be seen in this photograph.

Delivery of the Trinity Device to the base of the tower.

house, the master bedroom had been turned into a clean room for the assembly of the core. General Groves' deputy, Brigadier General Thomas Farrell, signed the receipt for the plutonium. He asked to hold the material he signed for and noted the sphere felt warm, which gave him "a certain sense of its hidden power." At one minute past midnight on 13 July, the explosive detonators left Los Alamos for Trinity. That afternoon, the plutonium core and explosives were delivered to the base of the tower, where final assembly of the bomb began. At first the core would not fit into the bomb. The scientists had to let the temperatures of the core and casing equalize. Then, the plutonium slid smoothly into place. The next morning, the bomb was hoisted to the top of the tower and the crew began installing the detonators.

During the night of 15-16 July there was a thunderstorm. Lightning flashed in the sky, and everyone nervously eyed the steel tower containing the gadget with its explosive charges in place. Fortunately, lightning did not strike the tower. The test was scheduled for 4:00 AM, but rainy conditions forced a delay. Low clouds and rain would, it was feared, increase the potential for radioactive fallout. At 4:45 AM, the weather report at last looked favorable—calm to light winds with broken clouds for the next two hours. The countdown started at 5:10 AM, and at 5:29:45 AM Mountain War Time, July 16, 1945, the world's first atomic bomb exploded.

United States Navy Captain R. A. Larkin observed the test from a distance of twenty miles. The terrain between his observation point on Campania Hill and the Trinity site was flat, so he had a clear view of the explosion. Observers were issued goggles with dark filters so the flash would not harm their eyes. Even with the goggles, at the instant of the detonation he looked down at the ground to avoid eye injury.

Larkin later reported his first impression was of "sudden brilliant lighting of the surrounding landscape, accompanied by a momentary flash of heat." After raising the dark filter on his goggles

he looked towards the explosion. Although the filter blocked 99% of the light, the intensity of illumination was such that there was a momentary sensation of blinding similar to that following a close flash of lightning on a dark night. Within two seconds, he could distinguish details of the explosion without the filter. Larkin recalled seeing a ball of light about three or four hundred yards in diameter about a thousand feet above the ground. Beneath this ball there appeared to be a column of red flame about 150 or 200 yards in diameter. He also noted flickering red reflections on the clouds above the ball of light.

As the fireball diminished "a smoky, grayish-brown ball took shape." The column beneath the ball darkened until it looked like "a dense dark pillar under the grayish brown ball." About ten seconds after the explosion, the ball began to flatten, so it and the column "took on the shape of a vast mushroom." The mushroom cloud continued to rise before beginning to fade after about fifteen minutes. The cloud faded completely from view about half an hour after the detonation.

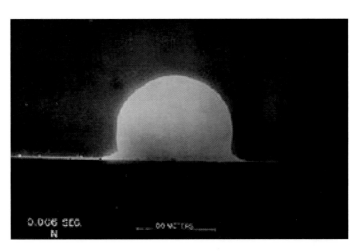

Detonation plus 0.005 seconds – the fireball is rapidly expanding.

The flash from the explosion was seen in Alamogordo, about 90 miles away, and the blast broke windows 120 miles away. People as far as 160 miles from the explosion reported feeling it. The explosion had a power equivalent to the detonation of 18 kilotons; that is, 18,000 tons of TNT. To cover the true nature of the test, the military issued a release stating an ammunition dump on the Alamogordo Bombing and Gunnery range that contained a large number of phosphorus bombs exploded just before dawn.

To the south, Lieutenant Colonel Harold R. Turner knew nothing about the Manhattan Project and Trinity (in fact, he was in his room at the Amador Hotel in Las Cruces when the detonation occurred), but he knew something extraordinary had occurred on the military installation he was in charge of. A week before the detonation, the Alamogordo Bombing and Gunnery Range became part of the White Sands Proving Ground, and Turner was appointed its first commanding officer.

Detonation plus fifteen seconds – the characteristic mushroom cloud is forming.

Ground zero after the detonation; the footings are all that remained of the 100-foot tall tower.

The tower as it appeared before the blast.

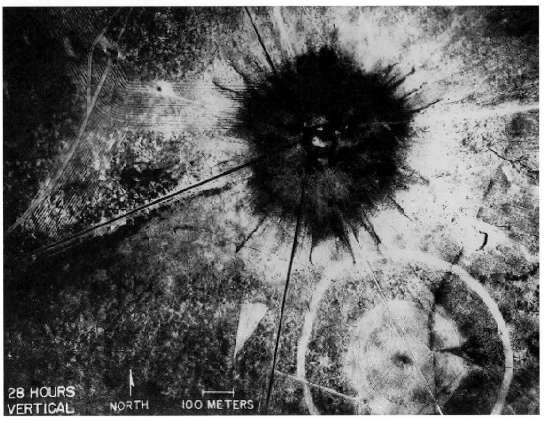

Aerial view of ground zero of the Trinity test.

3

Creating a Range at White Sands

On September 6, 1944, the Germans unveiled their newest weapon, a long-range ballistic missile. Reich Propaganda Minister Joseph Göbbels dubbed the missile the *Vergultungswaffe Zwei* (Vengeance Weapon Two), or simply V-2. Fueled by alcohol and liquid oxygen, the V-2 delivered a one-ton warhead to targets up to two-hundred miles away. Because it struck at supersonic speeds, the V-2 arrived without any warning, and there was no way to intercept or deflect it. The only way to combat the V-2 was to attack it while it was still on the ground, but even this was nearly impossible, because it was fired by mobile field batteries.

Germany's Vengeance Weapon One had been in service for three months by the time the V-2 arrived. Nazi leaders deployed the V-1, an explosive-laden pilotless aircraft or cruise missile, in June 1944. Armed with a one-ton warhead, at least the V-1 could be shot down, because it flew in a straight line at a constant altitude towards its target. To counter this threat, the British deployed a series of air defenses that integrated antiaircraft guns, fighters, and barrage balloons. Crude in comparison to the V-2, what it lacked in sophistication the V-1 made up for in sheer numbers. Thousands crossed the English Channel during the summer of 1944. While the defenses brought down most of the flying bombs, quite a few still managed to hit London. Now there was this new weapon to contend with.

Actually, the Allies had expected the arrival of the V-2 for some time. Early in the war an anonymous benefactor mailed a remarkable document to the British embassy in Norway. Called the "Oslo Report," this document contained details of German advances in radar and guided missiles. The Oslo Report even specified the locale for the missile program as being near Peenemünde, a small fishing village on the Baltic Coast. This was the first hint the British received regarding missile development in Germany, and the Oslo Report seemed too good to be true. Some members of the British government suspected it was a plant that provided false information to fool the English so they would waste important resources developing countermeasures for weapons that didn't exist. Dr. R. V. Jones believed the Oslo Report was genuine and kept an eye on German activities around Peenemünde. Even when reconnaissance photos of Peenemünde showed V-1 and V-

2 missiles on the ground, there were still those in Britain's War Ministry who refused to believe the Germans were building such weapons. The most notable disbeliever was Lord Cherwell, Prime Minister Churchill's chief scientific advisor.

Evidence continued to mount until there was no question about the missile's existence. One of the most compelling pieces of evidence was a secret recording of a conversation between two captured German Generals. Unbeknownst to them, Generals Wilhelm von Thoma and Ludwig Cruewell were being taped while they talked to each other in March 1943. Both had been captured in North Africa. General von Thoma knew about the V-2 project, and expressed surprise that rocket attacks on London had not already begun. Since he did not know their conversation was being monitored, von Thoma's remark was taken as genuine.

Clearly something had to be done to disrupt the German rocket program. On the night of August 18-19, 1943, the British launched a massive air strike against Peenemünde. Code named "Operation Hydra," the raid incorporated nearly the entire strength of the Royal Air Force Bomber Command. The British bombers had three major targets: the production works; the laboratories; and the housing area where the scientists and engineers lived. Locating the targets proved more difficult than expected, and the first pathfinder aircraft were slightly off course when they dropped their markers. Therefore, many bombs missed these three targets. Only two key people were killed: Dr. Walter Thiel, who headed the propulsion branch, and Chief Engineer Erich Walther. Most of the 750 casualties occurred in the foreign workers camp and a barracks for German girls who worked in support positions at the center. Critical facilities like the supersonic wind tunnel and liquid oxygen plant were barely harmed. Hydra damaged the German research station but did not knock it out completely. General Walter Dornberger (who headed the project) later contended in his memoir book *V-2* that the raid delayed the program four to six weeks.

To fool the Allies and give the impression the facility had been abandoned, Dornberger ordered that buildings be left in their demolished condition. Undamaged buildings were to be camouflaged with black and white paint to create the illusion they

German V-2 missiles undergoing test at Peenemünde, ca. 1943.

were burned out. This ruse bought the development center a nine-month respite before it was bombed again. Before the war ended, American and British bombers hit Peenemünde several more times, but never again on the scale of Operation Hydra.

Not only did missile development continue, but the Germans began field trials at an overland range established in Blizna, Poland. Launches over a land range were important to collect ballistic data on dispersion of the missiles and their behavior at the terminal portion of their flights. Up until that time all launches had been over water. Dye packets placed in the rockets gave a general indication of where they impacted in the Baltic, but for the V-2 to be fielded as a weapon, more precise data was needed.

The Polish underground reported on V-2 tests in Blizna, and even managed to recover missile components that were smuggled back to England. The reports and components smuggled out of Poland were important, but the courageous actions of the Poles were overshadowed by an even more spectacular intelligence victory. In June 1944, an errant missile launched from Peenemünde crashed in Sweden. Although officially neutral, the Swedish government let the British recover the wreckage. The British assembled the pieces and had a good idea of what to expect when the next V-weapon entered the war.

For example, they determined the V-2 stood 46 feet tall and weighed 28,000 pounds at launch. From the smell that accompanied the pieces, analysts could tell it used alcohol as a fuel. It contained five major subassemblies: warhead; control section; midsection; tail section; and propulsion unit. Known as the A-4 to its builders, it was a ballistic missile; that is, it flew a preset course during powered flight. Internal controls kept the missile on the desired path. This was the only aspect of the V-2 that the British got wrong. The missile that crashed in Sweden had been launched to test guidance equipment for the *Wasserfall* antiaircraft rocket.

Finding these components, British analysts concluded the missiles were radio controlled during powered flight.

The control section housed the gyroscopes that kept the missile on course, the accelerometer that told the engine when to shut down, and the mixing computer that controlled onboard functions. The midsection consisted of a pair of aluminum tanks held by a steel body shell. The tail section had four fins attached to an ogival boat tail. Graphite vanes in the engine exhaust and tabs on the outer corners of the four fins guided the missile towards its target. The propulsion section burned liquid oxygen and alcohol to generate a thrust of 54,000 pounds. A turbopump driven by high temperature steam fed the propellants into the combustion chamber. The steam came from the decomposition of concentrated hydrogen peroxide.

With a one-ton high-explosive warhead, the V-2 could hardly become the decisive weapon Hitler hoped for. Even firing at their maximum rate, the V-2 batteries could hardly match the effects of a single raid by British and American bombers. Hitler hoped the psychological effect of these weapons, which arrived and exploded with no advance warning, would break the will of the British to continue fighting. He misjudged the Allies' resolve, so the V-2 was not an important weapon that affected the outcome of the war, even though thousands were launched against Allied targets in England and Continental Europe. What was important, though, was what the V-2 represented. Through it, military planners envisioned a day when ballistic missiles would play an important strategic role in warfare.

Recognizing the importance of rockets in any future conflict, Major General Barnes initiated Project Hermes on November 15, 1944, for research and development of ballistic missiles. Hermes existed in parallel to the ORDCIT project. During December, it was decided to study the V-2 and conduct live launchings as part of Hermes. Hermes would unlock the secrets of German rocket programs and provide potentially useful information for the fledgling American efforts. This, of course, required that the American Army collect specimens of the V-2 and capture the people who created it. The General Electric Company received the Hermes contract. Studying the V-2 was only one facet of Hermes. Under the contract, General Electric was to research and develop both surface to surface and surface to air missiles.

As the war neared its end, General Dornberger and Wernher von Braun, who led the scientific and engineering team at Peenemünde, decided it would be best to seek out the Americans, particularly as they wanted to continue working on rockets after the war. It looked as though the Red Army would reach Peenemünde first. Surrendering to the Soviets was never an option, and they knew the British and French could not afford a major post-war rocket program. They concluded their best opportunity to continue building large rockets would be in America. Obviously, Dornberger and von Braun had to keep such intentions secret, because they would be construed as treason by the German high command. An excuse for leaving Peenemünde had to be found.

Even at this late stage of the war, Nazi leaders hoped to consolidate missile and aircraft designers at one place where

Wernher von Braun (with arm in cast) when he surrendered to the American Army. *Source: New Mexico Museum of Space History.*

allowed to fall into Allied hands. Then, one day the SS guards simply disappeared. Rumors spread through the group that the American Army was close. Wernher von Braun's younger brother, Magnus, was dispatched on a bicycle to contact the Americans because he spoke the best English among the group. On May 2, 1945, the rocketry group surrendered to the American 44th Infantry Division.

When von Braun and his group evacuated Peenemünde, they took their technical archives with them. Totaling nearly 14 tons, the archives contained the results of more than a decade of research. Acting on von Braun's instructions, Dieter Huzel and Bernhard Tessman stashed the documents in an unused salt mine near Goslar, in central Germany. During interrogation by the Americans they revealed the location of the mine. A recovery team was quickly dispatched to Goslar. This represented another major technological coup; not only did the United States have the rocketeers in custody, their written records had been recovered, too.

The United States Army also captured the underground factory near Nordhausen where V-2s were built. One of the effects of Operation Hydra was the decision to move missile production underground. Named Mittelwerk, the factory comprised two parallel tunnels that were more than a mile long with 44 connecting cross galleries. V-2 production did not need all the space in Mittelwerk, so the factory also produced V-1s and Jumo aircraft engines. The Americans found about 250 rockets on the assembly line in various degrees of completion, but no complete missiles. Since Nordhausen was in the area of Germany scheduled to be turned over to the Soviets, there was a hurried effort to remove as much hardware as possible. More than 640 tons of equipment was shipped from Mittelwerk.

The equipment was bound for southern New Mexico, where the Army had already set up a rocket testing center. When he created Hermes, General Barnes saw the need for a place to test missiles within the continental limits of the United States for it and the existing ORDCIT project. In the fall of 1944, Barnes appointed

they could continue to work, so von Braun's desire to evacuate Peenemünde fit nicely into these plans. After moving several times, von Braun eventually led a group of his top people to Oberammergau, near the Austrian border. At Oberammergau, the rocket scientists found themselves guarded by the SS. For several weeks the scientists feared they would be killed before being

An American Military Policeman looks at a partially assembled V-2 at the underground factory Mittelwerk, in central Germany. The American Army removed approximately 640 tons of missile components from the facility and shipped them back to the United States.

a committee to find such a place. This committee, which included officers and civilians from the Ordnance Department and the Corps of Engineers, conducted a careful survey of all open areas in the United States. They studied topographic maps and considered such factors as locations of highways, commercial air routes, and weather. Three of their main considerations were that the area be flat, sparsely populated, and have predominantly clear skies so testing could go on year round. Having a locale surrounded by hills or mountains for tracking stations was a plus. Committee members decided the site had to be alongside existing railroad tracks with access to water and electrical power. At the same time, railroad lines should not cross the site. If possible, it should be near a permanently established military base for support. The ideal place would also be close to communities that could provide for the off-duty needs of personnel and their dependents. The committee found few places that met even most of these requirements.

The Tularosa Basin presented the region that came closest to meeting these criteria. No air routes or rail lines crossed the area; there was no industry except for ranching and a few mines; and there were very few people there. The only drawback was the range would not be as large as they'd like. However, it was better than any other site they considered. In February 1945, the Army Corps of Engineers selected a locale adjacent to the White Sands National Monument. Fort Bliss and the city of El Paso, Texas, were nearby, as was the New Mexico College of Agriculture and Mechanic Arts (today known as New Mexico State University) at Las Cruces, and the city of Alamogordo. Even though the site was "only" 100 miles long and 40 miles wide, it would be the largest overland rocket and guided missile testing range in the United States. Lieutenant Colonel (LTC) Harold R. Turner, one of the members of the selection committee, is generally credited with naming the installation White Sands Proving Ground (WSPG) after the National Monument.

On February 8, 1945, the Corps of Engineers issued Real Estate Directive 4279, "Acquisition of Land for ORDCIT Range Facilities," to the Commanding General of the Army Service Forces. This Directive specified the tracts of land to be acquired for the WSPG. In most cases, procuring the land was not a problem since the government already had leases on much of it. The property comprised more than 2.6 million acres. It included the Alamogordo Bombing and Gunnery Range, Fort Bliss Antiaircraft Firing Range, Doña Ana Target Range, and Castner Target Range, all of which were already under military control.

The War Department also wanted to use the Jornada Experimental Range, which required an agreement with the Department of Agriculture and the White Sands National Monument. Department of the Interior Special Use Permit Number 30, dated April 30, 1945, covered the use of the White Sands National Monument. This permit allowed the Army to close the National Monument and all roads leading to it when necessary. These included U.S. Route 70, which crossed the southern end of the WSPG. The launch area was south of the highway; the impact area to its north. (In 1948 New Mexico state officials declared the road between Alamogordo and Las Cruces to be a military highway and agreed to let the Army close the road during missile firings. To

this day, Highway 70 is still subject to hour-long closures due to testing. Travelers are advised to call (575) 678-1178 in Las Cruces or (575) 443-7199 in Alamogordo before driving across the range to check for roadblocks.)

Army officials signed fifty-two co-use and full-use agreements with ranchers who already occupied portions of the land. These agreements allowed the ranchers to continue using their land, but upon written notice of an upcoming test, they had to vacate for the prescribed period of time. The ranchers received rental payments for the use of their land.

The original layout for the camp had been prepared in Washington in April and May 1945. Major Richard C. Crook of the Army Corps of Engineers submitted a memorandum to the District Engineer in Albuquerque on 12 June 12 outlining the buildings and roads that would be needed. The basic layout of the camp was in four quadrants established by the intersection of two main roads: one area to be for enlisted living quarters; the second for administrative functions and officer quarters; the third for maintenance, warehouse, and housekeeping facilities; and the fourth for technical requirements. With such a layout, the outer boundaries of any of the four quadrants could be expanded without seriously affecting the other elements. Construction began on 25 June.

Headquarters for the new testing center was near the foothills of the Organ Mountains, along the western edge of the Tularosa

Lieutenant Colonel Harold R. Turner, first Commanding Officer of the White Sands Proving Ground.

Basin and about 6.5 miles west of the Dona Aña – Otero County line. At the time, the Ordnance Branch did not know if this would be a permanent installation, so a number of Civilian Conservation Corps (CCC) structures at Sandia Base, near Albuquerque, were deemed adequate for movement to WSPG.

On July 13, 1945, Armed Forces Circular Number 268 established Headquarters of White Sands Proving Ground at Fort Bliss, effective 9 July. At the same time, the 9393rd Technical Services Unit was created to support activities at WSPG. The post had an initial complement of 136 officers and enlisted personnel. LTC Harold R. Turner was appointed the first commanding officer. Colonel Turner was born on June 30, 1898, at Waltham, Massachusetts. He graduated from Waltham High School in 1915 and Wentworth Institute at Boston in 1918. Later that same year he was commissioned a Second Lieutenant in the Air Reserve.

Turner was an engineering instructor at Wentworth from the time of his graduation until June 1922, when he accepted a position as a commercial engineer with the General Electric Company at Pittsfield, MA. In 1929, Turner transferred to the Ordnance Reserve. He remained at General Electric until February 1941. In April of that year he reported for active duty with the

Ordnance Department. He graduated from the Army Industrial College in Washington, D.C., three months later and was assigned as an Industrial Engineering Officer in the Office of the Chief of Ordnance (OCO).

In July 1942, Turner became chief of the Engineering Sub-Office at Cincinnati, Ohio; in February 1944, he returned to the Office of the Chief of Ordnance as an Industrial Engineering Officer with the Technical Division at Pinto, Maryland. He was again transferred in July 1944 to command the Research and Development Sub-Office (Rocket) of the OCO at Dover Air Force Base, Delaware.

On his first day at WSPG, LTC Turner felt "like Moses," because he walked through the empty, barren desert, placing sticks in the ground where he wanted facilities built. Water was a major concern, as would be expected for an installation in the New Mexico desert, so Turner decided the first order of business was well drilling. There was one well already there which had once provided water for cattle and ranch hands, but this would not provide enough for a new military base. Six wells were drilled to the south and east of the headquarters area. Construction engineers also found several abandoned mines in the Organ Mountains that had filled with water. Although this water was not potable, it sufficed for construction purposes during the early months of the base. Contractors used tanker trucks to move water from the mines to the construction sites.

The Army built a launch area six and a half miles south of the headquarters area. Construction at the firing facilities began on July 10, 1945. The area comprised a concrete pad where launch stands could be placed and a concrete "blockhouse." Assisted by the group from CALTECH, Dr. Del Sasso and LTC Turner designed the blockhouse. Construction of the blockhouse began on July 10, 1945, and was completed in September at a cost of $36,000.

The blockhouse was a squat building with a pyramid-shaped roof. Built of reinforced concrete, it had ten-foot thick walls. The roof was 27 feet thick at its apex, which made it (hopefully) able to withstand the impact of a V-2 falling from an altitude of 100 miles. The floor was eight feet thick, just in case an errant missile burrowed into the ground. The structure contained a 937-square foot control room that housed firing controls, along with monitoring and communications equipment for the test personnel. It had three viewing ports made of blast proof safety glass, a blast proof door, and a roof wash-down system to decontaminate the building in the event of a rocket explosion. The room was mechanically air conditioned and electrically heated. Three-inch diameter conduits provided wiring access to the launch pads.

The launch area was an L-shaped concrete apron where missiles could be erected. A 102-foot tall launch tower for the *WAC Corporal* was set up about 600 feet north of the blockhouse. It comprised a 77-foot triangular structural steel tower resting on a 25-foot tall tripod with a 26-foot base. Inside this tower were three launching rails spaced 120 degrees apart. The rails had an effective length of 82 feet. Consolidated Steel Corporation of Maywood, California, built the tower and erected it at WSPG.

The CCC buildings and a hangar from Sandia went up quickly. To house troops, Dallas-type hutments, measuring 16 by 16 feet,

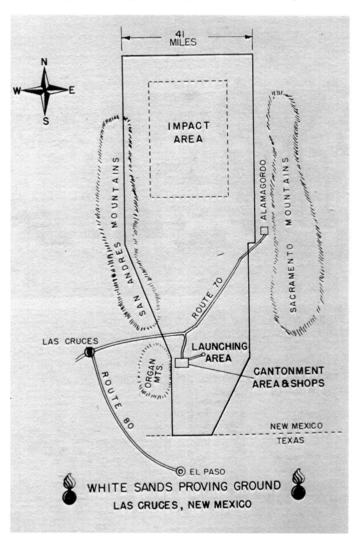

Layout of White Sands Proving Ground.

were built from plywood. By August 10, 1945, construction was far enough along that the first troops moved onto WSPG. Prior to this, personnel had been billeted at Fort Bliss. Battery C of the 69th Antiaircraft Artillery Battalion also moved from Fort Bliss to WSPG to support the emerging missile program.

The ORDCIT group fired the first rocket at WSPG at 10:00 AM on September 26, 1945. They launched a *Tiny Tim* rocket modified for use as a booster for the *WAC Corporal*. Later the same day, the group launched a second *Tiny Tim*. During the war, the Navy developed the *Tiny Tim* as an air to ground rocket. For use as a booster for *WAC Corporal*, a conical blast deflector replaced the warhead. Three rods attached to the blast deflector fit into recesses in the base of the *WAC Corporal*. After modification for use with the *WAC Corporal*, this rocket produced a thrust of 50,000 pounds for 0.6 second. (In its original form, the *Tiny Tim* produced a thrust of 30,000 pounds for 1 second.) This gave the rocket an initial acceleration of 37.3 gs and a velocity of 400 feet per second when it emerged from the launch tower. By the time the booster burned out, the rocket was traveling at about 720 feet per second. Overall length of the booster was 97 1/8 inches.

The second stage of the *WAC Corporal* consumed an oxidizer of red fuming nitric acid (RFNA) and a mixture of 80% aniline and 20% furfuryl alcohol as its fuel. The approximate weight ratio of oxidizer to fuel was 2.65:1. Compressed air forced the propellants into the combustion chamber to produce a thrust of 1,500 pounds for 47 seconds. An inertia valve in the compressed air circuit responded to the acceleration of the booster and started propellant flow to the combustion chamber. By the time the booster motor burned out, the sustainer motor was firing at its full thrust of 1,500 pounds. Because there was no hard connection between the *Tiny Tim* and *WAC Corporal* (an arrangement reminiscent of the earlier Private A and Private F rockets), the booster simply fell away after it consumed its ballistite propellant. Aerojet built the liquid-fuel engine for the *WAC Corporal*. The Douglas Aircraft Corporation assembled the missiles for the JPL.

There was a possibility that future *WAC Corporal*s carrying meteorological instruments might be launched near populated areas. Therefore, it was equipped with a recovery parachute. Deploying the parachute at the apex of the flight and bringing the rocket back presented a considerable challenge. For example, at that time nobody knew how hard the parachute's opening shock would be or how it would behave as it descended. The mechanism also proved more complicated than desired. Three explosive pins secured the nose section to the top of the rocket body. These pins were inserted through the skirt of the nose into lugs welded on the top of the propellant tank. The nose skirt was seated on a rubber ring seal that maintained atmospheric pressure inside the nose cone. Once the explosive pins were electrically detonated, internal pressure would force the nose and body apart. The parachute ripcord was attached to the nose. Despite its complexity, the nose release system worked fine during testing on the ground. Space was available in the nose cone for the Signal Corps to launch radiosonde units on several rockets. These units had their own parachutes, which were released at the same time the main parachute deployed.

WAC Corporal testing at WSPG comprised four phases. Phase 1 was the pair of launches on 26 September, and tested the *Tiny Tim* booster by itself. The second phase consisted of two *Tiny Tim* launches that boosted loads to simulate the weight of the *WAC Corporal*. These launches, designated Rounds 1 and 2, took place on 27 and 28 September. The first one lofted a 250-pound lead weight; the second consisted of the *Tiny Tim* and a cement-filled pipe that weighed the same as a fueled *WAC Corporal*. This rocket reached an altitude of 8,000 feet. On 1 October, the JPL group began testing the rocket with one-quarter of the fuel load in the second stage. Two of these rockets were launched, both of which reached 28,000 feet. Even though the nose release system did not work on either rocket, the tests were deemed successful, so the next flight would carry a full fuel load. The first fully fueled *WAC Corporal* (Round 5) lifted off on 11 October and reached 235,000 feet (43.5 miles.) At the time, this was a record for an American rocket.

ORDCIT continued the pace of launches with another rocket the next day. Radar tracking failed on Round 5, so Round 6 carried a "radar window," or beacon, in its nose. It also reached 235,000 feet. Despite the presence of the "window," there was no radar track on this rocket. Four days later Round 7 flew. At an altitude of 90,000 feet, the nose released prematurely and the rocket began spinning. Round 8 also suffered a premature nose release, but this time the rocket reached 235,000 feet. Radar tracking continued

Dr. Frank Malina with the *WAC Corporal*.

Loading a WAC Corporal in the launch tower at WSPG. *Source: U.S. Army photograph.*

to be a problem throughout the early flights, so Round 8 carried seven pounds of lamp black in its nose instead of the radiosonde equipment. The lamp black would, it was hoped, produce a cloud at the zenith of the flight. Like its predecessors, it reached an altitude of 235,000 feet; unlike its two most recent predecessors, the nose cone did not separate. As an additional enhancement for tracking, potassium nitrate had been added to the oxidizer to increase the density of the rocket's smoke trail. Rounds 9 and 10 were both fired on 25 October. Round 9 developed a fuel leak during charging, so it was launched with only a partial load of compressed air. Due to its low performance no data was obtained.

Since Round 10 was to be a night launch, a T-90 flare of 100,000 candlepower replaced the radiosonde equipment. The flare was supposed to be released at maximum altitude, but the nose failed to separate. This concluded the initial series of *WAC Corporal* flights. One *WAC Corporal* remained, but it would not be launched until more than a year later.

Meanwhile, General Electric personnel were busy inventorying and studying V-2 components. In August 1945, the missile components shipped from Mittelwerk arrived at White Sands. Originally, officials with the Santa Fe railroad told Colonel Turner to prepare to receive and unload ten train cars per day at Las Cruces. This was not the case, as all 300 arrived at once. To give some idea of the magnitude of the effort, every railroad siding from El Paso, TX, to Belen, NM, a distance of 210 miles, was full of cars bearing rocket hardware. Further complicating matters, the Army did not want to pay any additional fees for railroad cars that sat idle while waiting unloading. Turner's instructions were to unload the equipment and get it to WSPG as quickly as possible. Moving the materiel required hiring every flatbed truck in Doña Ana County. The task was completed in 20 days. The Army erected a large building along 3rd Street (Building T-1780) for the assembly and checkout of the V-2s. This was later joined by Building T-1740 for the assembly of other missiles.

General Electric Company employee L. B. Carter inspecting V-2 combustion chambers after their arrival at WSPG.

When the GE engineers inventoried the rocket components, they discovered a mixed lot of parts, some more useful than others. After the SS guards left Mittelwerk there was some vandalism and theft by German civilians and former slave laborers. Some critical parts just weren't present or were in poor condition. For example, only 50 control gyroscopes had been shipped from Mittelwerk, most of which were in poor condition. Each rocket required two gyroscopes. Seventy electrical distribution panels had been shipped, but most of them were without wiring and had to be overhauled by GE personnel. Project Hermes would be plagued by such parts shortages, particularly towards the end of the effort. In cases like the gyroscopes, American-made replacements were needed. Only two missiles could be assembled using originally matched parts from the factory. The others were built from the variety of subassemblies and individual components that had been gathered or manufactured in the United States.

The American Army offered contracts to just over 100 German missile scientists to work in the United States. Under the leadership of Wernher von Braun, they were first housed at Fort Strong, near Boston, Massachusetts. In October 1945, they began arriving at Fort Bliss to assist with V-2 launchings and answer questions by Army and General Electric personnel. At first, the exchange of information was hampered by language difficulties, but was overcome as the Germans learned English. While at Fort Bliss, the German engineers worked on a variety of projects. By March 1946, 39 members of the group were working at WSPG in support of the V-2 program. After that, the number decreased over the next year, by which time all the Germans working on the V-2 at WSPG had been replaced by General Electric and U.S. Army personnel.

Scientists were eager to use rockets to loft instruments that would probe the upper atmosphere and near space environment. They had their chance with the V-2. If launched straight up, the V-2 could reach an altitude of more than 100 miles. Hermes V-2 flights did not carry explosives. Because the V-2s were designed to carry one-ton warheads, they needed ballast to compensate for the missing explosives to remain stable. The Army reasoned if the rockets had to carry weight in their nose cones, why not let that weight be scientific instruments?

In January 1946, the Army Ordnance Department held a conference for military and university personnel to discuss the possibility of placing instruments on V-2s. Attendees included representatives of the Rocket Sonde Research Section of the Naval Research Laboratory (NRL) and the Applied Physics Laboratory (APL) of Johns Hopkins University. Realizing the potential benefits of inter-service cooperation, Lieutenant Colonel J. G. Bain of the Ordnance Department extended a special invitation to the Rocket Sonde Research Section to participate in the upper atmosphere research program.

The NRL decided, in late 1945, to develop a liquid fuel research rocket to probe the upper atmosphere, and created the Rocket Sonde Research Section to coordinate the effort. At first it looked as though the Navy would have to develop its own rocket to accomplish its research goals. When the Army extended the offer to allow scientific payloads aboard the V-2s, NRL scientists jumped at the opportunity. (The Navy took full advantage of the offer to participate in the V-2 flights while developing their own rocket.) At the conference, it was explained that the Army's V-2 program had three goals: to gain experience handling and launching large liquid fuel rockets; to obtain ballistic data; and to make measurements of the upper atmosphere. Initially, the Army planned to fire 25 missiles over a time as short as five months. (With the number of rockets available, this was later extended several times.)

The participants in the meeting created the "V-2 Upper Atmosphere Research Panel." (This became the "Upper Atmosphere Research Panel" when other rockets became available.) They mapped out a program of research that included research in:

radio frequency propagation and absorption in the ionosphere;
ionic density;
composition of the upper atmosphere;
structure of the upper atmosphere including pressure and temperature;
cosmic radiation studies;
ultraviolet radiation absorption;
meteorology;
propagation of sound and shock waves;
spectroscopic studies; and
biological research.

The V-2 assembly building at WSPG.

Each agency reported on the work it was doing or intended to do, which helped eliminate duplication of effort. The panel determined which agency would use each rocket. By cooperating, each participating agency could benefit from the experience of the others.

Besides the launch area in the desert, the Army built a test stand into the side of the Organ Mountains where a complete V-2 could be erected and fired without leaving the ground. As one of their first tasks at WSPG, German engineers directed construction of this test stand. From a functional perspective, it closely resembled one they had at Peenemünde. Instrumentation allowed measurement of all aspects of the missile propulsion system, including thrust, propellant consumption rates, and the pressures in the combustion chamber and propellant lines. The test stand structure was essentially a heavy concrete shaft that was open at the bottom on the side away from the mountain. It could accommodate rockets with thrusts of up to 100,000 pounds.

On March 3, 1946, the first American assembled V-2 was bolted to the recently completed static test stand and fired for 57 seconds. The force and heat of the blast ripped loose the heavy steel plates that lined the duct of the test stand. Caught in the rocket's exhaust, these plates were blown over the surrounding area. The hot exhaust gases ignited brush and grass up to 250 yards away from the stand, but since this was an unoccupied portion of the desert, no great damage was done. Major General Barnes was present at WSPG to witness this first test of a V-2 in America.

In March 1946, the Ballistic Research Laboratory of the Aberdeen Proving Ground in Maryland established a permanent presence at WSPG. The White Sands Annex – Ballistic Research Laboratory (WSA – BRL) provided instrumentation to collect trajectory and flight performance data; telemetry systems for measuring missile performance; and the creation and distribution

WSPG Test Stand 1. Built into the side of the Organ Mountains, the test stand could accommodate rockets with thrusts of up to 100,000 pounds. *Source: U.S. Army photograph.*

Loading WSPG V-2 #1 on the German *Meilerwagen* after assembly in the main post area. *Source: U.S. Army photograph courtesy of Bill Beggs.*

WSPG V-2 #1 on its way to the test stand. *Source: U.S. Army photograph courtesy of Bill Beggs.*

Placing the V-2 on the test stand. *Source: U.S. Army photograph courtesy of Bill Beggs.*

Final placement of WSPG V-2 #1 on Test Stand 1. *Source: U.S. Army photograph.*

of time signals that provided a reference for recording performance data. Some of the instrumentation for tracking missiles at WSPG came from the Army Signal Corps.

With the activation of WSPG, the Ordnance Department requested support from the Signal Corps Engineering Laboratories (SCEL) at Fort Monmouth, New Jersey, to provide communications, tracking, and other electronic facilities at the range. As a result of this request, a detail of ten men and two SCR-584 radar units arrived at WSPG on April 2, 1946. Initially, the detail was on temporary duty at WSPG. They established a tracking site, dubbed "A Station," a mile south of the launch area. Final preparations were underway for the first V-2 launch at WSPG.

Inventory of V-2 Hardware
Received at White Sands Proving Ground

Component: Warhead

    Quantity: Approximately 50

    Condition: Good

    Comments: Very few German warhead sections were used because they weren't suitable for housing scientific instruments. The Naval Gun Factory in Washington, D.C., built replacement warhead sections that were more suitable for carrying scientific instruments.

Component: Control Section

    Quantity: Approximately 115

    Condition: Varied from good to very poor

    Comments: Considerable repair needed to secure enough to complete flight program. Plywood bulkheads, which provided most of the structural strength of these sections, had to be replaced.

Component: Mid Section

    Quantity: Approximately 127 sets

    Condition: Varied from good to poor

    Comments: Some repair work needed to secure enough to complete flight program.

Component: Thrust Frame

    Quantity: Approximately 100

    Condition: Generally good

    Comments: There were enough frames in serviceable condition to complete the flight program. Very few repairs were needed on the frames that were used.

Component: Tail Section

    Quantity: Approximately 90 in usable condition

    Condition: Good to poor

    Comments: Considerable repair work needed on many; to complete the flight program, Douglas Aircraft built eight units.

Component: Propellant Tanks

    Quantity: Approximately 180 of each tank

    Condition: Generally good

    Comments: Some welding repairs were needed, particularly around support attachments. Overall, the level of workmanship was excellent, with no deterioration noted after seven years.

Component: Turbine and Pumps

    Quantity: Approximately 200

    Condition: Generally excellent

WSPG V-2 #1 on Test Stand 1 prior to the first static test of a German rocket at WSPG. Portions of the missile skin have been removed so the missile's internal mechanisms can be observed. *Source: U.S. Army photograph.*

    Comments: Only minor repairs needed, although turbine blades needed extensive cleaning after calibration runs.

Component: Combustion Chamber

    Quantity: Approximately 215

    Condition: Varied from good to unusable

    Comments: Inventory included obsolete types, unfinished units, and factory rejects. Overall, there was very little deterioration despite the units having been stored outdoors for several years. Considerable effort was required to remove scale and accumulated dirt from inside chambers.

Component: Hydrogen Peroxide Tanks

    Quantity: Approximately 200

    Condition: Excellent

    Comments: These tanks were made from steel, which is not suitable for use with hydrogen peroxide. Therefore, the tanks had to be lined with a special protective coating during manufacture. The Germans suspected this coating would deteriorate with age, but this never happened at White Sands.

Component: Permanganate Tanks

    Quantity: Approximately 200

    Condition: Excellent

The Army blockhouse. *Source: U.S. Army photograph.*

Comments: All the tanks were in excellent condition and required very little cleaning for use.
Component: Heat Exchanger
 Quantity: Approximately 100
 Condition: Good to poor
 Comments: Some units required considerable repair, but none malfunctioned during any of the flights.
Component: Air Bottles
 Quantity: Approximately 115 sets
 Condition: Generally good, but rusted inside. Accompanying manifolds were frequently in poor condition, and some had to be manufactured in the United States to complete flight program.
 Comments: Rust was removed from inside the bottles by rotating them while they were partially filled with abrasive fragments. There were no problems with the air bottles during the flight program.
Component: Steam Generator
 Quantity: Approximately 200
 Condition: Excellent
 Comments: Very little repair was needed and all performed well during the flights.
Component: Oxygen Valves
 Quantity: Approximately 200
 Condition: Varied from good to unusable
 Comments: After the best valves had been used, considerable effort was needed to provide acceptable units. There was excessive leakage past the rubber seal of this valve, and there were a few

instances where these valves were suspected of contributing to propulsion system failures. Various corrective methods were tried, but none were particularly successful.
Component: Alcohol Main Valves
 Quantity: Approximately 200
 Condition: Varied from fair to poor
 Comments: Many were rejected. Among those accepted for flight use, there were no known problems caused by these valves.
Component: Alcohol Preliminary Valves
 Quantity: Approximately 190
 Condition: Generally good
 Comments: Many required minor repairs, but there were no known failures in flight.
Component: Oxygen Vent Valve
 Quantity: Approximately 80
 Condition: Generally fair
 Comments: Some adjustments and minor repairs were needed. It was necessary to manufacture additional units in the United States to complete Project Hermes.
Component: Gyroscopes
 Quantity: Approximately 50
 Condition: Generally good
 Comments: Each missile required two gyroscopes. It was necessary to have 140 units built in the United States, which were essentially copies of the German units with minor improvements and changes to bring them to American standards.
Component: Mix Computer (Auto-pilot Servo Amplifier)
 Quantity: Approximately 70
 Condition: Varied from fair to unusable
 Comments: German units required test, adjustment, and replacement of defective components. The tubes in particular were prone to failure during vibration tests. It proved necessary to have 80 computers built in the United States. These were copies of the German units; the only design change was a reduction in maximum voltage in the American computers.
Component: Time Switches
 Quantity: Approximately 350
 Condition: Good
 Comments: There were two types of switches. Overall, they were in good condition and only needed minor repair, mostly of corroded solder joints.
Component: Main Distributors (Missile Relay and Junction Box)
 Quantity: Approximately 70
 Condition: Good to unusable
 Comments: Some units were unwired, and all required modification. Workmanship was good, but the Germans originally used small, single-strand wire that was subject to breakage. Approximately 30 units had to be manufactured in the United States. The most significant difference between the originals and the American copies was the use of more durable stranded wire.
Component: Electrical Cables
 Quantity: An adequate supply for 100 missiles
 Condition: Fair
 Comments: Connectors and workmanship was good, but the original cable sets used a small-gauge, single strand wire that was

prone to breakage. In 1947, the original cables were scrapped and replaced with stranded wire.

Component: Jet Vanes

    Quantity: An adequate supply for 100 missiles

    Condition: Varied from good to unusable

    Comments: Three different types were received. Many were rejected during tests, but vane failure was suspected in only two flights.

Component: Inverters

    Quantity: Approximately 600

    Condition: Good

    Comments: Each rocket required at least two inverters. With the quantities available, very little repair work was needed. Occasionally an inverter had to be replaced when a missile was on the launch pad, but these problems were due to dust and sand.

Component: Regulators for Inverters

    Quantity: Approximately 600

    Condition: Good

    Comments: Each inverter required one regulator. Very little repair was necessary and the Americans judged the design to be excellent.

Component: Servos

    Quantity: Approximately 500

    Condition: Varied from fair to unusable

    Comments: After the best units had been used, it was necessary to install new motors and completely overhaul the remaining servos. Most of the servos received showed signs of usage. Cylinders, gear pumps, and pistons showed wear and leakage. An aircraft-type motor of American manufacture was modified to replace the German motors and worked well with the overhauled units.

4

V-2s in the Desert

lace with missile #2 ... e was a multi-step ... nwheel-like igniter ... unted horizontally ... er. The propellant ... hol began flowing ... were gravity-fed ... did not generate ... liminary stage."

The propulsion engineer observed the rocket from inside the blockhouse to see that the engine was burning evenly. After seeing that everything was functioning normally, he pushed the "main stage" switch on the firing panel. This brought the turbopumps up to full speed and increased the thrust level to 56,000 pounds. With the motor producing its full thrust, the rocket lifted off.

V-2 #2 seemed fine during the preliminary stage, so the main stage switch was pushed. The rocket started flying erratically almost immediately after take off, lost a fin, and began to arc over.

Liftoff of V-2 #2 on April 16, 1946. This was the first V-2 flight in the United States. *Source: U.S. Army photograph courtesy of Bill Beggs.*

V-2 #2 on the launch stand. The trailer in the foreground was used to load hydrogen peroxide in the missile. German engineers assisting with the flight probably affixed the logo visible between the fins; it was common practice at Peenemünde to place such emblems on test missiles. *Source: U.S. Army photograph.*

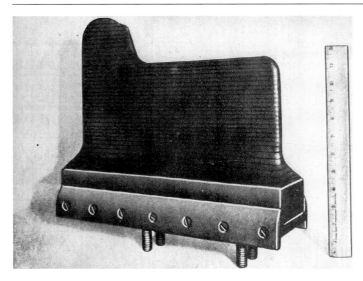

Situated in the exhaust jet below the motor nozzle, 4 graphite vanes like this helped steer the V-2 during powered flight. On WSG V-2 #2 one of the vanes failed, which led to the crash of the missile. *Source: Summary Report on V-2 Control and Stability.*

Aerial view of the Army launch area, about 600 feet north of the blockhouse. This is one of the first V-2s fired at WSPG, as evidenced by the use of German field equipment. All the WSPG-launched V-2s used the *Meilerwagen* for transport from the assembly building to the launch pad. The trailer closest to the missile contained liquid oxygen; the tank in the bed of the truck located slightly right of center transported alcohol. A German-made extendable ladder is being used to reach the control compartment. The *WAC Corporal* launch tower is visible on the right. *Source: U.S. Army photograph.*

V-2 #3 in a vertical position. *Source: U.S. Army photograph courtesy of Bill Beggs.*

V-2 #3 on the *Meilerwagen*, being erected into place on the launch pad. The *Meilerwagen* was a combination transporter/erector/servicing tower. Rockets rode in the lift frame, which elevated to a vertical position at the pad. Once the missiles were on the launcher, the lift frame became the servicing gantry. *Source: U.S. Army photograph courtesy of Bill Beggs.*

Base of V-2 #3. Once the missile was fueled and ready for flight, the *Meilerwagen* lift frame was lowered and the trailer taken away. *Source: U.S. Army photograph courtesy of Bill Beggs.*

The engine was shut off by radio command after only 19 seconds of powered flight and the missile, which still carried most of its propellants, crashed a short distance from the launch pad. Careful analysis of the photographic records revealed one of the graphite jet vanes broke off soon after ignition. With the steering vane gone, the rudder on the tip of the fin tried to compensate. This, in turn, placed unusually large loads on the fin and caused it to fail. One theory as to why the graphite vane broke was that a piece of the igniter hit it when the engine started. Another plausible explanation was there had been a flaw in the vane material. As a result of this failure, the graphite vanes on subsequent rockets were inspected using X-ray photographs. As an additional safeguard, cardboard covers that would burn away once the engine ignited were placed over the vanes to protect them from pre-launch damage.

Three weeks after the unsuccessful flight of the second White Sands V-2, missile #3 flew successfully. The onboard integrating accelerometer shut down the engine after 59 seconds. Missile #3 then coasted to an altitude of 70 miles. It impacted the desert and left a large crater about 31 miles from the launch area. Representatives from the press were invited to witness this flight.

Optical tracking was critical to assessing the performance of the rockets launched at WSPG. Initial results were poor, so in 1946 the Aberdeen Proving Ground (APG) invited Dr. Clyde W.

Tombaugh to evaluate the potential of a missile tracking telescope which had been adapted to a WWII M-45 machine gun mount. The tracking telescope system was built at the Ballistic Research Laboratory of the U.S. Army Ordnance Corps, Aberdeen, Maryland, to support the rocket testing program at WSPG. Tombaugh is best remembered for his discovery of Pluto in 1930.

Tombaugh accepted the challenge and soon began development of a family of long-range tracking telescopes that could observe missiles throughout their flights. By careful analysis of the photographic record, rocket designers could determine how a particular missile performed. Under Tombaugh's guidance, successful results with the telescope revealed previously unknown details of the way V-2s behaved in flight. Dr. Tombaugh eventually established a system of optical tracking stations on the range.

By the time of the first V-2 flights at WSPG, the United States' War Department was conducting a major review of the country's post-war military structure. The War Department Equipment Board conducted a study of how America might best organize its armed forces for the post-war world. This Board is frequently referred to as the Stilwell Board after its chairman, General Joseph Stilwell. In its report, the Stilwell Board made sixteen recommendations, chief among them that the "development of more potent or improved atomic weapons and suitable carriers thereof and the development

In the early 1950s engineers used instruments like this, called the Intercept Ground Optical Recorder (or IGOR), to track missiles at WSPG. This instrument was built on top of a Navy 5-inch gun Mark 19 mount. Optical tracking was important because it could provide valuable data about missile behavior. *Source: U.S. Army photograph.*

of defensive measures against atomic weapons be accorded priority over all other National Defense projects." At that time, "suitable carriers" meant aircraft, because existing missiles (i.e., the V-2) were not powerful enough.

While the Stilwell Board favored a strong nuclear-capable air arm as the best defense against attack, it also recommended that the Army be transformed into a highly mobile combined arms force. Such a transformation required the development of new weapons, so the Board suggested the adoption of a procedure where scientific research would be accorded a major role in the postwar defense structure. The War Department Chief of Staff approved the Stilwell Board report as a "policy document" on 29 May 1946.

World War II ended after the United States dropped atomic bombs on the Japanese cities of Hiroshima and Nagasaki. Military strategists concluded the air-delivered atomic bomb represented the ultimate weapon, and that the United States could maintain peace through the threat of its use. Intelligence specialists predicted the Soviets would not have an atomic bomb until 1952. Operating on these assumptions, having such a weapon in its arsenal allowed the United States to drastically shrink its armed forces. The general feeling at the time was that all enemies had been defeated, so a large military structure wasn't needed. Presumably the threat of "massive retaliation" with atomic weapons would deter any potential aggressors. This fit nicely with President Truman's desire to return to a state of normalcy as soon as possible.

As recalled by Truman in his *Memoirs*, "No people in history have been known to disengage themselves so quickly from the ways of war." By the end of June 1946, the Army's strength had been reduced from more than 8.2 million service members when the war ended to less than 1.9 million. The other services experienced similar reductions in force as the country demobilized. Combat divisions were deactivated; ships were mothballed; and billions of dollars worth of aircraft and equipment languished at storage depots.

While the Stilwell Board's recommendations called for the transformation of the military supported by continued scientific research, the War Department had to accomplish this in an austere fiscal environment. Desiring to fuel postwar economic growth by keeping taxes low, President Truman imposed strict fiscal limitations on government agency spending, particularly the War Department.

The emerging Air Force became the premiere branch of the military as postwar national strategy evolved. Abandoning its traditional isolationist position, the United States sought collective security through the United Nations and cooperation with its Western European allies. American forces were "forward deployed" in both the Atlantic and Pacific. Augmented by well-organized Reserve and National Guard forces, the standing Army was greatly reduced. At the same time newer, more advanced weapon systems had to be developed. These conditions set the stage for work at WSPG for the next few years. Namely, the American military was expected to transform itself into a nuclear-capable force and conduct basic research in a variety of areas, including missiles, within a limited budget.

Following the launch of *WAC Corporal* Round 10, work began to improve the design. The first series of rockets became known as the *WAC Corporal A*, while the improved versions bore the designation *WAC Corporal B*. Overall, the new rockets were 4 inches longer to provide more room for instrumentation. Propellant weight was reduced by 40 pounds, and the gross weight was reduced by 100 pounds in an effort to obtain higher altitudes.

Improvements in the rocket motor shortened it from 73 to 61 inches. It also weighed less than 12 pounds, rather than the 50 pounds of the motors used on the *A*-model rockets. The biggest change, though, was in the arrangement of the propellant tanks. On the original series of rockets, the compressed air tank was located aft of the propellant tanks, and the fuselage comprised a single long tank partitioned into three compartments. For the *B*-series rockets, each tank was a separate assembly. The compressed air

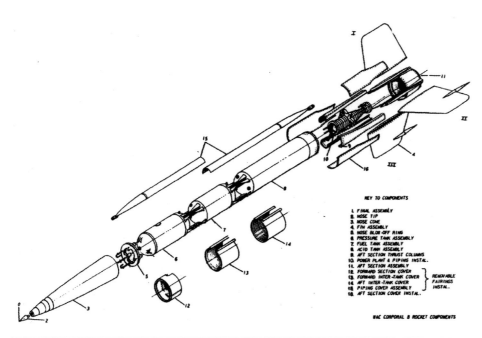

WAC Corporal B schematic. *Source: Development of the Corporal: The Embryo of the Army Missile Program.*

tank was placed above the propellant tanks. Using separate tanks offered several advantages to the *WAC Corporal B*. Separating the tanks meant dissimilar materials could be used, and removed the potential for explosions from intertank leakage. X4130 chrome molybdenum steel was used for the fuel and air tanks. The new oxidizer tank was made from 61ST aluminum.

The fins were extended by 2 inches each to improve stability, increasing the fin circle diameter by 4 inches. To save weight on the larger fins, skin thickness was reduced from 0.081-inch to 0.051-inch. While the aft section structure remained virtually unchanged from the *WAC Corporal A* rockets, the skin gauge was lightened. Static tests showed the fins and aft section skin still had sufficient strength to tolerate the stresses of flight.

The first *WAC Corporal B* was static tested at the Muroc Test Station. This was the first time a complete vehicle using burst-diaphragm starting valves was tested in the United States. The combustion chamber reached the 95% level in a half-second. Post firing examination of the motor showed it was in near perfect condition. After the prototype's testing, it was returned to the Douglas plant for refurbishment and conversion to flight configuration. This rocket was subsequently flown in December 1946.

On the *A*-series rockets, the nose release system never worked very well. For the *WAC Corporal B*, a ring of primacord inserted beneath a band of magnesium sheet which fastened the nose to the fuselage replaced the explosive pins. A blasting cap that could be fired by either an onboard timer (referred to as a "fuze" in the reports) or ground command detonated the primacord. An observer monitored the rocket trajectory on a plotting board linked to the radar tracking station. When he saw the rocket was at its peak, he sent the signal to detonate the blasting cap. The timer provided a backup in case of a radio failure.

The ORDCIT team returned to WSPG in early May 1946 to fire a series of nine *Tiny Tim* rockets. Eight of the *Tiny Tim* boosters carried *WAC Corporal B* nose cones to test the new parachute deployment system. Launched between 20 and 29 May, they reached an average altitude of 14,000 feet. While this was far short of the altitude reached during a full-scale *WAC Corporal* flight, it was sufficient to evaluate the new system. After these tests, further flights by the *WAC Corporal* were delayed for six months to develop better optical tracking techniques and to devise a fuse timer that would work in a vacuum.

Although the *WAC Corporal* had been designed as a meteorological rocket, its payload capacity was very limited. The V-2s could carry a much larger payload and became a workhorse for early space science research. From the beginning of the Hermes program, the captured German missiles carried scientific instruments. For example, WSPG V-2s #2 and #3 carried cosmic ray experiments in their warheads. The nose of each rocket contained a single Geiger tube shielded by an inch-thick lead cylinder. Power for the tube was supplied by an assembly of fifty-two 22.5 volt hearing aid batteries set in wax. In addition to the Geiger tube, each rocket carried a roll of 35-millimeter film in its nose. The film would record the passage of radiation particles through the warhead. A gravity switch, set to function when the rocket reached an acceleration of 4 gs, was used to turn on the flight data recorder.

Cosmic radiation was an area of great interest at the time. Comprised mainly of high-speed charged particles, nobody was sure how much of a health risk they posed to future space travelers or even high-altitude aircraft pilots. Balloon flights in the 1930s studied the structure and nature of cosmic radiation. In the years after the Manhattan Project, scientists were interested in the intensity and effects of cosmic radiation.

WSPG V-2 #2 did not reach a sufficient acceleration to turn on the data recorder, so even though the warhead was recovered, there was no data. In any event, it's unlikely that the instruments would have recorded any cosmic radiation because this rocket only reached an altitude of five miles. Rocket #3 achieved a high enough acceleration to turn on the data recorder, and its altitude (70 miles) should have been high enough to observe significant cosmic radiation activity. Unfortunately, the rocket created a large crater on impact and no trace of the warhead was ever found. This flight showed the need for further work in the area of payload recovery. Telemetry was in its infancy at the time, so the only way to reliably obtain data from the instruments was to record the information for recovery after the flight. Therefore, devising ways to recover the instruments became a priority.

Another problem area identified on these flights had to do with the warhead structure itself. The German warheads were generally unsuitable for scientific work, and instruments were inaccessible once placed inside the casings. The Naval Gun Factory in Washington, D.C., manufactured new nose sections designed specifically for scientific use. They were fabricated from 1/8 inch thick cast steel and contained a volume of 19.6 cubic feet. Three gasketed ports allowed access to the payload before launch. A pressure of one atmosphere was maintained inside the nose cone throughout the flight. The overall length of the new warhead sections was 7 feet, 6 inches, and they weighed 1,055 pounds.

Instruments carried aboard early V-2s at WSPG were often buried deep in the craters the missiles made when they impacted the desert. *Source: U.S. Army photograph.*

As evidenced by V-2 #3, even without explosive warheads, the missiles fired at White Sands made craters nearly as big as those fired during wartime. To enhance the probability that experiments would survive the landing, it was suggested that the missile be separated into two aerodynamically unstable sections before it reentered the atmosphere. In theory, the unstable pieces would tumble and fall slow enough for the instrument recordings to survive. Explosive charges were used to break the V-2s apart.

Although this sounds like a simple idea, its execution proved very challenging, and it took a number of flights before it was perfected. This was very much a trial and error process. Explosive separation was first attempted with V-2 #5. Lengths of primacord explosive were attached to the missile about a foot aft of the joint between the midsection and the tail. Launched on June 13, 1946, this missile reached an altitude of 73 miles. The explosives cut through the skin, but the plumbing that connected the propulsion unit to the midsection held the rocket together. It hit the desert more or less intact and none of the experiments survived.

Missile #6, which flew on 28 June, carried a one-pound block of TNT on each of the four main struts of the control compartment. Although the TNT detonated according to plan, the warhead did not separate. V-2 #9 (launched on 30 July) carried one-pound blocks of TNT and nitrostarch on each strut. The nose separated, and the body crashed in the desert without leaving a crater. No trace of the nose was ever found—apparently the explosives worked a little too well.

V-2 #12 contained two-pound blocks of TNT (without the nitrostarch) in the control compartment. This time the payload section separated and was recovered after reaching an altitude of 108 miles, but the problem of recovering the nose was still not solved. On the next missile, only the badly punctured base plate of the warhead was ever found. The explosives were cut in half on V-2 #23. The payload was recovered, but the base plate was badly bent.

Scientists began considering placing their instruments elsewhere in the missile. As discovered with V-2 #9, without the nose section, the body of the rocket tumbled as it fell, and it struck the ground at a speed of only a few hundred miles per hour. If properly packaged, instruments could survive such an impact. V-2 #12, launched on October 10, 1946, carried a solar spectrograph in a conical housing built into fin II. Two spectrographs had already been flown on previous rockets (in the nose sections) but had not been recovered. This time the instrument was recovered and returned measurements of the solar spectrum in the ultraviolet wavelengths that are normally absorbed by the atmosphere. Damage to the instrument was so slight that it was flown again.

As previously discussed, some critical components like gyroscopes and electrical junction panels were in short supply, so replacements had to be built in the United States for Hermes. American firms generally duplicated the German designs. In some cases the Americans improved the components. This was particularly true with the wiring harnesses. Early in the Hermes program, wiring throughout the missiles proved problematical. The Germans had used single strand copper wire that broke easily. By 1947 General Electric personnel replaced the original single strand copper wire with more durable stranded wire. Even if there were sufficient quantities on hand, missile components had to be thoroughly inspected, cleaned, and tested before use. This often required they be dismantled and rebuilt.

WAC Corporal flights resumed in December 1946. Over an 11-day period, JPL conducted 6 launches from WSPG. The first of this series, another test of the *Tiny Tim* booster with a *WAC Corporal B* nose section and a 10-foot glass fabric parachute, was on 2 December. The last *WAC Corporal A* blasted off the next day. Actually, this was a hybrid vehicle that comprised the *A* model airframe with the newer *WAC Corporal B* fins and nose section. This rocket, the 22nd *WAC Corporal* launch at WSPG (counting the booster tests), only reached 94,000 feet. The lightweight fins failed

By separating the nose section with explosives the body often tumbled, so it hit the desert at only a few hundred miles per hour. Onboard instruments generally survived such an impact. *Source: U.S. Army photograph.*

In 1947, the V-2 launch pad was moved to a site about 200 feet east of the blockhouse. A movable gantry crane was moved to the new pad area to provide work platforms for missiles up to 54 feet tall. This view shows, from left to right, the blockhouse at the left, a V-2 on the pad, the *WAC Corporal* launch tower in the background, and the movable crane. *Source: U.S. Army photograph.*

and the vehicle went unstable. The first *WAC Corporal B* launch occurred on 6 December. Again, there was a fin failure followed by instability, and Round #23 (also known as Missile #12) only climbed 92,000 feet, far short of what it was capable of. At least the parachute worked this time and the rocket was recovered. Missile numbers 13 and 14 (flights 24 and 25) both took place on 12 December.

The fins remained intact on Missile 13; the apex of its flight was 105,000 feet. Like its predecessor it was recovered, but suffered slight damage on landing. Flight 25, with Missile 14, peaked at 160,000 feet. Only the telemetry unit was recovered. The prototype vehicle that had been static tested at Muroc finally flew on 13 December. This was the most successful of the series—it reached 175,000 feet—but the parachute tangled and did not open, so the rocket was a total loss.

None of these flights lived up to expectations, yet none showed there was anything fundamentally wrong with the *WAC Corporal B* design. With the inventory of spare parts on hand and the recovered rockets, project personnel found they could assemble three more rockets for launch in February 1947. There was one complication to this plan; only two modified *Tiny Tim* boosters remained. The engineers at JPL decided to use the remaining *Tiny Tims* for the first two flights of the series, then switch to the Mk. I Mod I rocket motor. It was the closest motor in the inventory to the *Tiny Tim* in terms of performance, but it was slightly longer and heavier, which would reduce the altitude of the *WAC Corporal B*. On February 17, 1947, a Mk. I, Mod. I motor was fired with 680 pounds of ballast to provide burning time and acceleration data.

Because of the fin failures suffered on the December flight series, the skin thickness was increased from 0.051-inch back to 0.081-inch, which had been used on the original rockets. A tip casting was also incorporated in the fins as a further measure

to prevent the fins from warping and failing. None of the *WAC Corporal B* motors had delivered the expected power, so some modifications were made to the propellant injectors. Previously, the orifices in the injectors had been drilled. For the new rockets, the injectors were provided with screw-in orifice inserts that had rounded and polished ends. The new orifices prevented "cavitation" and resulted in a more efficient combustion. All three rockets were static tested at JPL, then shipped to Douglas Aircraft for refurbishment and flight preparation.

WAC Corporal flight #28 blasted off on 18 February. Again, the rocket did not live up to expectations and only reached 144,000 feet. Round #28 carried a 21-foot diameter silk ribbon parachute and was successfully recovered. This time the problem was traced to a malfunction in the air line disconnect coupling. Compressed air, which was needed to force the propellants from the tanks into the combustion chamber, had apparently leaked away, which reduced the performance of the engine. An additional check valve in the air-fill line aboard Rounds 29 and 30 corrected this problem.

Round 29, which was launched on 24 February, achieved the highest altitude of any *WAC Corporal B* (240,000 feet). Unfortunately, the parachute failed to open and the rocket crashed after an otherwise highly successful flight. Round 30, which used the Mk. I Mod. I booster, reached 206,000 feet and was successfully recovered on 3 March. The final *WAC Corporal B* launch—a re-launch of a recovered and refurbished rocket—occurred on 12 June. This time the rocket climbed to 198,000 feet. The parachute

In 1947, General Electric built a propulsion unit Calibration Stand behind the V-2 Assembly Building in the main post area. *Source: U.S. Army photograph.*

A V-2 propulsion unit undergoing calibration. This view shows the missile midsection with tanks, which were permanently affixed to the stand, and a propulsion unit undergoing testing. *Source: U.S. Army photograph.*

found German test results on enough turbopumps and combustion chambers to assemble 30 missiles. Complete test data was not available for the steam units, so these had to be tested at WSPG to determine the settings for their gas pressure regulators.

The first thirty missiles were assembled and adjustments made according to the German test data. The Americans soon discovered that assembling rockets using the data produced inconsistent results. For example, V-2s #15 and #17, launched on November 21 and December 17, 1946, respectively, both weighed virtually the same at liftoff. Yet, missile #15 achieved an altitude of 63 miles while #17 achieved 116 miles. In any event, the first 30 rockets, which had German calibration data, would be exhausted by the middle of 1947. The ideal way of testing the engines would be to static fire each one, but this was too expensive and time consuming, so the General Electric engineers settled on "cold" propellant tests. They decided the best way to calibrate the engines was to test the entire unit rather than using the German method of testing individual components. The German system worked adequately in a mass production situation, but for the relatively small number of missiles at WSPG eliminated any potential advantages of doing it this way. For the cold tests water was used to simulate liquid oxygen, but alcohol was still circulated through the fuel lines.

By restricting some of the orifices in the combustion chamber injectors, pressures inside the chamber could be simulated to provide accurate data on overall system performance. Using alcohol presented a fire hazard, plus it created objectionable fumes. They tried to recover the alcohol, but some always leaked and spilled on

deployed but broke loose. The rocket was never recovered. Battery D of the 1st Guided Missile Battalion provided the launch crew for this flight. This was the first American rocket launch by an all soldier crew.

Beginning in 1947, General Electric devoted a great deal of effort towards calibrating the V-2 propulsion units to achieve optimum output. To obtain optimum missile performance, it was necessary to ensure that the propellants were supplied to the combustion chamber in the proper quantities and proportions. Slight variations in component production could have large effects on the performance of the engines. The most common sources of variations were differences in pump characteristics and the pressure drop in the fuel as it circulated through the double-walled motor jacket.

At Mittelwerk, the Germans tested hydrogen peroxide steam units, turbopumps, and combustion chambers separately. Based on the turbopump and combustion chamber test results, they placed various size orifices in the main propellant lines to regulate propellant mixture ratio. The total flow rate to the combustion chamber was adjusted by varying the pressure of the gas provided to the steam unit. From the steam unit test data and the size of the orifices selected, a calculation determined the gas pressure needed to produce the desired flow rate and thrust. General Electric

Brigadier General Philip G. Blackmore, second Commanding Officer of White Sands Proving Ground. *Source: U.S. Army photograph.*

Operation Sandy V-2s being delivered to the USS Midway. Source: U.S. Navy photograph.

Liftoff of the Operation Sandy V-2 from the deck of the USS Midway. Source: U.S. Navy photograph.

the ground. This was particularly objectionable because GE set up the calibration stand in the main base area behind the V-2 assembly building. The first calibration test of a V-2 propulsion unit took place on May 23, 1947. For the next fourteen months, the engines were tested in this manner.

With the V-2 flights in full swing, Brigadier General Philip G. Blackmore arrived at WSPG on August 4, 1947, to become the next Range Commander. Blackmore was born on January 18, 1890, in Bristol, Virginia. He graduated from the Virginia Military Institute with a degree in electrical engineering and commissioned as a Second Lieutenant in the Coast Artillery Corps in 1911. Over the next five years he served at a variety of posts, including Fort Monroe, Virginia, Fort Hamilton, New York, and Fort Hancock, New York. In October 1916 he was transferred to Hawaii, where he served with coast artillery units at Fort Kamehameha and Fort DeRussey. By that time, he was a First Lieutenant.

On May 15, 1917, he was promoted to Captain, and a year later was elevated to Major (Temporary) and was reassigned to Fort Worden, Washington, with the coastal defenses of Puget Sound. The following year he transferred to the Ordnance Corps. Blackmore continued his military career in a variety of stateside assignments until February 1943, when he was assigned to be the Ordnance Officer for the newly created Sixth Army in Australia. By the time of his assignment to the Sixth Army he was a Colonel. In the three years following he was stationed at New Guinea, the Philippines, and Japan. While serving in the Far East, Blackmore was promoted to the rank of Brigadier General.

General Blackmore returned to the United States in February 1946 as the Ordnance Officer for the reactivated Sixth Army. From there, he was reassigned to WSPG and became its second commanding officer in August 1947. With General Blackmore's arrival, LTC Turner became the post Executive Officer. Turner departed WSPG in October 1947 for temporary duty at the Office of the Chief of Ordnance in Washington, D.C. In January 1948,

Turner was assigned to the Research and Development Division of the Office of the Chief of Ordnance. Three months later he was promoted to Colonel, Regular Army (Permanent).

Seven missiles were assigned to the Air Force's Cambridge Research Laboratory. One of the main objectives of the flights was to develop parachute recovery methods, so the Air Force sponsored flights were given the name "*Blossom*." Working under contract to the Cambridge Research Laboratory, the Franklin Institute Laboratories for Research and Development modified the missiles. The midsections were lengthened by one caliber (about 65 inches) and they carried larger warhead sections. These modifications increased the weight of the *Blossom* V-2s substantially. A typical Hermes V-2 weighed about 8,800 pounds without propellants. The

Operation Sandy V-2 in flight. The missile crashed a short distance from the aircraft carrier, but the test was considered a success. Source: U.S. Navy photograph.

lightest *Blossom* V-2 weighed 9,781 pounds; the heaviest 10,683 pounds. These missiles were modified so they would break apart in the air and have the nose sections return via parachute. Of the seven *Blossom* V-2s, four flew successfully.

The United States Navy also conducted two experiments with V-2s. The first, *Operation Sandy*, was a launch of a missile from a ship. Three V-2s were provided for *Sandy*. They were shipped from White Sands to Norfolk, Virginia, where they were loaded on the aircraft carrier *USS Midway*. The Army assembled the missiles and trained the Navy launch crew. Navy Commander P.G. Holt directed the launch team. On Saturday, September 6, 1947, one of the *Sandy* V-2s was launched from the deck of the *Midway* while it was several hundred miles off the East Coast of the United States. The launch itself was successful, but shortly after leaving the deck, the missile went out of control, caught fire, and exploded at an altitude of about 12,000 feet after a flight of six miles. Immediately after the launch, the *Midway* was able to launch its aircraft. Since the objective of *Sandy* was to see whether or not a large missile could be fueled and launched from a ship that was underway, and if the ship could resume normal operations immediately after launch, *Operation Sandy* was termed a success.

The second Navy experiment was one of the most spectacular American V-2 tests. Dubbed *Operation Pushover*, it was exactly what its name implied. A fully fueled V-2 was toppled over at White Sands to obtain data for estimating how much damage such a mishap would cause aboard a ship. During a second test, the motor was ignited and allowed to reach preliminary stage before the missile was tipped over. Both tests were sobering experiences to Navy personnel as to the amount of damage a large liquid-fuel rocket could cause to a ship.

Biological rocket flights began in the United States on July 9, 1946, when investigators from Harvard University provided packets of special strains of corn seeds that would (hopefully) show any signs of genetic mutations from cosmic radiation after being germinated. As described previously, the payload was not recovered. A second packet of seeds flew on V-2 #8, launched ten days later. This rocket exploded 28.5 seconds after lift off. There weren't any more of the special genetically controlled seeds left, but researchers figured after two successive failures, their chances

Operation Pushover V-2 on the pad. To assess the potential damage an accident with a liquid-fuel missile might cause on a ship, the pad was placed on a section of simulated deck. One of the results of this test was the decision to use only solid-fuel missiles on Navy ships, which ultimately led to the Polaris submarine-launched ballistic missile. *Source: U.S. Navy photograph.*

of recovery were slight anyway. A package of ordinary seeds was purchased at a store in Las Cruces and placed aboard V-2 #9. As luck would have it, the missile reached an altitude of 104 miles and the seeds, located in pouches tied to the structure inside the body, were recovered. There is no record as to what, if any, results were achieved from these seeds.

V-2 #17, launched on December 17, 1946, carried five Lucite cylinders containing fungus spores from the National Institutes of Health (NIH). Scientists hoped the spores would show if cosmic radiation caused genetic mutations or other abnormalities. The missile reached an altitude of 116 miles, the highest attained by any *Hermes* launch. Unfortunately, the experiment was not recovered.

Two months after the NIH experiment, *Blossom I* carried fruit flies, rye seeds, and cotton seeds in a cylinder which also contained a radar beacon, a device to measure parachute opening shock, and a camera. Launched on February 20, 1947, the rocket reached an altitude of 60 miles before it ejected the *Blossom* canister. The 14-foot diameter nylon ribbon parachute worked and the payload landed intact. No radiation induced mutations or other changes appeared in the test subjects or their offspring.

Fruit flies and plants seemed to show no ill effects from rocket flights, but what about primates? Would the accelerations and

Operation Pushover V-2. *Source: U.S. Navy photograph.*

vibrations encountered during a rocket flight be tolerable? What effects would weightlessness have? In April 1948, the Parachute Branch at Wright Field invited the Aero Medical Laboratory Acceleration Section to launch a monkey aboard *Blossom III*.

Dr. James P. Henry, who headed the Acceleration Section, supervised the experiment while Captain David G. Simons assisted him. Henry was already well known within the aviation community as the developer of the partial pressure suit for high-altitude flight. Simons, a 1946 graduate of Jefferson Medical College in Philadelphia, requested a research assignment when he entered the Air Force on August 17, 1947. First Lieutenant Simons was assigned to the Aero Medical Laboratory Acceleration Section. This assignment let him combine medicine with his other long-time interest, electronics. Promoted to Captain in 1948, Simons designed and built electronic devices for the laboratory centrifuge. One day, Dr. Henry asked Simons if he would like to help launch a monkey aboard one of the *Blossom* rockets. He estimated the monkey would be exposed to about two minutes of weightlessness. After Simons' enthusiastic and unqualified yes, Henry appointed him Project Officer for the experiment.

Blossom III had a special nose cone; one that had a fairing added that resembled the cockpit of the planned X-2 supersonic research airplane. The Air Force wanted to collect data on the aerodynamics of the shape and test the airplane's separation system for pilot escape. Because the X-2 would travel at three times the speed of sound, the pilot could not safely bail out or eject in an emergency. To provide a system of pilot escape, the X-2 had a detachable nose with a drogue chute. Once the aircraft nose slowed enough, the pilot was supposed to jump clear and land with a personal parachute. Bell Aircraft, builders of the X-2, provided a nose cone separation system for *Blossom III* that was like the one planned for the supersonic airplane.

Henry and Simons had only two months to design and build the capsule. They selected a nine-pound American-born Rhesus monkey for their passenger. Someone in the Parachute Branch nicknamed the monkey "*Albert*" and the name stuck. Because it was added to the flight so close to the launch, the capsule had to fit in space left over by other experiments. This resulted in an odd, irregular shape that was difficult to fabricate. The resulting capsule had numerous leaks when pressurized. Simons tried to patch the leaks by dabbing rubberized sealant over them.

Another problem was that the capsule wasn't as large as the doctors would have liked. Simons then discovered that when pressurized, the capsule bulged and wouldn't fit in the nose cone. To solve this problem, he had to weld reinforcing bands inside the capsule, which further reduced the interior volume. Simons had to scrape the sealant off the capsule before the welding. It proved impossible to remove every last bit of the rubber compound. What remained was reduced to a sticky, foul-smelling mess during the welding process. After the welding was finished, he once again tried to seal the leaks. At last, Simons managed to make the capsule more or less airtight. The only remaining problem was getting the monkey in the capsule. *Albert* had to be placed in a very awkward position, with his chin against his chest, to fit in the tiny capsule. The launch was set for June 11, 1948.

Above: *Blossom III* (V-2 #37) carried a monkey named Albert I in its nose. Note the fairing on the side of the nose cone that was added to simulate the canopy shape of the *Bell X-2* research airplane. *Source: U.S. Army photograph.* Right: Albert I capsule flown aboard *Blossom III*. *Source: U.S. Air Force photograph.*

The night before the flight, Simons anesthetized *Albert* with sodium phenobarbital and attached biosensors that would measure his pulse and respiration. As a further protective measure, Simons injected *Albert* with Luminal, a muscle relaxant, to help him endure a hard landing. The respiration sensor, which was a mechanical lever attached to *Albert*'s chest, stopped working after Simons sealed the capsule, but the heart sensor continued to work.

When Dr. Simons climbed the launch tower to load the capsule in the nose of the missile, he noticed someone had written "Alas, poor Yorick, I knew him well" across one side of the rocket. After Simons loaded the capsule in the missile, the heart sensor showed no activity. Either the sensor failed or *Albert* had suffocated in the cramped confines of the capsule. Simons and Henry surmised the latter was the more likely possibility. In any event, *Albert* would not have survived the 38.7-mile high flight, because the parachute tore away from the nose cone.

The next attempt to launch a monkey aboard a V-2 took place on June 14, 1949, on *Blossom IV-B*. With a year to prepare for *Albert II*, Henry and Simons built an improved capsule and instrumentation system. The new capsule was a 36- by 12-inch diameter cylinder and offered plenty of room for the passenger. The breathing sensor that had proven so balky on *Albert I* was completely revamped. *Albert II* wore a miniature oxygen mask. A heated wire inside the mask registered each breath the monkey took.

Henry and Simons also refined their test procedures. Two monkeys were selected for the flight, a primary and an alternate. For several weeks before the flight blood was drawn from both to provide a baseline from which to measure any effects of cosmic radiation. On the morning of the launch, the doctors sealed *Albert II* in his capsule and loaded it in the rocket by X-45 minutes. (The early White Sands launches used the term "X" to denote launch time.)

Albert II reached 83 miles. There was no telemetry; heart and respiration rates were registered on an internal recorder, so recovery of the payload was critical. Unfortunately, the parachute again failed. The nose section created a crater ten feet across and five feet deep. Some pieces were buried 12 feet, and only a few fragments could be identified. Fortunately for the scientists, those fragments included the precious pulse and breathing recordings. *Albert* survived the launch and weightless portions of the flight with no ill effects. During powered flight, *Albert*'s pulse rate slowed from 190 to 110 beats per minute and his respiration went from 90 to 60 breaths per minute. Twenty seconds after motor burnout, as the rocket coasted to its apogee, the heart rate returned to 190, but the respiration rate rose only to 65 breaths per minute.

After *Albert II*, Simons left the Aero Medical Laboratory to attend the School of Aviation Medicine at Randolph Air Force Base, Texas. He graduated from the Advanced Course in Aviation Medicine as a certified Flight Surgeon in 1950. His next assignment was at Yakota Air Force Base in Japan as a Flight Surgeon for the Far East Air Force. Dr. Henry continued flying biological payloads aboard V-2s. *Albert III*'s V-2 exploded in midair on September 16, 1949. Three months later, on 8 December, the parachute (again) failed when *Albert IV* flew. Results were the same as *Albert II*; the data recordings showed the monkey tolerated acceleration and weightlessness.

With only one *Blossom* V-2 remaining, Dr. Henry decided to try another line of research and placed a mouse aboard the missile, which flew during the summer of 1950. No attempt was made to measure the rodent's physiological response to rocket flight. Instead, a camera recorded the mouse's reaction to weightlessness.

(left to right) John Addison and Louis Padderson of the New Mexico School of Mines; Lieutenant Colonel Harold Turner, Commanding Officer of WSPG; and Dr. James Van Allen and Arthur Coyne of the Johns Hopkins University Applied Physics Laboratory. Padderson is explaining to Turner how modified M-7 rifle grenades will be fired from a V-2 to create artificial meteors. *Source: U.S. Army photograph.*

Lieutenant Colonel Harold Turner, Commanding Officer of White Sands Proving Ground, demonstrates how M-7 rifle grenades were placed aboard V-2 #17. *Source: U.S. Army photograph.*

The rocket reached 85 miles, but the parachute failed again. At least the film survived, because the camera was heavily armored. It showed the mouse retained "normal muscular coordination" throughout the weightless portion of the flight, and it "...no longer had a preference for any particular direction and was as much at ease when inverted as when upright relative to the control starting position."

One of the more unusual experiments to be carried aboard the V-2 flew in late 1946, when attempts were made to create artificial micrometeorites using rifle grenades fired from the missiles. Dr. James Van Allen from the Johns Hopkins University Applied Physics Laboratory calculated that the velocity of a jet from a shaped-charge rifle grenade was comparable to the lower range of meteor velocities. If an M-7 grenade was fired from a missile and detonated at a high enough altitude, then Van Allen theorized it might produce artificial meteors. Since the mass, velocity, and composition of the matter ejected by the detonation was known, data from this experiment would help scientists in their studies of natural meteors. The experiment would also yield data on the physical properties of the upper atmosphere. Two flights were planned for this experiment.

V-2 #12, launched on October 24, 1946, was the first in the meteorite experiment series. Black powder charges were substituted for the grenades in order to test the ejection system. It was expected the charges would, when ignited, produce puffs of smoke that would be visible from the ground. As a bonus, the puffs of smoke would provide a means of observing high altitude winds. The charges detonated as planned, at altitudes of 100,000, 160,000, and 200,000 feet, as the rocket climbed to an altitude of 102 miles, but did not produce the desired results. The black powder burned slower than expected and did not produce the discrete puffs the scientists had hoped for. Instead, the charges created smoke streamers that indicated there were high winds aloft, but could not be used to quantify the conclusions.

Modified M-7 grenades were placed on V-2 #17, which was launched at 10:12 PM MST on December 17, 1946. One observer on the ground reported seeing a streak of light from the rocket, but he was the only person who saw anything, and this was suspect. Post flight analysis indicated the ejection mechanism probably failed; subsequent tests revealed the jet from an M-7 grenade was too weak for this application anyway.

The V-2 became the booster for the world's first two-stage liquid fuel rocket. In June 1946 (then) Colonel Holgar N. Toftoy, Chief of the Research and Development Division, Office of the Chief of Ordnance, suggested using a V-2 to boost a *WAC Corporal*. This would provide a two-stage rocket capable of reaching extreme altitudes and would greatly increase the possibilities of upper atmosphere research. This project, which was dubbed *Bumper*, was inaugurated to investigate launching techniques for a two-stage missile and separation of the two stages at high velocity to conduct limited investigation of high-speed high-altitude phenomena, and to attain velocities and altitudes higher than ever reached.

JPL was assigned responsibility for the theoretical studies of the feasibility of *Bumper* and the performance that might be expected from such a missile. Simultaneous with the work at JPL,

the German engineers at Fort Bliss also conducted a preliminary study of the vehicle. Wernher von Braun and Ludwig Roth led the German study, which considered stability, performance, and terminal trajectory of the combination. Even before these studies were finished, the Army Ordnance Department authorized *Bumper*.

Overall responsibility for these missiles was given to the General Electric Company, and *Bumper* was added to the *Hermes* Project. In addition to the theoretical studies, JPL had responsibility for the design of the second stage and separation system. The Douglas Aircraft Company built the *WAC Corporal* and the special V-2 parts required. Design work began in May 1947.

JPL personnel studied several configurations, including placing a *WAC Corporal* with its solid fuel booster in the nose of a V-2. They also looked at simply standing a *WAC Corporal* on top of the V-2 nose cone, leaving the smaller rocket fully exposed throughout the flight. Eventually, JPL concluded the best approach would be

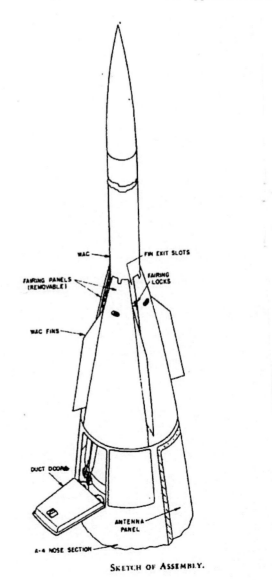

Project Bumper V-2 nose section schematic showing the WAC Corporal. Source: Development of the Corporal: The Embryo of the Army Missile Program.

to use the *WAC Corporal* without its booster and to imbed the base of the small rocket inside the V-2 nose section.

The normal fins of the *WAC Corporal B* were large enough to stabilize the rocket up to Mach 5, which was near the velocity that would be reached by the V-2. Beyond that, it was necessary to increase the *WAC Corporal's* fin area for stability. This could be done most easily by giving the smaller rocket a fourth fin. Merely adding a fourth fin only increased the area by 33%; more was needed for stability, particularly at staging. The four fins were enlarged to give a 50% increase over the original vehicle, but during the latter portion of the *WAC* powered flight, even this would not be enough.

As the *WAC* climbed out of the sensible atmosphere, the fins lost their effectiveness and the slightest asymmetry of thrust would make the missile tumble. The answer would be to spin the *WAC* so the effects of any asymmetry would be cancelled out. A spin of about 500 RPM would be enough to stabilize the rocket. Two small solid-fuel rocket motors mounted perpendicular to the *WAC's* long axis would produce the desired spin after staging. These motors were imbedded inside the fuselage between the fuel and oxidizer tanks, at the rocket's center of gravity. A switch in the V-2 ignited the solid motors as the *WAC* slid out of the nose section. In tests, these motors would produce a spin of 540 RPM in less than half a second after ignition. The fins were mounted at a slight angle to provide a zero angle of attack as the rocket spun. The new, larger fins were made from 24ST aluminum, rather than the J-1H magnesium alloy previously used.

The V-2 nose housed the guide-rails used as a launcher for the *WAC Corporal*. The simplest method of separation was to use the *WAC's* engine. Obviously a new warhead section would be needed, but this required extensive modification to the V-2 instrument section as well. A conical pressure bulkhead had to be added to the forward portion of the instrument section, about 8 inches beneath the second stage motor, to protect the mechanisms it contained. Provisions also had to be made to duct the exhaust gases from the *WAC* once it ignited. Vent doors were placed in instrument compartment quadrants II and IV. Doppler antennae were built into the doors over compartments I and III, so they could not be altered.

Firing the *WAC* motor had to be timed with the V-2 cutoff so the launching duration was kept to a minimum. If the *WAC* lingered inside the guide rails it could damage both vehicles. A way had to be found to precisely sequence the ignition of the *WAC Corporal* and shutdown of the V-2. The first step in the process was to use the V-2's own integrating accelerometer to trigger a reduction of the booster's thrust from 28 tons to 8 tons. (This system had been used for the combat missiles to precisely control the cutoff velocity.) Once the desired velocity had been reached, the final signal from the accelerometer opened the vent ducts in the V-2 instrument compartment and started the *WAC* motor. The exhaust jet from the *WAC* burned through a wire that triggered the final shut down of the V-2.

Eight missiles were assembled during the *Bumper* program, and the first six were launched at WSPG. *Bumper 1*, a test of the separation system, flew on May 13, 1948. It had a short-duration

solid propellant motor in the second stage, and the *WAC* attained only slightly more speed and altitude than the V-2. This was the first large, two-stage rocket launched in the Western Hemisphere. The *WAC* carried ballast to simulate the weight and center of gravity of a fully fueled rocket.

Bumper 2 was fired on August 19, 1948, and like *Bumper 1*, contained only a partial charge. The velocity of the V-2 was about ten percent below normal, but the steering was good. Up to 28 seconds the propulsion system performed normally, but at 33 seconds the turbine malfunctioned. The *WAC* separated at a lower velocity than intended and the booster actually reached a higher altitude than the upper stage.

On September 30, 1948, the third missile was launched. The second stage used a liquid propellant but only carried enough for 32 seconds' burning time. Operation of the V-2 was successful, but the second stage motor exploded just prior to separation. The fourth *Bumper*, like the third, used a liquid propellant with 32 seconds burning time for the second stage. The flight appeared normal at first, but a break in the alcohol piping resulted in an explosion in the V-2 tail section at 28.5 seconds. *Bumper 4* went out of control and crashed into the desert.

Despite the problems encountered in the first round of *Bumper* flights, it was decided to press on with a full flight. *Bumper 5*, fired on February 24, 1949, was the first one with a fully tanked second stage. This allowed 45 seconds burning time with the *WAC*.

Upon its delivery to WSPG, the *WAC* was taken to the *Nike* hangar for cleaning and final testing. After reassembly, the *WAC* was loaded with its aniline/alcohol fuel and installed in the nose of the V-2. Originally the launch was scheduled for 7:15 AM, but

Project Bumper liftoff. Source: U.S. Army photograph.

this was delayed for nearly 8 hours due to cloud coverage and the failure of an electrical lead in the V-2 midsection. *Bumper 5* finally lifted off at 3:14 PM. The 8-ton thrust signal was given at 61 seconds, followed by the *WAC* start signal at 63.8 seconds. The V-2 shut down at 64.5 seconds, by which time the missile had attained an altitude of 18.3 miles and a speed of 3,600 miles per hour. The *WAC Corporal* separated cleanly from its booster and continued on its way. With its power added to that of the V-2, the *WAC* attained a speed of 5,150 miles per hour and an altitude of 244 miles. This was the highest altitude ever reached by a man-made object, but was still slightly below predictions.

The V-2 velocity was about 150 feet per second less than the setting on the integrating accelerometer, which was probably due to the combined effects of integrator error and slightly low thrust. *WAC* burnout occurred 107 seconds after launch. Based on pre-flight predictions, everyone expected prevailing high-altitude winds to make the *WAC* drift towards the east during the powered portion of its flight. However, as the *WAC* climbed, it abruptly changed direction and began heading in a westerly direction.

The nose cone carried instruments to measure temperatures at extreme altitudes. In addition, the *WAC* carried telemetry that transmitted technical data about the rocket itself back to the ground. This was the first time radio equipment had ever operated at such extreme altitudes. Although the missile had been tracked by radar for most of its flight, it wasn't found until September 1949. Indications from the wreckage were that the rocket fell in a flat spin, because it did not produce any appreciable crater. The leading edges of the fins showed erosion caused by the elevated temperatures encountered during the flight. Most interestingly, the combustion chamber had burned through at the throat. This likely caused the lower than expected performance.

The sixth V-2/*WAC* combination missile was launched on April 21, 1949. This missile also had a fully tanked second stage, and it was hoped that the performance of *Bumper 5* could be surpassed. The nose cone was instrumented to record data on cosmic radiation at altitudes greater than could be reached by other missiles. Performance was normal for 47.5 seconds when the cut-off relay was operated by some malfunction in the control system. The *WAC* did not separate from the V-2. Excessive vibration, due to structural changes made to accommodate the *WAC Corporal*, most likely caused this failure. It was also concluded vibration caused the failures of missiles 2 and 4, as well.

It was decided to use the remaining *Bumper* rockets to conduct aerodynamic investigations in the vicinity of Mach 7 at relatively low (120,000-150,000 feet) altitudes. To accomplish this, the rockets would be guided to essentially flat flight paths after launch, which would result in their traveling 250 miles. This, of course, was more than could be accommodated at WSPG, so another launch site was needed. The Air Force had recently created the Joint Long-Range Proving Ground (LRPG) at Cocoa Beach, Florida, where missiles could be fired out over the Atlantic Ocean. This would be the launch site for *Bumpers 7* and *8*.

Preparations at the LRPG began in September 1949. Because these would be the first firings at the LRPG, virtually all the required facilities, personnel, and equipment were not present. At

first, the flights were planned for January 1950, but necessary funds were not available. Funding did not come through until April, at which time the launches were scheduled for July. *Bumper* missiles 7 and 8 were shipped from White Sands Proving Ground to Florida by standard Army tractors and flatbeds. The rockets arrived on 18 June.

Since the V-2 missiles previously shipped to Norfolk, Virginia, for *Operation Sandy* had been damaged in transit, modifications were made in the shipping cradles for *Bumpers 7* and *8* to prevent such damage. The rigid tail support in each cradle was replaced by a partially inflated truck tire to provide a non-rigid support for the tail. The Army vehicles were driven with extreme care, and the missiles arrived in excellent condition.

At least one person at the Long-Range Proving Ground was very familiar with the V-2 and its launching requirements: Colonel Harold Turner. Following his assignment to the Research and Development Division of the OCO, he was posted to the Joint Long-Range Proving Ground on October 1, 1949. Colonel Turner assumed command of the Advance Headquarters when he arrived in Florida; he became the Proving Ground's Deputy Commander upon its activation.

For the most part, conventional V-2 ground equipment was used for the *Bumper* launches in Florida, all of which had to be shipped from WSPG. The one major change at the LRPG was in the type of working platform used to service the upper levels of the missiles. Rather than construct a permanent gantry like the one at WSG, the Army decided to use iron pipe scaffolding of the type commonly used by painters. These assemblies were mounted on casters. Rising about 55 feet above the concrete pad, the scaffolds had sufficient strength and rigidity for the purpose.

The first attempt to launch *Bumper 7* took place on 19 July. This launch had to be cancelled due to moisture that collected within the missile after it was held on the pad for over nine hours. The countdown was plagued by a series of problems. First, fueling was delayed because of leaks in the alcohol truck. Later, an acid

Bumper 7 being towed to the launch area at the Long-Range Proving Ground, Cape Canaveral, Florida. *Source: U.S. Army photograph.*

overflow occurred which required a detailed inspection of the entire vehicle. The missile's Doppler unit had to be replaced at about X-4 hours. Failures in the firing circuits of the WAC spin rockets caused further lengthy delays. Finally, it was decided to launch without the spin rockets.

By the time *Bumper 7* was ready, liquid oxygen had been in the V-2 for over seven hours. Two oxygen refills were required before the launch signal was given at 5:20 PM. The rocket did not respond to the firing signal. Coastal Florida is more humid than the deserts of New Mexico. The presence of super cold liquid oxygen in the oxidizer tank led to condensation inside the rocket which impaired the insulation of the main fuel valve control electromagnet. It was necessary to return *Bumper 7* to the hangar, where it was dried and rechecked. Two steps were taken to reduce the probability of further condensation troubles: (1) silicone grease was applied at vulnerable points, and (2) the loading sequence was reversed to load liquid oxygen after loading hydrogen peroxide.

Postponing *Bumper 7* created major problems for the Army Ordnance Branch. Both firings had to be finished by 1 August because of prior commitments of personnel and equipment. Launch preparations were further complicated by the loss of many specialists due to the recent start of the Korean War. Rather than wait until *Bumper 7* was ready, work went on with *Bumper 8*. Launched on July 24, 1950, this was the first missile firing from Cape Canaveral. The launch had to be held twice: once to replace the telemetry transmitter, and then once more to replace the fuel cut-off receiver. Launch occurred at 9:28 AM, nearly an hour and a half later than planned. Cloud cover was about 50%, which impaired optical coverage of the rocket. At first everything looked normal, but subsequent analysis showed the trajectory had been shallower than intended. Staging was supposed to occur with the missile at an angle of 20 degrees from the horizontal. Instead, *Bumper 8* was at an angle of only 13 degrees. Separation altitude and velocity were both lower than desired because of the flattened flight path. Shortly after staging the Doppler transmitter in the *WAC* failed, presumably because of a structural failure in the nose cone. The *WAC* did not accelerate after it separated from the V-2.

Launch of *Bumper 7* on July 29, 1950. This was the final flight of the series. *Source: U.S. Army photograph.*

Bumper 7 was successfully fired on July 29, 1950. Project engineers took advantage of the time it was sent back to the assembly hangar after the first launch attempt to make some improvements. Because of the failure of the nose cone on *Bumper 8*, they strengthened the junction between the nose and fuselage. They also added packets of green dye in the V-2 instrument compartment to mark its impact point in the Atlantic Ocean. Hopefully, some pieces of the missile could be recovered if the impact point was known.

When it was being transported back to the launch pad, the missile was damaged while being placed on the Meilerwagen. After careful examination, the engineers decided it was still flight worthy and went ahead with the launch. Operations at the launch pad had improved to the point where some activities, particularly loading acid in the *WAC*, took less time than planned. The cut-off receiver failed during preliminary checks and had to be replaced, but even this did not delay the countdown. *Bumper 7* lifted off at 6:44 AM, 16 minutes ahead of schedule. This proved fortuitous, because the weather was changing for the worse.

Once again the trajectory was too shallow, and the *WAC* separated at an altitude of only 48,000 feet. This time, the *WAC* performed well and the engine delivered the expected thrust until burn-out at 103 seconds. The shallower than expected trajectory

Bumper 7 on the pad. *Source: U.S. Army photograph.*

took the missile through denser portions of the atmosphere than intended, so the *WAC* encountered higher than anticipated drag forces. (Aerodynamic drag is a function of velocity and air density.) Despite the increased drag, the upper stage reached Mach 9, which was the highest speed ever attained in the Earth's atmosphere. Doppler and telemetry records were obtained throughout the entire flight. The search aircraft found the dye pool at the V-2 impact point, but only a few fragments of wood could be found floating in the water. No trace of the *WAC Corporal* was ever recovered.

The fact that both rockets exhibited shallower than anticipated trajectories indicated there was a systemic cause, so GE engineers began looking at the V-2 guidance system. The General Electric Report on these firings stated:

"This trajectory required a relatively rapid turn during the powered flight of the V-2. Both missiles made the turn successfully and the general performance appeared good. A closer examination of the trajectory data showed, however, that the program had been greater than desired. Trajectory data showed the separation angle for Bumper 7 to be approximately 10 degrees and that for Bumper 8 to be about 13 degrees. The fact that the two trajectories showed the same type of discrepancy indicated a systematic rather than a random fault. Since it seemed highly improbable that the pitch device itself would fail in such a fashion as to increase the program, precession of the pitch gyro circuits had been modified to obtain a much larger than normal program, these circuits were among the first investigated. This investigation turned up a "sneak-circuit" which caused the erecting motors of the pitch gyro to be energized after take-off. This in turn caused a procession which operated to increase the program angle. This fault appeared to answer fully the observed discrepancy."

For the Operation Paperclip scientists, this was a particularly frustrating time because they felt underutilized. They were housed at Fort Bliss, and most of them did not participate in the V-2 firings at White Sands. The number of Germans at White Sands reached its peak of 39 in March 1946. After that General Electric personnel replaced the Germans, and by the following spring the process had been completed. Rather than being involved in any new programs, many of the German group found themselves answering questions about the V-2. Their fortunes changed on April 15, 1950, when the Army created the Ordnance Guided Missile Center (OGMC) at Redstone Arsenal in Huntsville, Alabama. Most of the Paperclip group moved to Huntsville, where they continued working on Army missile programs. The *Hermes II* project was transferred to the OGMC. By November 1, 1950, all research and development activities at Fort Bliss had been transferred to the OGMC.

General Electric's participation in the V-2 program ended on June 30, 1951, after 72 launches, counting the *Hermes*, *Hermes II*, *Bumper*, and *Sandy* flights. As *Hermes* progressed, scientists placed more and more instrumentation aboard the rockets and began making modifications to the basic missile. In 1946, the White Sands V-2s weighed an average 150 pounds over their design weight, and none incorporated major contour modifications. By 1949 the missiles weighed an average 1,036 pounds over their basic weight, and three quarters of them had significant contour modifications.

When the V-2 phase of *Hermes* ended, Brigadier General George G. Eddy was commander of WSPG. General Eddy was born on July 4, 1895, in Norwich, Connecticut. He graduated from the United States Military Academy in 1918 and was assigned to the Cavalry as a Second Lieutenant. In October of the same year he was promoted to First Lieutenant, and was assigned to the Infantry School at Fort Benning, Georgia. A year later, he entered the Ordnance School of Application and the Ordnance School of Technology at Watertown Arsenal, Massachusetts.

Upon completion of the course in June 1921, his next posting was to the OCO in Washington, D.C. Eddy served in a number of Ordnance assignments over the next several years before earning a Bachelor of Science degree from Colgate University in 1928 and a MBA from Harvard University in 1931. After receiving a promotion to Captain on November 1, 1934, he became the Assistant Ordnance Officer and Ammunition Officer for the Hawaiian Department. As Ammunition Officer, Eddy created the first Field Inspection Manual for all weapons to be used in the Hawaiian and Philippine Departments.

Reaching the rank of Lieutenant Colonel in July 1941, Eddy served with various commands in the European Theater. In November 1948, he returned to the States and became the Deputy

Brigadier George G. Eddy, third commander of WSPG. *Source: U.S. Army photograph.*

Commander of WSPG. He was appointed WSPG commander on February 1, 1950. While serving at WSPG he was promoted to Brigadier General.

The conclusion of Hermes was not the end of American V-2 flights. The White Sands launches had been supported by the Army's 1st Guided Missile Battalion, which had been formed on October 11, 1945. In January 1951, a V-2 Section was added to the Battalion's organizational structure. The V-2 Section comprised about 35 personnel under the command of Lieutenant Allen C. Metzger. After the *Hermes* V-2 flights, the 1st Guided Missile Battalion fired four rockets.

As part of their training program, personnel from the V-2 Section were in the blockhouse during the launch of V-2 #55 on June 14, 1951, as observers. This rocket carried instruments to measure solar and cosmic radiation for the Naval Research Laboratory. At first, everything looked normal as the motor ignited. Then, just as the missile lifted off, the engine faltered and it settled back down on the pad after lifting only an inch or so. Once clear of the launch pad the rocket shifted slightly, less than an inch. When it dropped back on the pad, contacts in the tail of the rocket reconnected, but because the rocket had shifted, they were out of alignment. This caused a short circuit in the nose separation system. The primacord at the base of the control compartment detonated and triggered an explosion of the fully fueled rocket. The blockhouse, with its reinforced concrete construction, kept everyone safe.

To gain further experience, the V-2 Section conducted two static firing tests of the missile propulsion system. The rockets were tested without the aft body section and fins. Anticipating larger missile programs in the future, the Army built a second static test stand on the side of the mountain about a mile south of the original test stand. This stand could handle rockets of up to 500,000 pounds' thrust. Personnel referred to the test stand as "Shangri La" because of its physical resemblance to the structure in the movie "Lost Horizons." Planning for the larger facility began in 1946; construction was finished in 1950. The V-2 Section used this larger test stand for the static firings. The first test, SF-1, took place on July 2, 1951. SF-2 occurred on 7 August. For these tests, the rockets were mounted at a 30-degree angle in the stand.

Two weeks later, on 22 August, the 1st Guided Missile Battalion launched their first rocket, designated TF-1. On this flight, TF-1's engine was allowed to fire until all the propellants were exhausted in a test to see how high an altitude could be attained by a six-year old German rocket launched by American soldiers. Army personnel made several modifications to the rocket in an effort to reduce its weight and maximize its altitude. This rocket used pressurized nitrogen rather than compressed air for the pneumatic controls, and the tanks were moved from the propulsion section to the nose compartment. This shifted the center of gravity without adding ballast to the nose for stability. The Army personnel concluded the air vanes were not needed to guide the rocket; in other words, the

Members of the 1st Guided Missile Battalion loading a V-2 engine in the 500,000-pound test stand. *Source: U.S. Army photograph.*

The 500,000-pound capacity test stand. *Source: U.S. Army photograph.*

TF-3 launch preparations. Source: U.S. Army photograph courtesy of Bill Beggs.

Launch of *TF-1*. Source: U.S. Army photograph.

graphite vanes in the engine exhaust were sufficient to stabilize the missile. This meant the mechanisms—the gears, chain drive, and servos—for the vanes could be removed to further reduce weight. The vanes were welded in place.

On the first attempt to launch the missile, the igniter blew out of the combustion chamber before the propellants ignited. Someone had to leave the safety of the blockhouse and install another igniter in the fully fueled missile. On the second attempt, the motor ignited and the rocket lifted off. TF-1 reached an altitude of 132 miles, the highest attained by a V-2. Missile #59, which was also identified as TF-2, flew on May 20, 1952, and climbed 64.3 miles. TF-3 reached 48.5 miles on 22 August; TF-4 never flew. The last American V-2 flight took place on September 19, 1952, when the 1st Guided Missile Battalion launched TF-5.

Officially, 68 percent of the V-2 flights were successful; that is, they flew with no malfunctions. Of the remaining 32 percent, though, many were still scientifically useful. As an example, one missile was classified as a failure because the steering mechanism malfunctioned. Despite the malfunction, this particular missile reached an altitude of 99 miles and returned excellent scientific results. Overall, the percentage of fully successful flights compared to unsuccessful ones does not give a clear picture of the results of *Hermes*. For America, the V-2 provided the first experience in handling and firing large missiles and laid the foundation for future rocket development. By taking advantage of the work done at Peenemünde, the United States saved at least a decade and billions of dollars that would have had to have been spent to reach the same level of technology.

JB-2 Loon. In 1944, shortly after the Germans began firing V-1 Buzz Bombs towards England, the Americans obtained one that failed to explode. The Army Air Force decided to copy the cruise missile. Republic Aircraft received the contract for the airframe, and Ford received the contract for the pulse-jet motor. The *Loon* was considered for use during the expected invasion of Japan, but when it was realized the amount of cordite needed for the launchers would have exceeded the supply these plans were abandoned. When the war ended *JB-2* production was halted. While most were launched at Eglin Air Force Base in Florida, a *JB-2* launch ramp was constructed at Holloman Air Force Base as well. A limited number were flown at WSPG to test guidance equipment. *Source: U.S. Army photograph.*

5

Project *Hermes* Missiles

While *Hermes* is most frequently associated with the V-2 firings, it actually covered a much larger effort and involved several different rockets. In general, work on the *Hermes* project can be divided into the *A-1* and *A-2* series; the *A-3* rockets; and other missiles and supporting research. Among the last category, the most notable was the *Hermes II*. In June 1946, the General Electric Company received an amendment to the original *Hermes* contract for a test vehicle for a two-stage surface to surface missile using a V-2 as the first stage. This became the *Hermes II*. The second stage of the *Hermes II* was a dummy ramjet propelled cruise missile capable of reaching an altitude of 66,000 feet and a speed of 2,100 miles per hour.

In theory, ramjets are the simplest propulsion system devised, comprising little more that an open tube containing fuel injectors and a flame holder with no moving parts. Air enters the front of the tube and mixes with fuel. The fuel/air mixture ignites, and the hot combustion gases exit from the back of the tube. Despite their seeming simplicity, in practice ramjets are very difficult propulsion systems to design. One of the challenges with harnessing a ramjet as a propulsion device is that it cannot operate while sitting still. As its name implies, a ramjet relies upon ram effect to build up the pressure of the air entering the engine. Before it can operate, a ramjet has to be accelerated to a high enough speed, typically greater than Mach 1, so that the shape of its inlet helps compress the air for combustion. Part of the complexity comes from the way air behaves at supersonic and hypersonic velocities. Shock waves that form at the inlet or within the tube can choke the engine and block its operation. Likewise, the exit nozzle must be carefully designed for the engine to work. Results from the *Hermes II* series of experiments added to the existing body of knowledge on how to design and build ramjets.

The first *Hermes II* test, missile 0, was launched on May 29, 1947. This was a standard V-2 with the proposed *Hermes II* guidance system. Four seconds after launch, the missile was supposed to head north at an angle of 7° off the vertical. At first, no pitch was evident. Observers at the emergency cut-off station soon noted it was headed slightly south. They judged the angle was so slight that the missile would land within the confines of WSPG, so

they let it continue on its course. As the missile flew, they noticed its southward angle was steeper than first thought and realized it would overshoot the range.

With this realization came the fear that it might hit the City of El Paso if they shut off the engine too soon, so they let it continue. Cut-off occurred 46 seconds after launch, which was long enough to take it past El Paso, across the Rio Grande River, and into Mexico. The rocket hit just outside Ciudad Juarez, in a cemetery that was next door to a site where a construction company stored dynamite. Fortunately, the rocket was not close enough to detonate the explosives and there were no injuries. Within minutes Mexican entrepreneurs were offering fragments of the missile for sale. (Some of the fragments looked suspiciously like tin cans.) This incident caused a major re-evaluation of range safety rules at WSPG.

The next test in the *Hermes II* effort was WSPG V-2 #44. This missile, which was launched on November 18, 1948, carried a

Hermes II, which had a modified V-2 booster and a dummy ramjet upper stage. *Source: U.S. Army photograph.*

ramjet diffuser in its nose. Aerodynamic data collected during the flight agreed with wind tunnel and theoretical studies as the missile accelerated to Mach 3.6. This rocket topped 90 miles altitude. With this successful flight, the General Electric team was ready to move on to flight tests of the two-stage configuration.

The *Hermes II* rockets were unusual looking, comprising a V-2 body with a pair of large canards near the nose and enlarged fins near the base. It was ultimately planned to place a ramjet propulsion system in the canards. The ramjets themselves were somewhat unusual, being rectangular in shape. The canards, or "wings," had a span of 183.86 inches. A cap over the leading edge of the wings protected the inlet and reduced drag during the ascending part of the trajectory. Having such large surfaces near the nose of the V-2 affected its stability, so the fins were enlarged by 30%. The canards were also rotated 45° relative to the fins so the air flow off the forward surfaces did not disturb the fins.

Hermes II missile #1 flew on January 13, 1949. *Hermes II* #1 weighed 32,597 pounds at launch. The flight was postponed twice; once due to an onboard instrumentation problem and a second time for weather. On 13 January the skies were overcast, but the winds were within the narrow limits allowed by the peculiar *Hermes II* configuration. The decision was made to launch regardless of the overcast. Radar and radio problems delayed the launch, but the missile finally lifted off at 1:26 PM. Twenty-two seconds after launch the rocket disappeared in the heavy clouds. At 33.4 seconds into the flight something happened and the rocket broke apart. Debris from the shattered rocket landed about seven miles north of the launch pad and were scattered over an area about a mile in diameter. There were two more *Hermes II* rocket flights on October 6, 1949, and November 9, 1950.

Initially, *Project Hermes* included antiaircraft missile development. As a starting point for this line of research, GE built

V-2 number 19, which carried guidance equipment for the *Hermes A-1*. *Source: U.S. Army photograph courtesy of Bill Beggs.*

upon prior German experience. One of the most promising missiles developed at Peenemünde during the war was the *Wasserfall* (Waterfall) anti-aircraft rocket. Looking very much like a half-scale V-2 with short, stubby wings in the midsection, the Germans tested about 35 *Wasserfalls* by the end of the war. General Electric engineers copied the *Wasserfall* airframe and designated it the *Hermes A-1*. Copying the *Wasserfall* design allowed the *Hermes* project to take advantage of German aerodynamic data.

The *Hermes A-1* was 35 ½ feet long and 34 ½ inches in diameter. Like the *Wasserfall*, it burned liquid propellants, but it had a completely new propulsion system. The *Wasserfall* had consumed a hypergolic fuel mixture of nitric acid and *visol*, a byproduct of petroleum production. For the *Hermes A-1*, General Electric engineers opted to use a more familiar and easier to handle combination of liquid oxygen and alcohol. The *Hermes A-1* engine had a thrust of 16,000 pounds and would give the missile a maximum velocity of 1,800 miles per hour. Like its German predecessor, *Hermes A-1* was highly maneuverable.

V-2 #19, launched on January 23, 1947, tested the telemetry unit intended for the *Hermes A-1*. Other V-2s launched in 1947 and 1948 carried *Hermes A-1* telemetry and guidance equipment. On May 18, 1950, the Army shifted the emphasis of *Project Hermes* away from antiaircraft missiles to focus on surface to surface weapons. The Army found it had too many research projects competing for

Hermes A-1 prior to launch. The *Hermes A-1* was an experimental surface to surface missile that outwardly resembled the German *Wasserfall* antiaircraft missile design. *Source: U.S. Army photograph.*

too few dollars, so something had to be discontinued. Even though the *Hermes A-1* was no longer considered for tactical use, it still served as a test bed for guidance and control research. Six were built; the first flew on 19 May, the day after the Army's decision. (Of the six missiles built, only five flew. One was damaged beyond repair during a static test.)

On the first launch, the rocket lifted off smoothly, but it lost thrust within 10 to 20 seconds and crashed a little more than a mile and a quarter from the pad after a flight of 39 seconds. It only reached an altitude of 2,980 feet. Data records indicated there were three individual failures on board the rocket. About one second before launch, the emergency oxygen dump valve opened and released the helium used to pressurize the tanks at four times the normal rate. The main alcohol valve opened early, which caused the oxygen valve to also open prematurely. Because of the early valve openings the preliminary stage did not occur. Two seconds after take off, the inner wall of the combustion chamber burned through. Despite these multiple failures, the guidance system worked well, with only small variations in roll and yaw.

The second rocket, launched on September 14, 1950, turned in somewhat better performance. Six or seven seconds after launch the rocket began to roll, but otherwise remained stable until 41 seconds, when the engine exhaust burned through the hydraulic servo covers. *Hermes A-1* #2 lost control, then exploded at 81 seconds.

Round #3 did not get off the ground. The motor ignited but did not achieve main stage, so it was shut down after a few seconds. The vehicle was disarmed and shipped back to the General Electric plant at Malta Test Station, New York. Subsequent examination showed fouling of the alcohol feed line after the cadmium plating in the combustion chamber jacket failed. This rocket was repaired and returned to WSPG for launch in 1951. The remaining *Hermes A-1* flights occurred on February 2, March 18, and April 26, 1951, with one of these being the refurbished Round #3. None of the rockets were completely successful, but they demonstrated the functional capability of the missile system.

Although work stopped on the *Hermes A-1*, development of the *Hermes A-1E-1* and *A-1E-2* continued. Designed as a tactical surface to surface missile, the *Hermes A-1E-1* was 25 feet long and carried a 1,450-pound warhead. *Hermes A-1E-2* was four feet longer, but carried the same payload. On November 10, 1950, Army Ordnance authorized the construction of 12 *A-1E-1s*. Two months later, the Joint Chiefs of Staff approved development of *Hermes A-1* type missiles for interim tactical use and ordered the construction of twelve *A-1E-2* rockets. The Army had another vehicle being considered for the interim missile role—the *Corporal*. The *Corporal* showed better results, so the *Hermes A-1E-2* was cancelled in April 1952 because the Army could not need it. The *Hermes A-1E-1* survived until it, too, was cancelled on October 25, 1952.

At first, the *Hermes A-2* did not progress beyond the drawing board. As initially proposed, *Hermes A-2* was a wingless version of the *A-1* missile. When work halted on the *A-1*, it stopped on the *A-2* as well. Then, in December 1948, the *Hermes* Project incorporated a study to develop an "inexpensive guided missile" to

lob a 1,500-pound payload to a range of 75 miles. Solid propellants were chosen for this missile, which received the *A-2* designation before it finally became the solid fuel *RV-A-10* test vehicle. It used guidance components from the *Hermes A-1*. GE work on the *A-2* was confined to work on the propulsion system, and the motor was test fired twelve times at Redstone Arsenal and flown four times at the Air Force Missile Test Center in Florida. A hybrid propulsion system using polyethylene plastic as the fuel and concentrated hydrogen peroxide as an oxidizer was tested, but work on this design was discontinued in 1953 because no immediate application for it could be found.

Development of the *Hermes A-3* surface to surface missile began in 1947. At 29 feet, it stood about 2/3 as tall as the V-2 and could deliver a 1,000-pound warhead across a range of 150 miles. Its engine burned liquid oxygen and alcohol to produce a thrust of 18,000 pounds. The *A-3A* had an unusual fuselage shape; its maximum diameter was in the lower half of the fuselage. The airframe then tapered down to the base, and the rocket had four triangular fins. Twelve *A-3AE1* missiles were ordered on November 10, 1950. The *A-3AE1* test missiles evolved into the *A-3AE2*, which was planned for the 1,500-pound Type B atomic warhead.

In 1951 the *A-3A* was cancelled as a tactical missile, but work continued on the rockets. The completed airframes became test beds for the *A-3B*. As a test vehicle, the designation of the *A-3A* became *RV-A-8*. In the end, there were eight *RV-A-8* (or *A-3A*) rockets completed. The first exploded on August 7, 1952, during a

Liftoff of *Hermes A-1* number 5. *Source: U.S. Army photograph courtesy of Bill Beggs.*

The *Hermes A-3A*. Source: U.S. Army photograph.

static test at GE's Malta Test Station in New York. WSPG missile #1 flew on March 13, 1953. Things went well at first, but the turbopump failed 23 seconds after liftoff and the rocket exploded. Round #2, launched on June 13, 1953, reached a velocity of 4,450 feet per second at burnout.

The remaining rockets of the series produced mixed results. Round #3, launched on 13 August, reached a speed of 4,150 feet per second. This rocket carried a redesigned tail section to correct some problems detected with the second vehicle. Problems with the turbopump on Round #4 resulted in a higher than expected cutoff velocity. The excessive velocity was blamed for roll instability that occurred at 161 seconds. Round #5 operated as planned until 75 seconds, when the batteries failed, which resulted in a loss of flight control from the ground. The tail section of this missile was not recovered so no reason was ever found for the battery failure. Round #6 went well until 20,000 feet before impact when it went out of control and it spun out of its trajectory. The final *A-3A* flight, on January 15, 1954, went out of control 53 seconds after launch. Despite the failure, it returned extensive data on the performance of the guidance system.

Launch and handling equipment for the *A-3A* included a modified Meilerwagen. (Originally, the Meilerwagen had been built in Germany for the V-2.) The launch stand provided stability and support to the missile in winds of up to 50 miles per hour. This equipment was modified for the *A-3B*.

In September 1953, the Army established a requirement for a missile capable of carrying a 3,000-pound atomic warhead. This requirement brought about the *Hermes A-3B*, essentially a hurried redesign of the *A-3A*. The *A-3A* motor was redesigned to produce a thrust of 22,000 pounds, which was 10% greater than the motor built for the *Corporal*. Other changes were made to simplify the system, improve its efficiency, and reduce its cost. The *A-3B* was slightly bigger than the *A-3A*: it was 400 inches long, 47 inches in diameter, and had a fin span of 100 inches.

The *A-3B* flight test program created in 1953 comprised a series of 28 launches. Flights 1 through 6 were to be test fired to perfect the operating system. Missiles 7 through 12 were accuracy tests, while the remaining twelve rounds were to provide performance data under simulated field conditions. By mid-year, the number of *A-3B* missiles authorized for testing was reduced to six. These were to fulfill the original objectives for the first six missiles to demonstrate the feasibility of the guidance system concept. The *A-3B* inertial guidance system comprised a stable platform, range and azimuth unit, and a timer.

A-3B Flight #1 was launched on May 11, 1954. The inertial guidance system performed well until 141.5 seconds when the power supply failed. Round #1 continued flying until 192 seconds when the rocket broke apart. It reached an altitude of 106,000 feet, which was slightly below the planned 118,000-foot altitude. Major pieces of debris were found 42 miles from the pad. Missile #3, the second *A-3B* launched, lifted off on 20 July. This rocket reached 117,600 feet. Round #2 finally flew on 26 August. Its guidance system malfunctioned and it began veering away from the planned trajectory, so the engine was shut down after 30 seconds.

Missiles 4, 5, and 6 flew about a month apart, on 21 September, 19 October, and 16 November, respectively. Round #4 broke apart a few seconds before impact. The fifth *A-3B* achieved a range of 55 miles and was stable when it hit the ground. *A-3B* #6, the final missile in the program, broke apart at 204 seconds. Peak altitude was 113,000 feet; range was 47 miles; and the flight lasted 206.6 seconds.

The *Hermes A-3B* was designed to carry a 3,000-pound warhead. This missile was seriously considered for tactical deployment. *Source: U.S. Army photograph.*

Work on *Project Hermes* ended on December 31, 1954. At its peak in 1952, *Project Hermes* directly employed more than 1,250 people. Technologies developed during *Hermes* advanced the state of the art in such areas as guidance, tracking, and propulsion. When the project ended, *Hermes* was responsible for the development and flight testing of what was then the highest performance large liquid fuel rocket in the United States. One phase of the project, the *Hermes C*, led directly to the development of the *Redstone* ballistic missile, which launched the first American satellite in 1958 and the first American astronaut in 1961.

The Army's *Redstone* began with the *Hermes C* design studies. Although most *Redstone* testing took place at Cape Canaveral, Florida, a limited number were fired at WSPG beginning in 1956. *Source: U.S. Army photograph.*

6

Projects *MX-774*, *NATIV*, and *GAPA*

The late 1940s were a busy time for the Army Air Force (AAF) in the Tularosa basin, with three separate missile development programs. While none of the three directly resulted in an operational missile, each contributed to the growing pool of knowledge concerning guided missiles.

On October 31, 1945, the AAF Air Technical Command issued a request for proposals (RFP) to the aviation industry for a ten-year study on guided missiles. At this stage the RFP was very broad, asking for ideas for missiles with ranges between 20 and 5,000 miles. The Consolidated Vultee Aircraft Corporation submitted proposals for two types of missiles capable of ranges of 1,500-5,000 miles with an accuracy of 5,000 feet. The Corporation's Vultee Field Division in Downey, California, produced the designs. One was a subsonic jet-propelled cruise missile; the other was a supersonic ballistic missile. The AAF awarded a $1.4 million contract to Vultee on April 19, 1946, for a one-year study of the designs under contract *MX-774*.

Karel J. "Charlie" Bossart was Vultee's lead engineer on the project. Bossart graduated from the University of Brussels in 1925 with a degree in mining engineering. He subsequently won a scholarship from the Belgian-American Education Foundation to attend the Massachusetts Institute of Technology (MIT). At MIT he switched his field to aeronautics, and specialized in structures. Bossart remained in the United States, and by 1945 was Vultee's Chief of Structures.

Bossart's team produced three designs. An additional rocket was needed to test some of the ideas they had for the ballistic missile. They nicknamed the subsonic cruise missile the *Teetotaler*, since it used jet fuel, rather than alcohol. The second design was called the *Old Fashioned*, because it was a supersonic test missile that outwardly resembled the V-2. Because it was intended to deliver a nuclear warhead, design C was dubbed the *Manhattan*, an allusion to the atomic bomb project. By the end of the year, the AAF asked Vultee to stop work on the cruise missile because the service preferred one created by Northrop Aircraft. The Northrop design became the SM-62 *Snark*.

The AAF awarded Vultee another contract, this one for $493,000, in June 1946 to construct ten test missiles. The Air Force

named the missile *HIROC*. Bossart studied the V-2 designs, and the *HIROC* ended up looking like a small version of the German rocket, including the shape of its fins. This saved time and money by utilizing captured German wind tunnel data. After all, everyone reasoned, the Germans must have had a good reason for choosing that particular fin shape. A visiting German engineer who worked on the V-2 laughed when he saw the *HIROC*. It turned out the Germans utilized that particular shape because it would fit through railroad tunnels.

It seemed to Bossart the German missile was structurally very inefficient, with aluminum propellant tanks encased in a steel body shell. He reasoned it would be better to devise a way for the tanks to become primary structural members, a technique that is also described as "integral tanking." The tanks needed slight pressurization to keep them from collapsing as propellants were burned. (The V-2 used ram air pressure through an inlet in the warhead casing for the alcohol tank and pressure from vaporizing liquid oxygen in the oxidizer tank.) Why not increase the pressure in the tanks to make them rigid? That way, the tanks could be made from thinner and lighter material than would otherwise be possible. Even more weight could be saved by having a common bulkhead between the tanks. Using vanes in the engine exhaust like the V-2 was not the best way to steer the missile. Instead, the Vultee engineers proposed that the engine be gimbaled, or swiveled. Interestingly, at around the same time, the Glenn L. Martin Company in Baltimore was looking at integral tanking and gimbaled engines for their *Neptune* rocket.

Another idea Bossart wanted to test with the *HIROC* was having a detachable warhead. The V-2 hit its target in one piece—warhead and body together. For a long range missile, he thought it would be better to separate the warhead from the rest of the rocket. Since the rocket body did not have to survive the rigors of atmospheric reentry, it did not have to be as rugged as the warhead. This helped further reduce overall weight. Eliminating the drag caused by the rocket body had the added benefit of increasing the range of the warhead. Before being incorporated in the long range missile, this concept needed to be tested so the *HIROC* had a detachable nose section.

Because the *HIROC* was primarily a test bed for structural concepts, the Vultee engineers looked for an existing engine they could use. They settled on the four chamber *XLR-11* built by Reaction Motors, Inc. (RMI), in New Jersey. Used on the Bell *X-1* research airplane, the XLR-11 had a proven record of reliability. The *XLR-11* burned ethyl alcohol and liquid oxygen. In the *X-1*, propellants were pressure-fed to the four combustion chambers. Each chamber produced a thrust of 1,500 pounds, giving the engine a combined total of 6,000 pounds. For *HIROC*, a pair of turbopumps fed the propellants to the chambers more forcefully and increased the thrust of each to 2.000 pounds, which gave the rocket a thrust of 8,000 pounds. Since it utilized four separate combustion chambers, each one could be adapted to swivel to steer the rocket. Moving two opposing chambers back and forth in one axis controlled pitch; the other two controlled yaw. Deflecting all

The *MX-774* being raised into the static test stand. *Source: U.S. Army photograph courtesy of Bill Beggs.*

four chambers at once caused the *HIROC* to roll. Actuating rods linked to the rocket's gyroscopic guidance system swiveled the chambers.

Fabrication of *HIROC* components began in August 1946. Then, on July 1, 1947, the AAF abruptly cancelled the contract. As part of the continued draw-down of the American military after World War II, AAF commanders had to choose between near-term weapon systems like aircraft and cruise missiles or long-term projects like ballistic missiles. With the cancellation of the contract, the Downey team moved to San Diego as part of a Consolidated-Vultee (Convair) plant consolidation. The hardware that had been fabricated included three tank sections and other fuselage components, all of which was moved to San Diego.

Bossart convinced the AAF to allow Convair to complete three test rockets using remaining contract funds and existing hardware. The resulting rocket became known as the RTV-A-2 *HIROC*. It is also frequently referred to by the contract name, the *MX-774*. The rocket stood 31 feet, 7 inches tall and had a body diameter of 30 inches. Its fin span was 82.24 inches. One concession Bossart had to make was that the alcohol and liquid oxygen tanks had separate bulkheads, rather than the common one he wanted. However, this resulted in a negligible weight penalty. As a testament to Bossart's skill at eliminating unnecessary structure, the *MX-774* had an empty weight of less than 900 pounds! Instrumentation, flight test equipment, and a recovery parachute added another 277 pounds. Gross weight at launch, with all propellants, was just under 4,100 pounds.

Reaction Motors, Inc. *XLR-11* engine. This motor was originally developed for high-speed aircraft, but was adapted for the *MX-774*. For the *MX-774*, turbopumps forced liquid oxygen and ethyl alcohol to the four combustion chambers. By using turbopumps, the thrust of the XLR-11 was increased to 8,000 pounds rather than its original 6,000 pounds.

The *MX-774* is nearly at its vertical position in the static test stand at Point Loma, California. *Source: U.S. Army photograph courtesy of Bill Beggs.*

Bossart's group finished the first rocket in the fall of 1947. Convair built a static testing facility at Point Loma, California, overlooking the Pacific Ocean. The facility included a tower to hold the *MX-774* and a blockhouse. On 20 November the rocket was ready for firing. It was suspended 17 feet above the ground and was itself in a gimbaled rig that allowed observers to see the effect of swiveling the engine. Just before it was time to fire the engine, the engineers discovered corrosion on the igniters. This forced a 24-hour postponement of the test while the igniters were cleaned.

The second firing attempt went smoothly. When the count reached zero, the firing button was pressed and that's when problems started. Only two chambers ignited. Suddenly there was an explosion and flames engulfed the rocket! The water deluge system quickly doused the fire, and once it was safe, the accident investigation began. The fault was traced to the igniters, only two of which worked. Fumes from the chambers that did not ignite were detonated by the two operating ones. It took two months to repair and rebuild the *MX-774*.

Finally, in January 1948 the engine successfully fired for 30 seconds. There were five more static firings in February and March. The final static test took place on 26 May, after which the *HIROC* was cleared for flight. The Air Force and Convair decided

to launch the rockets at WSPG. That way, the entire flight could be observed and the payload recovered. *HIROC #1* arrived in New Mexico on 2 June.

A launch pad for *HIROC* was set up about 600 feet north of the WSPG blockhouse. WSPG-provided range support for the launch included radar tracking; Askania Cine theodolite coverage; two Mitchel and three Bowen-Knapp cameras; sky-screen observers; and four tracking telescopes. The Proving Ground also furnished shop, weather, photo lab, communications, and transportation facilities; housing for Convair personnel; the use of the gantry crane for pre-flight checkout; guards and fire crew; and recovery crews. Convair personnel prepared and launched the rocket with assistance from WSPG and the Air Force Project Officer.

The command center was located in the blockhouse, its crew receiving instructions via telephone line from the Flight Control Director and Range Safety Officer in the WSPG radar tracking station three miles to the south. Convair also set up Doppler tracking stations one mile west and one mile south of the pad. The rocket carried a 40-foot diameter recovery parachute, which would return it safely to the ground after reaching an apogee of 100 miles.

The *MX-774* used the same servicing gantry as the V-2 at White Sands. This photograph shows the missile being erected on the launch table. The four chambers of the *XLR-11* engine can be clearly seen in the base of the rocket. *Source: New Mexico Museum of Space History.*

HIROC #1 stood ready on the pad on July 13, 1948. The sky was cloudy, which would have prevented optical tracking of the rocket, so the liftoff had to be postponed several times throughout the day. Finally, a little past 5:00 PM, the launch crew began loading liquid oxygen in the forward tank. Weather forced yet another delay, but at 6:05 PM, the *MX-774* finally lifted off. The rocket lifted cleanly from the launch pad, and the umbilical cord pulled free with no apparent disturbance to the craft.

Several observers opened the blockhouse door and ran outside to glimpse the missile as it climbed. For 12.8 seconds everything worked as it should, then the engine quit. The safety officer yelled over the loudspeaker: "Burnout… She's falling… Heading straight for the blockhouse." The rocket coasted upward to an altitude of 6,200 feet, then fell back to earth. The observers hurriedly scrambled back into the blockhouse and pulled the door shut. Everyone waited for the explosion, which came 48.5 seconds after *HIROC* #1 blasted off. The rocket impacted just 415 feet from the pad and left a crater that was 30 feet wide and 10 feet deep. The recovery parachute was never deployed by the operator.

Miraculously, the film from the instrument recording camera in the nose survived the flight. The film record showed the engine functioned normally until it stopped. No cause was ever found, but indications were that there was a short circuit in the engine control circuit. If this was the case, it would have caused the valves controlling the flow of oxygen and alcohol to the engine to close.

The second *MX-774* was launched on September 27, 1948. Like the first missile, it lifted cleanly off the pad, but there were small oscillations in all three axes during the flight. By the time the rocket reached 54,000 feet it was accelerating at 2.8 gs, and had reached a velocity of 2,350 feet per second. Then, 48 seconds after launch, the engine quit. *HIROC* #2 coasted to a maximum altitude of 24 miles.

Approximately 98 seconds into the flight the onboard battery failed, and the recording camera, telemetry, and radar beacon ceased working. The battery failure also meant ground control could not deploy the recovery parachute or trigger the detonation system, which was located between the tanks. As the rocket plunged through the atmosphere, friction with the air heated it. By the time *HIROC* #2 reached 20,000 feet, it was falling at 1,900 feet per second. Suddenly the missile exploded. Residual liquid oxygen in the tank boiled as the *HIROC* heated during its descent. The internal pressure became too great for the tank and its aft bulkhead burst. This, in turn, detonated the explosive charges between the tanks.

It was actually fortuitous that the rocket broke apart, because the pieces tumbled, and were only traveling a few hundred miles per hour when they impacted the desert. Because the rocket did not streamline in the photo recorder in the nose survived. The film recorded the rocket's performance until the battery failure. Analysis of the film data and flight performance led to the conclusion

Also known as the *HIROC*, the first *MX-774* on the launch pad at White Sands Proving Ground. *Source: New Mexico Museum of Space History.*

Lift-off of the first *MX-774* at White Sands Proving Ground. *Source: New Mexico Museum of Space History.*

that the engine quit because the oxygen propellant valve closed prematurely. Convair engineers conducted several tests, but could not identify the reason for the valve closure by the time the third rocket blasted off on December 2, 1948. The third rocket was 34 inches taller than its predecessors to provide additional payload space.

Fifty-one seconds into the flight, a radio command was sent to the rocket to have it tilt 7 degrees towards the north. The rocket received the command and the pitch gyroscope began the ordered tilt, but the engine quit less than one second later and the *MX-774* never deviated from its flight path. The rocket was at an altitude of 56,214 feet and traveling at a velocity of 2,653 feet per second. Just 51.6 seconds had elapsed since *HIROC #3* began its flight. At 132 seconds, the rocket reached a peak altitude of 30 miles. Its deviation from the vertical was only 2,800 feet north and 4,600 feet east, showing how effectively the guidance system performed during powered flight.

Ground command ordered the parachute to deploy 138.2 seconds into the flight, but it did not open until 45 seconds later. A ring that held the detonating charge fouled the pilot chute and caused the delayed opening. When the parachute finally cleared the ring, the rocket was at 121,000 feet and was falling at 1,550 feet per second. Opening at such a high rate of speed tore the parachute from the rocket. The photo recorder camera was thrown clear and fell by itself to the ground. Careful analysis of the tracking data gave an idea of where to look for the camera, which was subsequently found.

Again, premature closing of the oxygen valve caused the engine to quit. The engineers were sure this had happened because they put an indicator light on the photo recorder panel that only came on when the valve was closed. They ultimately concluded a chain of events led to the premature valve closing. Vibration caused problems with the solenoid valves that controlled pressure in the hydrogen peroxide lines that fed the propellant turbopump. This allowed nitrogen gas to vent from the engine control lines. The resulting pressure drop affected the oxygen propellant valve and caused it to close.

Although all three of the *MX-774 HIROCs* suffered in-flight failures, a great deal was learned from the flights. Most importantly,

NATIV prior to launch at Holloman Air Force Base. There were six flight attempts with *NATIV* rockets. *Source: U.S. Air Force photograph.*

MX-774 recovery parachute. This is likely the parachute from Round #3, which tore away from the missile body after deployment, because the first two missiles crashed without releasing their parachutes. *Source: New Mexico Museum of Space History.*

they successfully demonstrated the concepts of swiveling the engines to steer a rocket and thin-wall construction were sound. In 1951, Convair received a contract from the Air Force that began development of the *Atlas* intercontinental ballistic missile. Concepts tested during Project *MX-774* were incorporated into the *Atlas*.

At around the same time that Convair was working with the *MX-774* project, North American Aviation, Inc., was also conducting rocket research in the Tularosa Basin. Near the end of the Second World War, the Germans tried to double the range of the V-2 by giving it wings. Two of these were launched from Peenemünde, but both failed. The second missile at least transitioned into a supersonic glide before breaking up.

In July 1946, North American received an Army Air Force contract, designated *MX-770*, for missile development. Under the terms of the contract, North American had access to V-2 components and other German information. North American even built a duplicate of the V-2 engine. This was never "hot fired"; rather, it was used for "cold flow" testing with water to study how it operated. (This engine is in the collection of the National Air and Space Museum in Washington, D.C., and at the time of this writing is on display in the "Rocketry and Spaceflight" gallery.)

As a further part of its effort under *MX-770*, the company decided to build a technology demonstrator to test various ideas. This became known as the North American Test Instrument Vehicle, or *NATIV*. Initial plans for the *NATIV* called for a liquid-fuel copy of the German *Wasserfall* anti-aircraft guided missile. This proved too ambitious, so North American built a simpler solid-fuel rocket without the mid-fuselage wings.

The *NATIV* was not launched at WSPG; instead, the Air Force built a launch pad with a small blockhouse and tower at Holloman Air Force Base. There were six launch attempts, two of which never made it very far off the pad; three that made it some distance aloft; and only one that was considered somewhat

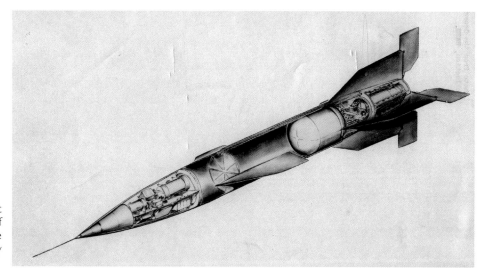

Early concept for North American Test Instrument Vehicle (*NATIV*). The *NATIV* began as a copy of the German *Wasserfall* design. By the time the missiles were built, however, the central body wings were deleted.

NATIV in the hangar prior to launch. The fins retain their similarity to those used on the *Wasserfall* and *Hermes A-1*. The large movable surfaces on the bottom edge of the fins would make the rocket very maneuverable. *Source: U.S. Air Force photograph.*

GAPA missile on a rail launcher at Holloman Air Force Base on September 17, 1947. *Source: U.S. Air Force photograph.*

Launch of a *GAPA* on September 17, 1947. The wooden fuselage of this missile shattered when it impacted the desert. *Source: U.S. Air Force photograph*

successful (reaching Mach 2.23 and an altitude of 18 km). Just like the *HIROC*, the experience gained with *NATIV* helped form the foundation for later missile projects. In the late 1950s North American built the *Navaho*, a rocket boosted intercontinental supersonic cruise missile. *Navaho* proved to be too complex and was never deployed. North American's Rocketdyne Division built the engines for *Navaho*, which led to the powerplants for other missiles, including the Convair *Atlas*.

Senior commanders in the AAF felt the aerial defense of the United States should reside with their service. Therefore, in January 1946 the AAF awarded the Boeing Company a contract to develop a surface-to-air guided missile. (It should be pointed out that this came at a time when the Army Ground Forces were working on two other antiaircraft missiles – *Loki* and *Nike*.) Boeing named the missile *GAPA*, an acronym for Ground-to-Air Pilotless Aircraft. The AAF designation for the project was *MX-606*.

On June 13, 1946, Boeing fired the first *GAPA* missile at a range in Utah, in an area of desert that is just outside of present-day Hill Air Force Base. Between 13 June and 1 July there were 38 firings in Utah. These initial rockets, which comprised the Boeing Model 600 series, were two-stage solid-fuel missiles. The following year *GAPA* tests were moved to Holloman Air Force Base.

GAPA testing at Holloman began on July 24, 1947. The first *GAPA* missiles fired at Holloman were little more than telephone poles with fins. For propulsion, solid-fuel JATO motors were attached to the fuselage. According to one project participant, when these rockets impacted in the desert, they resulted in "a large number of toothpicks."

Boeing progressed through two more versions of the *GAPA*— Models 601 and 602. The Model 601 version used a solid-fuel booster and a liquid-fuel sustainer. Firings of this model began in March 1948. They tested the proposed beam-riding, mid-course guidance system and a target seeker for terminal homing. The Model 602 variants were the most advanced, having a solid-fuel booster and ramjet sustainer for supersonic cruise. An even more

advanced Model 603 was on the drawing board, but it was never built. On November 15, 1949, a GAPA Model 602 reached an altitude of 59,000 feet, which was the highest altitude ever reached by a ramjet at that time.

By that time, the AAF was the United States Air Force (USAF). The USAF had plans for a large ramjet-powered interceptor, the BOMARC. This missile's name was an acronym for BOeing and Michigan Aeronautical Research Center, the contractors for the project. *GAPA* was terminated in December 1949, but its technology, especially the work done with supersonic ramjets, directly supported the BOMARC program.

One of the later *GAPA* variants, probably a Model 601. *Source: U.S. Air Force photograph.*

7

Korea

On June 25, 1950, Communist North Korea invaded its neighbor to the south. What followed over the next three years has been variously described as a "war," "conflict," or "police action." The Korean War had profound effects on the United States military, Army missile programs, and activities at WSPG.

At the end of World War II an uneasy peace existed on the Korean peninsula. Japan, which had occupied the country for the previous fifty years, was gone. Now, the United States and Soviet Union occupied Korea. The Soviet Union declared war on Japan on August 6, 1945, and invaded Manchuria. Four days later Soviet forces entered Korea. At the Potsdam Conference, the United States and Soviet Union agreed to partition the country along the 38th Parallel. According to the terms negotiated at Potsdam, Soviet Premiere Joseph Stalin agreed to not advance any further south than the 38th Parallel.

The American army arrived on the peninsula a few weeks later. Lieutenant General John R. Hodge formally accepted the surrender of Japanese forces south of the 38th Parallel on 9 September. Potsdam created a structure where the Soviets occupied the northern portion of the country, while the Americans were in the south. The plan stipulated that the occupying armies leave after four years, and the Korean people would be free to choose their own government.

On June 29, 1949, the last American occupation troops left the peninsula, leaving just 500 military advisors behind. The United States honored the agreement in spite of the major changes that had occurred in the world since Americans first landed in Korea. With the end of World War II, America demobilized and quickly switched to a peacetime economy, even though the Soviet Union expanded their military and maintained a menacing presence in Eastern Europe.

At Yalta, American President Franklin Roosevelt, British Prime Minister Winston Churchill, and Soviet Premier Joseph Stalin agreed to divide Germany into occupation zones, and to allow the Soviet Union to establish a buffer zone around its borders by establishing Communist governments throughout Eastern Europe. Communism spread into Yugoslavia, Albania, Romania, Bulgaria, Poland, Hungary, and Czechoslovakia. Stalin further espoused the inevitability of an eventual conflict between capitalism and communism, and embarked on a program to modernize and expand Soviet military forces. At the time, this did not overly alarm most Western government leaders. After all, the United States had the atomic bomb, and Russia did not.

In 1945, the most advanced bomber in the world was the Boeing B-29 *Superfortress*. With a nominal bomb load of 12,000 pounds, the B-29 was the heaviest combat aircraft in World War II. It flew at 357 miles per hour at an altitude of 30,000 feet. On August 6, 1945, a B-29 nicknamed *Enola Gay* dropped an atomic bomb on the Japanese city of Hiroshima. Three days later another B-29, *Bock's Car*, dropped a second atomic bomb over Nagasaki. One of these 4-engine bombers fell into Soviet hands during the war, and the Tupulov design bureau reverse-engineered it to build the Tu-4 *Bull*. In theory, the Soviets had an aircraft capable of delivering an atomic bomb, but they didn't have a bomb.

The lack of the atomic bomb did not keep the Soviets from trying to spread Communism throughout the world. Emboldened by its gains in Eastern Europe, the Soviet Union looked for ways to increase its influence. In one of the first confrontations of the Cold War, the Soviet Union tried to spread Communist doctrine southward, into Turkey and Greece. President Truman, who succeeded Roosevelt upon the latter's death on April 12, 1945, responded with a $400,000,000 aid package to help these countries recover from the war and resist Communist efforts to exploit their weakness. This program of providing aid to contain the spread of Communism became known as the "Truman Doctrine."

The first major post-war crisis that had the potential to escalate into an armed conflict came in Berlin. Like the rest of Germany, Berlin was divided between the Americans, British, French, and Soviets. From Stalin's perspective, this presented a vexing problem because Berlin was in the heart of Soviet-occupied Germany. Eager to force the western powers out of eastern Germany, Stalin blockaded Berlin in June 1948. The only western access to the isolated city was by three narrow air corridors. England and America responded to the blockade with the Berlin Airlift. For the next 15 months, American and British aircrews delivered everything the city needed to survive.

President Truman reinforced the Berlin Airlift by deploying 60 B-29 *Superfortress* bombers, theoretically carrying atomic bombs, to England. What Stalin did not know was that atomic bombs were in short supply. In fact, these B-29s had not even been modified to carry atomic weapons. The bluff worked. Unwilling to risk provoking a nuclear response, Stalin did not interfere with the supply flights. Throughout the rest of 1948 and into 1949, airplanes brought enough food and supplies (including coal) into Berlin to mitigate the effects of the blockade. Realizing he had underestimated President Truman's resolve, Stalin finally reopened the surface routes. On September 30, 1949, the United States Air Force flew its last supply flight into Berlin.

However, by that time, the Soviet Union had exploded its first atomic bomb. On August 29, 1949, Soviet scientists detonated a 22-kiloton device at the Semispalatinsk Test Site in Kazakhstan. Now the Soviets also had "the bomb," and Stalin continued his military buildup and occupation of Eastern Europe. At a speech delivered on March 3, 1946, at Westminster College in Fulton, Missouri, Winston Churchill had already described the "iron curtain" that had descended across the European continent. With the atomic bomb in its arsenal, Western leaders became increasingly uneasy about the threat posed by the Soviet Union.

After the first Soviet atomic test there was a greater emphasis on the development of a thermonuclear weapon, or hydrogen bomb. Edward Teller proposed such a weapon while working on the Manhattan Project at Los Alamos. Where atomic bomb yields were measured in kilotons, thermonuclear devices would result in megaton explosions. Teller became so engrossed in the "super" that he actually refused to work on anything else. In the wake of the Soviet detonation, President Truman announced the United States would pursue the hydrogen bomb.

Further fueling American concerns, Communist forces under Mao Zedong took over China in 1949. Communist doctrine espoused world domination, and it seemed like Stalin, Mao, and others were doing everything in their powers to bring this about. Despite world events, President Truman insisted on maintaining a $15-billion a year ceiling on defense spending. The situation in the Far East was especially troubling, but American military leaders hoped stability could be maintained in Korea through the deterrent effect of the United States' continued military presence in nearby Japan. Although Korea was supposed to be reunified, two governments existed in the country. The territory south of the 38th Parallel became the Republic of Korea (ROK). The northern portion of the peninsula became the Democratic People's Republic of Korea (DPRK).

Syngman Rhee, a fervent anti-Communist, became President of the Republic of Korea. Kim Il Sung became General Secretary of the Communist Party and leader of the DPRK. In accordance with terms of the Potsdam Conference, the United States called for elections to reunify the country and install a single government. South Korea had nearly double the population of the North, so Kim Il Sung would not agree, because he knew he could not win a free election. As President Rhee's government gained popularity and strength, it seemed to Kim the only way he could remain in power and reunite the country on his terms was through military action. Throughout 1949 and the first half of 1950, Kim Il Sung built the North Korean Army into a formidable force with materiel aid from the Soviet Union. The DPRK Army eventually had nearly half a million troops, 150 Soviet-made tanks, and approximately 300 airplanes (including trainers and reconnaissance aircraft.) The South Korean military, in comparison, comprised 150,000 soldiers, 40 tanks, 14 attack planes, and a few anti-tank weapons.

On June 25, 1950, the North Korean army poured across the 38th Parallel into the Republic of Korea. Outnumbered and outgunned, the South Korean army was routed. Three days after the invasion began, North Korean troops occupied Seoul, South Korea's capital. Without outside help, the Republic of Korea would cease to exist.

After the first reports of the invasion reached Washington, D.C., President Truman directed General Douglas MacArthur, commander of the American forces in Japan, to transfer munitions to the ROK Army and provide air cover for evacuating U.S. citizens. The next day, Truman authorized American forces to aid the ROK military. Truman also turned to the United Nations for an international mandate to aid the ROK. Primarily because the Soviet Union boycotted the meeting of the United Nations Security Council and did not have a member present who could veto the action, Truman obtained a resolution that called for military intervention to support the beleaguered ROK. On 5 July Task Force Smith, part of the American 24th Infantry Division based in Japan, engaged the North Koreans at Osan. American aircraft had already been battling the North Korean air force for over a week by that time.

American forces in the Far East were not prepared for combat. Total American strength in the region comprised just four infantry divisions and one regimental combat team. These units lacked about a third of their organic infantry and artillery and almost all of their armor. Most averaged just 70% strength, and they only had a 45-day ammunition reserve. American units were initially deployed to Korea in a piecemeal fashion in an effort to slow the North Korean advance. At the same time, the U.S. Seventh Fleet was ordered to protect Taiwan against possible action by China.

By August, South Korean forces and the U.S. Eighth Army had been forced into the southeast corner of Korea around the city of Pusan. With the aid of massive American supply shipments and air support the perimeter held. Weapons and soldiers poured into Pusan. Before the end of the month, ROK and UN forces outnumbered the North Koreans 180,000 to 100,000. UN forces launched a counterattack and broke out of the Pusan Perimeter in early September. The North Koreans were forced to retreat.

American air power played an important role in the breakout. B-29 bombers operating out of Japan pounded targets in North Korea. These aircraft were World War II vintage. More up to date B-50 bombers were being held to counter the Soviet threat in Europe. Most of the equipment used by the Army and Marines dated from the Second World War. Other than developing new jet aircraft, the government had done very little to upgrade America's military in the late 1940s. For example, American and South Korean soldiers had the 2.36" *Bazooka* antitank weapon to counter the Soviet-made North Korean tanks. The *Bazooka* was used during World War II with great success against German and Japanese tanks. Against the heavier armor of the Soviet tanks used by the North Koreans it was ineffective. The warhead just wasn't large enough. Fortunately, the Ordnance Department had a heavier 3.5" diameter *Super Bazooka* under development, and it was rushed into production.

To further help the breakout from the Pusan Perimeter, General MacArthur came up with a bold plan—an amphibious landing at Inchon. This would place United Nations forces behind the North Korean front lines. American and South Korean forces landed at Inchon on 15 September. MacArthur's plan put the North Korean Army in full flight. The UN force crossed into North Korea in early October and was soon on the banks of the Yalu River, which formed the border with China. Rather than allow their North Korean ally to suffer defeat, China entered the war.

American intelligence failed to detect the infiltration of nearly a million Chinese into North Korea until it was too late. The renewed Communist assault, which started on 1 November, pushed the UN Forces south of the 38th Parallel. Seoul fell again. The Communist advance continued until the Chinese outran their supply lines, at which time they had to withdraw. Throughout the offensive, American airpower made it impossible for the Communists to move supplies in daylight. In late January a major counterattack began, which culminated with the recapture of Seoul on 14 March. This was the fourth time the South Korean capital changed hands in less than a year. UN forces continued to advance a few miles north of the 38th Parallel where they stopped. They called this position Line Kansas.

Korea represented a new type of war. For the first time, American military leaders were not allowed to pursue and destroy an enemy. Fearing a Soviet response in Europe or a Chinese attack against Taiwan should the conflict spread beyond the territorial boundaries of Korea, President Truman embarked on a policy of limited war. General MacArthur wanted to continue the advance into North Korea and carry the war into China using atomic weapons if necessary. Truman would not allow this, and MacArthur openly criticized the Commander in Chief. President Truman relieved General MacArthur of his command on April 11, 1951, and installed General Matthew Ridgeway as Supreme Commander of the United Nations forces.

China launched yet another offensive and gained some ground, but was ultimately beaten back to Line Kansas. As before, the United Nations military force halted and did not advance further into North Korea. With that, the war entered a protracted stalemate that saw several pitched battles and offensives, but no major territorial gains until an armistice was negotiated in July 1953.

Within a month of the Korean armistice, Soviet scientists detonated their first thermonuclear device in Siberia. This test came a little more than nine months after the first American hydrogen bomb. At that time, the H-bomb was not ready for employment as a weapon. The American device, code named *Mike*, was the size of a house. Detonated on November 1, 1952, *Mike* had a yield of 10.4 megatons. The radioactive mushroom cloud from the explosion rose more than 25 miles into the sky, and the island of Elugelab, in Eniwetok Atoll, was vaporized. As fearsome as this device was, it had little impact on the war in Korea beyond its psychological value.

While the Korean War had a major impact on American military doctrine, it showed the limitations of atomic weapons and the effects of too much reliance on their deterrence effect. The threat of massive retaliation might prevent a large-scale general war, but atomic weapons were not useful in a limited regional conflict. The lack of preparedness of American military units also showed the false economy of post-World War II limitations on military spending. The introduction of Soviet-built T-34 tanks and MiG-15 jet fighters illustrated the need for American weapon development. Flown by Soviet pilots, the MiG-15 gave the Communists air superiority for a brief time until the introduction of the American F-86 *Sabre*. Fortunately, the *Sabre* entered service about a month after MiG-15s first appeared over Korea, and eventually established a ten to one victory ratio over the Russian jets.

In the early months of 1950, the Army Chief of Staff had already convened a panel to reexamine the Stillwell Report. Chaired by Lieutenant General John R. Hodge, who had accepted the surrender of Japanese forces in Korea, this panel performed a critical review of the Army's current equipment requirements. When the final report of the Hodge Board was approved on December 29, 1950, the Korean War was already six months old. The new "Army Equipment Development Guide" superseded the Stillwell Report.

White Sands Proving Ground base headquarters, ca. 1953. *Source: U.S. Army photograph.*

On-post housing, ca. 1953. *Source: U.S. Army photograph.*

To "win a war that may come at any time," the Guide recognized the "urgency for a high degree of concentration on those items from which the greatest benefit can reasonably be expected in the foreseeable future." Where the Stillwell Report emphasized development of more potent atomic weapons and strategic aircraft, the Hodge Report gave priority to modern equipment necessary to restore the Army's combat effectiveness.

With the outbreak of war in Korea, a number of Army projects, including the *Corporal* and *Nike* missiles, were placed on a crash basis to expedite development, production, and delivery. From 1944 to 1949, the total spent on missile research and development by all 3 services was $292.6 million; the Army share of that was just $56.5 million over the five-year period. In 1950, the total amount for all services was increased to $105.6 million, and the following year it climbed to $178.5 million. The Army allocation of that amounted to $22.8 million in 1950 and $55.4 million in 1951.

Construction at WSPG showed a similar pattern. For fiscal year 1949, the amount spent on construction amounted to only $402,702. The following fiscal year (which began on July 1, 1950) the figure more than tripled, to $1,515,976. After that it dropped to $1,037,070 in FY 1951, but then jumped sharply to $3,265,895 for 1952. After another slight dip in 1953, the upward trend started again as new missile programs began. For FY 1955, the amount spent totaled $5,078,038.

Under the command of General Eddy, facilities at WSPG underwent major expansion. The Wherry Housing Development was started in August 1952 to accommodate the influx of personnel. WSPG also received a new theater, Post Exchange, commissary, fire station, elementary school, and dispensary in the early 1950s.

Eddy directed the creation of the Flight Determination Laboratory (FDL) on November 1, 1951. The FDL, which officially came into being on February 15, 1952, absorbed the functions and personnel of the Aberdeen Proving Ground Ballistic Research Laboratory assigned to WSPG. In addition, Eddy presided over the establishment of the integrated test range, which combined control over WSPG and the Holloman Air Development Center (HADC). Holloman Air Force Base became the Holloman Air Development Center, an independent research and development center under the Air Research and Development Command in October 1952. HADC had the mission of research and testing of Air Force pilotless aircraft, guided missiles, and other programs. One of these "other" programs was the Aeromedical Field Laboratory, which conducted space biology research. The Navy had maintained a presence at WSPG since 1946 and had its own launch facility a few miles away from the original Army pad area. Now Army, Navy, and Air Force missile programs could use the same range and test facilities in a coordinated fashion.

Even before the North Korean attack the Army had reorganized its missile programs. On April 15, 1950, the Ordnance Department established the Ordnance Guided Missile Center (OGMC) at Redstone Arsenal in Huntsville, Alabama. During the Second World War chemical munitions were manufactured at Redstone. With the end of the war, activities at the base had been scaled back, and at one point the Arsenal was slated for closure. Now, with the transfer of missile programs there, the Redstone Arsenal had a new lease on life.

The OGMC replaced the Ordnance Research and Development Division Sub-Office (Rocket) at Fort Bliss. The *Hermes II* project was the first project to be moved to the OGMC. Facilities at Fort Bliss included test cells for ramjet, fuel injection, and combustion problems. These facilities were housed in mobile trailers on the Texas installation. Now, they could be moved into permanent structures. By 1 November all research and development activities at Fort Bliss had been transferred to Redstone. Most of the German personnel at Fort Bliss moved to northern Alabama as well. As of December 31, 1950, there were approximately 700 military, civil service, and contractor personnel assigned to the OGMC for guided missile research and development. Redstone Arsenal also housed chemical, mechanical, and electronic laboratories, as well as production and assembly shops to support OGMC projects. Responsibility and oversight for Army guided missile programs was transferred to OGMC.

In the wake of the crisis in Korea, the Army pushed ahead with the *Hermes C*. In July 1950, the Army directed the OGMC to begin studies for a 500-mile range ballistic missile. At first, this was seen as an extension of the *Hermes* project, and it was called the *Hermes C*. This later became the *Redstone*. Spurred in part by the Korean War, the OGMC had a number of missile projects underway, some of them operating on a "crash program" basis to get them to the field as soon as possible. Missiles being managed by OGMC during the early 1950s included *Corporal*, *Nike*, *Hermes*, *Loki*, *Lacrosse*, and *Honest John*. However, despite their accelerated development schedules, none of these missiles were ready for action when the armistice was signed that ended the Korean War in July 1953.

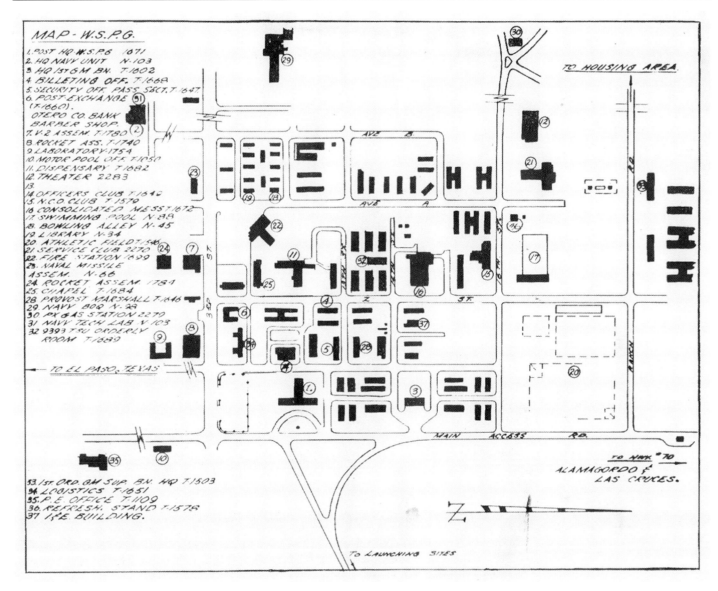

MAP - W.S.P.G.

1. POST HQ W.S.P.G 1071
2. HQ NAVY UNIT N-103
3. HQ 1st GM BN. T-1802
4. BILLETING OFF. T-1668
5. SECURITY OFF. PASS SECT. T-1647
6. POST EXCHANGE (T-1660).
   OTERO CO. BANK
   BARBER SHOP.
7. V-2 ASSEM. T-1780
8. ROCKET ASS. T-1740
9. LABORATORY T-1754
10. MOTOR POOL OFF. T-1050
11. DISPENSARY T-1682
12. THEATER 2283
13.
14. OFFICERS CLUB T-1649
15. N.C.O. CLUB T-1579
16. CONSOLIDATED MESS T-1672
17. SWIMMING POOL N-88
18. BOWLING ALLEY N-45
19. LIBRARY N-34
20. ATHLETIC FIELD T-500
21. SERVICE CLUB 2270
22. FIRE STATION 1699
23. NAVAL MISSILE
    ASSEM. N-66
24. ROCKET ASSEM. 1784
25. CHAPEL T-1684
28. PROVOST MARSHALL T-1646
29. NAVY BOQ N-28
30. PX & AS STATION 2279
31. NAVY TECH LAB N-103
32. 9393 TSU ORDERLY
    ROOM T-1689

← TO EL PASO, TEXAS

33. 1st ORD. QM SUP. BN. HQ T-1503
34. LOGISTICS T-1651
35. P.E. OFFICE T-1109
36. REFRESH. STAND T-1576
37. I.&E. BUILDING.

TO HOUSING AREA.

AVE. B.

AVE. A.

MAIN   ACCESS   RD.

TO HWY. #70 →

ALAMAGORDO &
LAS CRUCES.

N

TO LAUNCHING SITES

Street map of the main post area, ca. 1953. *Source: U.S. Army.*

8

Viking

During World War II, scientists at the Naval Research Laboratory (NRL) worked on a variety of projects, including the proximity fuse, radar, and missile guidance systems. With the end of the war, many NRL scientists returned to their pre-war positions, but a significant number remained and sought other projects. The NRL remained in business because the Navy recognized the importance of basic scientific research, particularly research that would eventually increase knowledge of the properties of the upper atmosphere. In the short term, such knowledge could potentially enhance the development of high performance aircraft. Flight through the stratosphere was already commonplace, and it only seemed a matter of time before humans ventured beyond that. At that time, knowledge of the structure and properties of the upper atmosphere and near space environment was lacking.

To explore these regions, Milton Rosen, an engineer who worked on missile control systems during the war, proposed the NRL build a rocket that could carry a 500-pound instrument load to altitudes of up to 500,000 feet. Initial response to the idea seemed lukewarm; Rosen's proposal was number eight on a list of eight. Gradually, though, he began winning converts to the project and eventually won over his boss, Ernst H. Krause. Rosen received approval to proceed.

The Army's offer to allow scientific instruments aboard the *Hermes* V-2s slowed the Navy's rocket program. The NRL had a means of lofting experiments, so the Navy did not have to develop their own rocket right away. NRL managers realized the supply of V-2s represented a finite resource, so Rosen's proposal remained an active project. Eventually the NRL settled on a multi-prong approach that fostered the development of two different rockets while the Navy launched instruments on the V-2. By April 1946, the NRL Rocket Sonde Research Branch established the specifications for both rockets.

The first was a small, lightweight, and relatively inexpensive rocket that became known as the *Aerobee*. Based on the Army *WAC Corporal*, *Aerobee* could carry a payload of 100 pounds to 100 miles. The Applied Physics Laboratory of Johns Hopkins University developed *Aerobee*, which was built in California by Aerojet. Its low cost meant a large number could be fired to carry a

cumulatively large quantity of instrumentation over time. Like the *WAC Corporal*, *Aerobee* was unguided and fin stabilized. It burned red fuming nitric acid (RFNA) and aniline. C. H. Smith led the NRL team that worked on the small rocket. (The *Aerobee* is more thoroughly covered in Chapter 10.)

The second rocket, championed by Rosen, was much larger and could carry a 500-pound payload. As a scientific platform, the V-2 had many disadvantages that Rosen's rocket would overcome. With the V-2, steering was possible only while the engine was burning, and nearly all rockets spun after thrust termination. As they neared the apex of their flights, a few missiles even tumbled end over end because the air was so thin their fins no longer stabilized them. Such motions limited the useful data returned from scientific instruments that needed precise pointing, like solar spectrographs and telescopes. The V-2 also had to carry a warhead section weighing a ton for stability. If the scientific payload was not heavy enough on a particular missile, lead weights had to be added to the nose section, which reduced the potential altitude for the missile. Despite its limitations, the V-2 proved to be a workhorse for science and lofted more than 20 tons of instruments into the upper atmosphere during the firings from WSPG.

Rosen's rocket, by comparison, represented a vast improvement from a scientific standpoint. Not only was it designed specifically to carry scientific instruments, it had systems to stabilize it in pitch, yaw, and roll, even after engine shutdown. This vehicle, which was first named *Neptune*, incorporated many innovative design elements. It used integral tanking—that is, the tanks themselves formed the missile structure. The V-2 had aluminum tanks carried inside a steel shell. While very robust and sturdy—characteristics you would want in an artillery weapon—it was structurally inefficient. *Neptune* dispensed with the external shell, resulting in a much more efficient structure. For stabilization, the new rocket had movable rudders on the fin tips and attitude jets. During powered flight the engine swiveled, or gimbaled, to steer the rocket. Again, this was a significant improvement in efficiency over the graphite steering vanes in the V-2 exhaust stream.

The Glenn L. Martin Company in Baltimore received the contract to build *Neptune*. The spirit and enthusiasm of the Martin

Company personnel impressed NRL managers, and was one of the reasons their company received the contract. Another factor affecting the decision to award the contract to Martin was the company's proximity to the NRL, which was in Washington, D.C. Competition to build the engine came down to two companies: Aerojet and Reaction Motors, Inc. (RMI). Again, geography was a factor and RMI won the competition.

Headquartered in New Jersey, RMI traced its origins to the American Rocket Society (ARS). Founded in 1930 as the American Interplanetary Society, the ARS conducted numerous tests of liquid fuel motors and flew several rockets. One of the organization's most prominent members was James Wyld, who developed the first rocket engine to use regenerative cooling in America. For his engine, Wyld circulated fuel through a jacket that surrounded the combustion chamber. A few days after the Japanese attacked Pearl Harbor, Wyld and fellow ARS members John Shesta, Hugh Pierce, and Lovell Lawrence created Reaction Motors, Inc., to market the engine to the military. The Navy awarded a contract to RMI to work on a liquid-fuel JATO rocket. (This was in addition to the JATO contract awarded to Goddard and the work being done by the group under Robert Truax.) This work led to other, larger rocket engines.

RMI received the contract for the *Neptune* engine, designated the XLR10-RM-2, in 1946. Initial engine development took nearly a year, and the first engine, Model A, was finished in October 1947.

The XLR10-RM-2

20,750 POUND THRUST

LIQUID PROPELLANT ROCKET ENGINE

This engine has powered a Navy RTV-N-12 VIKING high altitude sounding missile to a record altitude of 136 miles and a maximum speed of 4,100 miles per hour (Mach 6.8).

The engine has a variety of applications and is readily adaptable to a thrust range of 18,000 to 23,000 pounds at sea level.

Its light weight and safe, low-cost propellant combination contribute to make the XLR10-RM-2 a successful rocket engine whose reliability and durability have been checked by more than 200 test and flight firings.

The XLR10-RM-2 is a rated 20,750 pound thrust liquid propellant rocket engine which operates on ethyl alcohol and oxygen.

Reaction Motors, Inc. advertisement for the XLR10-RM-2 engine.

RMI set up a test stand where engines could be fired in Dover, New Jersey, next door to the Army's Picatinny Arsenal. During its first static test, which lasted fourteen seconds, Model A performed reasonably well, but did not develop full power. During the second run a portion of the nozzle burned through. This was repaired, and RMI tested the engine again. On the fifth test, the inner wall of the combustion chamber collapsed and destroyed the engine. Model B was ready in December. On its fourth firing the propellant injector exploded, but the nozzle portion was intact. This combustion chamber was subsequently repaired and became the workhorse of the engine development program. The third engine, Model C, exploded on its fourteenth firing due to a so-called "hard start," which shattered the combustion chamber.

About a year after the NRL selected *Neptune* as the name for the rocket, they were told it had already been claimed by an airplane that was under development. The NRL would have to find another name for their rocket. Thor Bergstralh, one of the scientists working on the project, suggested the name *Viking*, which was adopted in July 1948.

Motor number 4 became the prototype for the flight article. On September 21, 1948, RMI technicians fired it for 66 seconds, during which time it produced a thrust of 21,000 pounds. With this successful test, the Navy accepted the XLR-RM-2. By that time the first production motor was nearly finished. Once completed, it was fired several times on the RMI test stand before being shipped to the Martin Company for integration into the first *Viking* rocket.

The XLR10-RM-2 burned liquid oxygen and a mixture of 95% ethyl alcohol and 5% water. Production engines produced a nominal thrust of 20,750 pounds. Like the V-2, *Viking* had a turbopump powered by the decomposition of hydrogen peroxide that fed propellants to the combustion chamber. Concentrated hydrogen peroxide (90% concentration) passed over a catalyst of manganese dioxide to produce superheated (1,300° Fahrenheit) steam to drive the turbines. Pressurized nitrogen forced the peroxide into the gas generator. The steam produced by the hydrogen peroxide drove the turbopump at 10,000 RPM. Liquid oxygen was fed directly from the tank, through the pump, to the combustion chamber injector head. The alcohol fuel took a more circuitous route; it circulated through the cooling jacket that enclosed the combustion chamber before reaching the injector head. Once the firing switch was pushed in the blockhouse, it took three seconds for the engine to build up to its full thrust.

The thrust chamber was made from stainless steel and had a rolled sheet nickel inner jacket. Fuel entered the engine through four 1 ½-inch fittings at the nozzle end of the cooling jacket. It weighed 194 pounds and was 33 ¾ inches long. The mixture ratio of oxygen to alcohol was 1 to 1.11. The combustion chamber was attached to a gimbal ring that let it move to steer the rocket. During powered flight, hydraulic actuators attached to the ring swiveled the chamber plus or minus 5 degrees in the pitch and yaw axes.

Viking had four swept-back fins mounted equidistantly about the tail. The fins were labeled according to the cardinal points on a compass; that is, North, East, West, and South. Turbine exhaust steam from the propellant pump was diverted to nozzles in the East and West fins. These jets and trim tabs on the outer corners of the

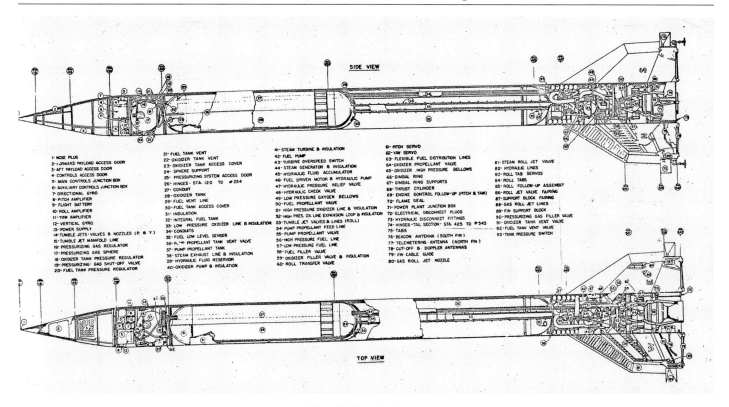

Viking RTV-N-12 cutaway.

fins kept the rocket from rolling during powered flight. Tabs on the North and South fins were adjustable before launch to correct fin misalignments, then remained fixed; the ones on the East and West fins were movable. After the motor stopped firing, pressurized gas jets eliminated any rotation around the pitch, yaw, or roll axes introduced at or after burning's end. This post-cutoff stabilization system operated for 20 seconds after the motor quit.

There were two versions of the *Viking*. The first version, the RTV-N-12 series, was frequently described as "pencil-thin," because the rockets were 32 inches in diameter and 45 feet long. The diameter was defined by the fact that aluminum sheet came in 100-inch widths that could be rolled into a 32-inch diameter cylinder with only one weld seam. The RTV-N-12 rockets weighed about 11,000 pounds at launch, including 8,000 pounds of propellants. After *Viking 7*, the design evolved into the 45-inch diameter RTV-N-12a vehicles, which will be described more fully in a later chapter.

During the early part of the *Viking* program, Rosen spent nearly a year at the Jet Propulsion Laboratory (JPL) in California, learning how to design, build, and test rockets. While there, he witnessed a series of static firings of the *WAC Corporal* to determine why the motors did not perform as well as predicted. The ability to observe the motor during an actual firing and collect data on its performance made quite an impression on Rosen, and he decided that every *Viking* would be bolted to the launch pad and static fired before it flew.

In the Fall of 1945, the Army Chief of Ordnance invited the Navy to participate in the activities at WSPG, because he felt both services could benefit from such cooperation. The Navy

accepted the invitation, and the Bureau of Ordnance (BurOrd) and Bureau of Aeronautics (BurAir) both provided funds to augment the facilities at WSPG. The concept of this working arrangement between services was to cooperate in order to avoid duplication and provide additional facilities to enhance the value of WSPG.

On June 14, 1946, the Navy officially established its presence at WSPG. Construction included living quarters, shops, and additional firing facilities. The Navy built their firing installation about two miles from the Army launch area. This was complete with a blockhouse similar to the Army's, firing ramps designed to handle Navy missiles, and several buildings. The recently constructed Navy firing area included an air-conditioned brick building with a 60' x 60' room that served as a hangar for rocket testing and assembly and several Quonset huts. The brick building was WSPG Building N-77. One of the Quonsets, Building N-76, contained a machine shop. It measured 40' x 100'. A storage area for parts and supplies was constructed in the rear of the building. Building N-75, a Quonset that measured 20' x 40', housed offices and administrative space for the rocket crew. Because the launch area was nine miles from the main base, every day the Navy brought a hot lunch to the remote site, and a fourth building was converted to a mess hall.

In another agreement, permission was granted by the Chief of Ordnance and the Chief of the Bureau of Ordnance for the Army and Navy to share property and equipment. Actually Krause, Rosen, and Smith had already established an informal presence at WSPG and the practice of sharing resources. In January 1946 they traveled to New Mexico to inspect the firing range. Upon their arrival they met Colonel Turner, who told them he had a range safety problem with the upcoming V-2 launches. He needed a way to shut off the engine in flight in case the missile's guidance system malfunctioned and sent it on a trajectory that would take it outside the range boundaries. Since Rosen had worked on guided missiles during the war, he knew the Navy had a radio apparatus that could be adapted for use in the V-2. After a few phone calls, the radio units were on their way from a Navy warehouse to the Army installation.

Krause also chaired the "V-2 Upper Atmosphere Research Panel," which the NRL organized after receiving the Army's invitation to place instruments aboard captured German missiles. The panel included representatives from the NRL; Army Air Force; Army Signal Corps; the Applied Physics Laboratory of Johns Hopkins University; Princeton University; Harvard University; CALTECH; and the University of Michigan. The panel assigned individual rockets to research organizations and served as a forum for discussing proposed experiments and results. This group later became the "Upper Atmosphere Research Panel" as other rockets entered service.

The first NRL personnel to arrive at WSPG were housed in Quonset huts erected in the main base area. Living conditions in the huts were primitive. Clothes were hung on nails driven into the walls. A single heater in each hut provided warmth. On cold nights, when the men in the lower berths adjusted the temperature so they were comfortable, it proved too hot for the men in the upper bunks. When the people in the upper bunks turned down the thermostat, it was too cold for those in the lower berths. No matter how much tape they put over every crack and seam, dust blew into the buildings. Such rugged living conditions engendered a strong sense of camaraderie among the Navy personnel at WSPG.

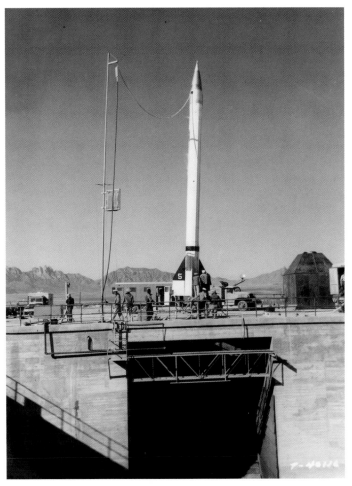

This view of *Viking 5* on the launch pad shows the 35-foot deep blast pit. The pit's walls were lined with two-foot thick reinforced concrete. Two-foot wide overlapping steel plates covered its rear wall. It also illustrates the way the early *Vikings* were angled slightly towards the north to take them downrange. *Source: U.S. Navy photograph courtesy of Bill Beggs.*

The *Viking* crew at WSPG included eight engineers from Martin, one from RMI, three people from the NRL, and twelve Navy personnel under the supervision of a Project Officer. Lieutenant Commander W. P. (Pat) Murphy, a former submariner, was the first commanding officer of the Navy crew. The civilian crew received training at both contractors' plants in assembly, bench testing, and operation of the rocket in late 1948. In December they completed their training and moved to WSPG, where they took up permanent residence. They, in turn, trained the Navy personnel. *Viking 1* left the Martin plant on January 11, 1949, bound for Orogrande, New Mexico. It arrived four days later. Three days after that, it was loaded on a truck and transported to the Navy technical area, where it was inspected for damage.

View of the Army launch area looking towards the northwest, as it appeared in late 1947. The blockhouse is clearly visible. To the right of the blockhouse there is the movable gantry, which at this time was surrounding a V-2. (The V-2 pad was moved from its original location adjacent to the *WAC Corporal* tower earlier in the year.) Following the tracks for the gantry, the blast pit is clearly visible along the right of the picture. No V-2s used the blast pit, but *Viking* did. The Viking launch pad was situated over the blast pit between the gantry tracks. *Source: U.S. Army photograph courtesy of Bill Beggs.*

Everything checked out, so the rocket was moved to the launch pad for the next round of tests. *Viking* engineer Irwin Barr created an interesting way to move the rocket over short distances. He designed a fixture that became known as the *Barr Cart*. The Barr Cart came in two parts: the forward portion was a single wheel that attached near the nose of the rocket, while the aft part was a frame with two wheels that bolted to the fins. All three wheels had aircraft-style shock absorbers. Before *Viking* left Baltimore, Barr demonstrated his creation by towing the rocket around the Martin plant at forty miles per hour.

Although the Navy had their own launch area, *Viking* used the Army pad. This was partly because a "blast pit" had been added to the Army complex in 1946. Formally called the "20,000-Pound Motor Test and Launch Facility," the pit directed the rocket's exhaust away from the blockhouse so the vehicle could be better observed during ignition. The 35-foot deep pit's walls were lined with two-foot thick reinforced concrete, and its back wall was further covered by two-foot wide overlapping steel plates. The platform over the pit had a seven-foot square opening where the launch stand could be erected. Exhaust gases passed into the pit and were redirected up and out across the desert. A sprinkler system sprayed water into the pit to help quench the rocket's exhaust.

Interestingly, no V-2 ever used the blast pit. The German launch pads had a built-in blast deflector, and a new launch stand would have been required. Rather than expend the time and expense to create a new launch table, the Army continued to fire V-2s from a concrete apron to the east of the blockhouse. Tracks had been laid from the V-2 launch pad to the blast pit so the gantry crane that had been built to service the German rockets could be used there, too.

On 1 February, *Viking* was moved to the launch pad for the first round of tests. After erecting the rocket on the launch stand, NRL, Martin, and RMI personnel conducted a series of preflight tests, servicing, and firing rehearsals. Since nobody had ever launched a *Viking* before, Martin Crew Chief J. Preston Layton timed how long it took to load alcohol, liquid oxygen, and hydrogen peroxide. After each propellant was loaded, it was dumped from the rocket before the next one was loaded. Layton incorporated the timing information into the countdown for an actual firing. On 5 February the rocket was taken back to the hangar for final preparation.

Because it was the first of the series, *Viking 1* carried minimal scientific instruments. The only scientific instruments it carried were sensors to measure atmospheric pressure and skin temperature. Otherwise, the majority of the instrumentation measured different aspects of the rocket's performance. These instruments had to be installed, tested, and calibrated. *Viking* carried a 30-channel matrix-type radio telemeter. The cycling range for all 30 channels was 312.5 per second, so ground stations received virtually continuous streams of data. A commutator allowed some channels to be used for more than one function. For example, on *Viking 1*, channel 1 telemetered data on pressures in both propellant tanks; turbine block pressure; hydraulic system pressure; gas sphere pressure; propellant pump inlet pressures for oxygen and alcohol; turbine exhaust pressure; and battery voltage. Each measurement was broadcast in sequence during the channel 1 signal. The transmitter radiated a 3-kilowatt peak power signal on a frequency of 1025 megacycles. While work was underway to finish installing instrumentation on the rocket, all the ground equipment used in the launching area was checked.

Structurally, *Viking 1* did not incorporate all the features later rockets would have. As the first missile, *Viking 1* did not have an integral liquid oxygen tank. In other words, the oxidizer was contained in a separate tank mounted inside the body shell.

The alcohol fuel tank employed the integral tanking construction technique.

Two new consoles, one to control the rocket firing and one for the stabilization system, were installed in the blockhouse, and cables were run to the launch pad. All these preparations were finished on 25 February, after which the rocket was painted and weighed. To aid visual tracking, the familiar black and white paint pattern was used. With one fin painted black, observers could see if the rocket rolled during its flight.

The first live firing was the static test. *Viking 1* was bolted to the launch stand, and the south fin and adjacent skin sections were

Viking 1 surrounded by the gantry crane. *Source: Martin Company photograph courtesy of Bill Beggs.*

removed so the interior of the entire tail section could be observed. A pipe structure replaced the south fin. Additional piping attached to this structure was used to spray carbon dioxide and water into the tail section. The carbon dioxide was used for normal shutdown procedures; the water was for use in an emergency. The missile was loaded with 1,500 pounds of alcohol, which was less than half the tank's capacity, but enough for a 30-second static firing. Even though the rocket was supposed to fire for only half a minute, the liquid oxygen and hydrogen peroxide tanks were fully loaded.

The first static firing attempt on 7 March was halted at X-minus 15 minutes due to electrical problems with the magnetic disconnect plug. In addition, there was no data coming through half the telemetry channels. The peroxide was dumped, and the gantry moved back around the rocket so the problems could be fixed. At around 5:30 PM, the static test was cancelled for the day. Most of the crew had been on duty since 2:00 AM.

A second attempt took place the next day. This time, at X-minus 35 seconds, the liquid oxygen tank vent valves wouldn't close, which resulted in a loss of the nitrogen gas used to pressurize the tank. Evidently the super cold liquid oxygen froze the valves. Henry Hardin, a NRL engineer who manned the firing console, thought he might get the valves to operate smoothly by ordering them to open and close several times. After four cycles the valves worked properly, but each time he operated them *Viking* lost more nitrogen, and now there wasn't enough left to pressurize the oxidizer tank. The nitrogen bottle would have to be recharged. Rosen moved the countdown back to X-minus 35 minutes to allow time to do this.

There was one major problem—they were out of high pressure nitrogen and there wasn't any on the base. A supply of high pressure helium was on hand, so this was used instead. Such a substitution should have been okay because *Viking* had been originally designed to use helium. Nitrogen had been substituted because it was safer to work with. Because of its low density, helium will leak past gaskets and fittings that would otherwise contain nitrogen. The charging process went smoothly for a few minutes, then a sound "like a pistol shot" came from the rocket. The helium supply was shut off, and Layton ordered the hydrogen peroxide and liquid oxygen be drained into the blast pit.

Upon examination, the firing crew discovered the pressure line between the first and second stage pressure regulators burst when high pressure helium leaked past the first regulator. In addition, when the line ruptured, it cut through six adjacent electrical leads and shifted the pressure sphere 1/8th inch. It would take at least two days to repair the damage. This aborted test created another problem for the *Viking* crew—their supply of hydrogen peroxide was running low. There was not enough on hand to conduct the static test and subsequent flight. Only one company in the United States, the Buffalo Electro-Chemical Company, produced the concentration of hydrogen peroxide needed. Because the chemical was so volatile, it could only be shipped via rail, and then with special handling. Officials in Buffalo told Layton it would take two weeks to get a shipment to WSPG.

Hydrogen peroxide is a colorless liquid, like water, and appears harmless. Appearances can be deceiving—at high concentration levels, it is anything but harmless. Concentrated hydrogen peroxide is extremely reactive, and readily causes fires or explosions on contact with many materials. Drugstore-variety hydrogen peroxide, which is used as an antiseptic, is 3% concentration. Thirty percent concentration can cause chemical burns if left on the skin long enough. During World War II, Germany fielded the Messerschmitt 163 *Komet* rocket powered interceptor. The *Komet* used 80% strength peroxide as an oxidizer, and pilots wore "acid proof" coveralls for protection against spills. Not that the coveralls helped that much; the propellants were so volatile the *Komets* had a nasty habit of exploding, especially during landing. *Viking* required 90% concentration.

Two Martin Company designers, Bill Webb and Jack Early, heard about the situation and offered a solution. They volunteered to drive a company station wagon to Buffalo, pick up a drum of peroxide, and then deliver it to White Sands! The pair had wanted to be on hand for the first launch, and this looked like their opportunity to travel to WSPG. Somehow, they received approval for the hazardous trip. The next day, Webb and Early picked up a fifty-gallon drum of concentrated hydrogen peroxide from the Buffalo Electro-Chemical Company and loaded it in the back of the station wagon. As a precaution, Webb brought along a large trash can that he filled with water to dilute any peroxide that might spill before it could set the vehicle on fire. It's doubtful this would have done any good if there had been a spill.

In St. Louis, they encountered a severe snow storm. In Tulsa, they stopped to have the station wagon greased, but didn't tell the mechanic about the dangerous cargo until the car was on the lift. The mechanic finished the grease job in record time. At last, Webb and Early reached New Mexico and called Layton from Roswell. Layton admonished them to drive no faster than 25 miles per hour for the remainder of the trip. Finally, on 14 March, after five days on the road, Webb and Early delivered the barrel of concentrated hydrogen peroxide.

While the peroxide was en route, the next attempt at a static firing took place. At the same time the ruptured pressure line was being replaced, work had been done on the oxygen vent valves. On 11 March—the day of the next static test—the valves worked, but the magnetic disconnect plug failed to drop away from the rocket as the engine ignited. The firing was aborted at X-minus 0. Someone came up with the idea of shorting out the plug security circuit so the rocket could be fired with it still in place. On the second attempt of the day the engine roared to life.

Thirty-one seconds after ignition, Layton ordered an emergency cutoff after observing smoke and fire near the top and bottom of the hydrogen peroxide tank. The nozzle spray put out the fire, and carbon dioxide was sprayed into the aft section of the rocket. Once it was safe to approach the *Viking* launch pad, the crew discovered the insulation on lines adjacent to the steam turbine that powered the propellant pump were burned and charred. The turbine housing comprised two halves that were bolted together. Pressure tests showed there were several leaks through the joint that sprayed high temperature steam into the aft section.

The obvious fix was to tighten the bolts holding the turbine halves together. This was not an easy task. To conserve space in the 32-inch diameter rocket, the hydrogen peroxide tank spiraled inside the aft section, surrounding much of the plumbing for the turbopump unit. The crew tried to reach the bolts, frequently having to work by feel, and managed to tighten most of them. Although everyone was sure the halves were now sealed, there was no conclusive test to prove this was the case. They'd been fortunate that the steam leaks and fire hadn't ignited the hydrogen peroxide tank. Rosen reached a painful decision: *Viking 1* had to be removed from the pad and taken back to the hangar where the turbine and fire damage could be repaired. These repairs took a month.

All the turbine gaskets were replaced and the unit was rebuilt. While it was being tested, a weld failed in the aluminum liquid oxygen bellows. A stainless steel replacement was installed. Most of the glass wool insulation in the tail section was removed and the wiring wrapped with asbestos tape. *Viking 1* was taken back to the launch pad on 22 April and prepared for another static test. Three days later, the rocket was once more loaded with 1,500 pounds of alcohol and the full quantity of liquid oxygen and hydrogen peroxide. Again, the oxygen vent valves were slow to close, but this time 12 full nitrogen bottles had been connected to the rocket through an external manifold. The count was recycled back to X-minus 10 minutes. On the second attempt, the engine ignited.

Twenty four seconds into the test Layton observed smoke in the upper portion of the tail section, so he shut down the engine. Post-firing examination showed no signs of damage, and the smoke was presumed to have come from residual oils in the glass wool insulation. On the first static test the engine generated a thrust of 20,450 pounds; during the second firing the average thrust was 20,390 pounds. Since everything appeared to be fine, *Viking 1* was cleared for flight.

Launches were generally scheduled for the morning, so much of the preflight activity occurred during the night before. The countdown began at X-minus 14 hours, with final instrument installation and testing. At X-minus 10 hours, WSPG personnel installed the tracking beacon and Doppler transmitters. When they were finished installing the transmitters, they turned them on to make sure outlying tracking stations received the signals. Around 4:00 AM the firing crew arrived. Range safety personnel tested the rocket cutoff system with the propulsion crew. They ran through several simulated launchings from the blockhouse, and every time a cutoff signal was sent to the rocket, a red light on the firing panel had to come on. This was necessary to make sure *Viking* did not stray beyond the boundaries of WSPG, so the test was performed several times. Fueling began at X-minus 3 hours. Alcohol was loaded first, followed by the hydrogen peroxide, then finally liquid oxygen. With the rocket fully fueled and ready, the gantry was rolled away from the rocket, to the north end of its tracks. Paul Smith, one of the launch crew, was the last person to leave the pad and enter the blockhouse, usually at X-minus 15 minutes. He held the safety key that had to be inserted in the launch panel to fire the rocket. In the final minutes, the control gyroscopes were "nulled" and the combustion chamber centered in its gimbal ring.

The first launch attempt on 28 April had to be cancelled due to weather. Weather forecasters said the situation would be better the next day, so everyone repeated the preflight process that night. The next day the oxygen vent valves misbehaved again, and the flight was aborted after two attempts. Technicians removed both valves from the rocket for inspection. A shattered "O" ring was found in one of them and replaced. Five-hundred watt heaters were also added to each valve to keep them from freezing. After the valves

Liftoff of *Viking 1*. Source: Martin Company photograph.

were reinstalled, the yaw servo bracket on the gimbal ring broke and had to be repaired. Finally, on 3 May, the rocket was ready for the next flight attempt.

Everything worked this time, and liftoff occurred at 9:14 AM MST. *Viking 1* lifted off cleanly, and was stable as it climbed into the sky. The mission proceeded smoothly until 53 seconds into the flight, when the motor quit. The rocket was at an altitude of 14.6 miles and traveling at 3,450 feet per second. Viking 1, which held enough propellant to reach an altitude of 98 miles, only achieved 50.4 miles 163.5 seconds after launch. Aerodynamic forces during descent tore the rocket apart after 290 seconds, when it was at an altitude of 5 miles. Debris was scattered over an area of 4 square miles, centering 10 miles north and 2.5 miles west of the launch site. Looking for an explanation for the premature engine shutdown, it appeared *Viking 1* exhausted its supply of hydrogen peroxide prematurely. At the time, the most probable explanation for this seemed to be that some of the hydrogen peroxide was spilled while filling the tank. The turbine ran until all the peroxide had been consumed.

Attention turned to *Viking 2*, which arrived at Orogrande on July 16, 1949. *Viking* was an evolutionary program, where lessons learned from one rocket were applied to the next. For the first *Viking*, the nitrogen pressure bottle took about 25 minutes to charge, and the system required that four men be positioned near the rocket. During the time it took to fill the spherical-shaped bottle some of the liquid oxygen boiled off, reducing the rocket's potential altitude. An improved system that pressurized the bottle in 10 minutes was devised for *Viking 2*. Ten high pressure nitrogen tanks, charged to 3,500 pounds per square inch, were placed behind the blockhouse. A pressure line ran from the tanks, through the blockhouse, and then to the launch pad. The new procedure involved equalizing the pressures in the tanks and rocket pressure bottle. In addition, the charging line had a quick disconnect fitting that separated from the base of the rocket at liftoff. This meant the bottle could be continuously topped off if there was a launch delay.

Viking 2 carried instruments to measure air pressure and the skin temperature of the nose cone. It also carried four cameras: two 16-mm gun cameras in the base of the rocket and two K-25 aerial cameras in the nose. The gun cameras looked rearward, and were aimed 10 degrees off the rocket's axis. This rocket had an explosive nose separation system. By separating the nose at the right time during the descent, the rocket was no longer a sleek, aerodynamic projectile, and the pieces would hit at "only" a few hundred miles per hour. Heavily armored packages could survive such a crash. This technique was well tested, and had been successfully used on many of the White Sands V-2s. Hopefully, the cameras would survive the flight and their film records would return high altitude photographs of the earth. The Naval Ordnance Test Station, Inyokern, California, designed and manufactured a shaped charge to cut through wiring going to the nose cone.

The static firing took place on 16 August. After 30.3 seconds, the alcohol level sensor indicated *Viking 2* had exhausted its 1,500-pound load of fuel and shut down the engine. Just before shutdown, a fire appeared near the helical hydrogen peroxide tank. The carbon dioxide fire extinguishing system put out the flames and minimized the damage. Otherwise, the engine performed well and produced an average thrust of 19,890 pounds. Inspection of the tail section showed the insulation around the turbine was burned and charred. Pressure checks of the system showed the turbine casing was leaking steam, just like it had on *Viking 1*.

Components in the aft section had been rearranged on *Viking 2* and made the turbine more accessible. Instead of having to take the rocket back to the hangar for repair, the engineers could make the necessary repairs on the pad. This took just two days, but problems with the Doppler and beacon units delayed the launch until 26 August. On the first attempt, everything went smoothly until Hardin threw the ignition switch. The disconnect plug dropped away and the igniter fired, but the engine refused to light. After ten seconds he switched the rocket controls to the cutoff positions. By this time, there was a lot of oxygen vapor coming out of the turbine exhaust lines.

Throughout the engine testing program, RMI personnel observed a small leak of liquid oxygen past the seal between the pump and turbine. A small leak didn't affect the turbine performance, so this was acceptable. This time, though, enough liquid oxygen leaked into the turbine to fill it and the steam system all the way up to the hydrogen peroxide valves, which froze shut. This was something that could not be repaired on the pad, so *Viking 2* had to go back to the hangar.

Technicians worked around the clock to disconnect the tail unit, remove the turbopump, and replace the oxygen pump seal. The repair was completed in three days; on 31 August *Viking 2* was back on the launch pad. Two days of tests took place, and the launch was set for 6 September.

Viking 2 lifted off smoothly, just like its predecessor, and thundered into the New Mexico sky. This rocket was expected to reach an altitude of 100 miles. Then, the engine quit at 49.5 seconds. Powered flight was supposed to last 66 seconds. *Viking 2* was only 11.1 miles up, traveling at 2,675 feet per second. It continued to coast upward and reached a peak altitude of 32.3 miles 133 seconds after liftoff.

Ground control sent the command to detonate the nose separation charges once the rocket was back down to 30 miles. The nose separated cleanly, and aerodynamic drag kept both fragments from falling too fast. The nose landed in the desert 394 seconds after launch; the main body impacted after 506.2 seconds. Ground cameras and radar tracked both pieces, so the recovery teams knew where to look. The nose was 8.5 miles north and 0.2 miles east of the launch pad. Winds apparently made the main body drift slightly, as it was found 8.4 miles north and 2.4 miles east of the launch site.

It looked as though there was still considerable alcohol and hydrogen peroxide in the rocket when the main body hit because it exploded on impact. The explosion blew the thrust chamber and fins about 50 yards from the rest of the body. Surprisingly, the rocket motor and gas pressure sphere were both in usable condition! All four cameras were recovered. Usable film was obtained from one of the K-25 units and both gun cameras. Of course, the obvious question was what caused the premature shutoff?

Forty seconds into the flight, telemetry indicated the turbine nozzle block pressure dropped. At the same time, pressure in the hydrogen peroxide tank began dropping at a greater rate than could be normally accounted for, which indicated venting of the tank. Film records from the tracking telescopes showed a great deal of smoke coming from the base of the rocket for at least 60 seconds after the engine quit. The final evidence was uncovered in the wreckage of the rocket itself. Insulation on many electrical leads in the tail section was charred, and had even burned completely away in some places. While this could have been due to the explosion when the main body hit the desert, the pattern of charring indicated the damage occurred before impact.

Finally, the fault was placed on the turbine seals, which failed and leaked superheated steam into the tail section. This also explained the premature shutdown of the *Viking 1* engine. Since there was no reason to disassemble the turbine once it was installed, RMI decided to weld the casing halves together. This eliminated the problem and was incorporated on *Viking 3*. RMI also redesigned the oxygen pump seal to eliminate leakage into the turbine.

The third *Viking* included additional improvements over the first two rockets. For the first time, an integral tank was used for the liquid oxygen, a change that reduced structural weight and increased the available volume of oxidizer. To take advantage of the extra oxidizer, the fuel tank was lengthened by 12 inches. These changes increased the thrust duration and potential altitude. Electrical wiring, pneumatic control, and plumbing lines previously arranged internally were now placed in two conduits on the exterior of the rocket body. Earlier rockets had problems with "noise" in the control system during vertical testing, so changes were introduced to the system to eliminate this and give better flight performance. The Rocket Sonde Branch invited the NRL Mechanics Division to participate in *Viking 3*. The Mechanics Division provided instrumentation to measure vibrations in the motor and nose section.

Viking 3 was also the first of the series to carry a full suite of scientific instruments. Scientists hoped to record the solar spectrum in the ultraviolet region, measure cosmic radiation, record cosmic radiation particles in packets of film emulsion, and measure ambient air pressure. The payload weighed 483 pounds. The post-cutoff stabilization system was still untested because the motors on the first two rockets shut down at such low altitudes, so the engineers looked forward to demonstrating this on *Viking 3*.

The rocket arrived at Orogrande on Sunday, January 8, 1950. The next day it was delivered to the hangar, where it underwent several weeks of checkout. During this period, the crew installed a system at the launch pad to top off the liquid oxygen tank right up to tank pressurization. This involved adding a 125-gallon liquid oxygen container to the gantry. Because *Viking 3* had an integral tank with no exterior insulation, it was expected that liquid oxygen would boil away from the rocket before launch at a faster rate than on previous vehicles. Therefore, having a way to replace the lost oxidizer was necessary to achieve maximum altitude.

On the static firing test, the combustion chamber pressure gage malfunctioned, so Hardin shut the engine down after only 14 seconds. The engineers also discovered some of the vibration sensors did not work because the super cold liquid oxygen froze them. The gauge was repaired, vibration sensors insulated, and the rocket prepared for another static firing. This test took place on 6 February. The engine produced a thrust of 20,300 pounds and fired for 67.3 seconds. *Viking 3* was cleared for flight.

February 9th was selected as the launch date. Having solar observation instruments on board meant the angle of the sun above the horizon became a factor in determining the launch time. The best times for that date were at 10:15 AM and 2:30 PM MST. The weather forecast for the morning launch window looked poor but was expected to clear by 3:00, so the launch was scheduled for that time in the afternoon. Everything went smoothly with the countdown, so smoothly that an extra fifteen minutes was gained during fueling. Even the weather cooperated; it cleared a little earlier than predicted, and *Viking 3* lifted off at 2:44 PM.

As usual, the rocket separated cleanly from the launch pad. Then things began to go awry. The turbine worked perfectly; this time the problems were in the guidance system. The combustion chamber oscillated in the pitch and yaw axes plus or minus 5 degrees at a frequency of 1.5 to 2 cycles per second. *Viking* began drifting to the west as it ascended. After 59.5 seconds it looked like *Viking 3* was headed off of WSPG, so the engine was ordered

Viking 3 liftoff. This view clearly shows the deflection of the exhaust flame due to a guidance system problem. *Source: U.S. Navy photograph courtesy of Bill Beggs.*

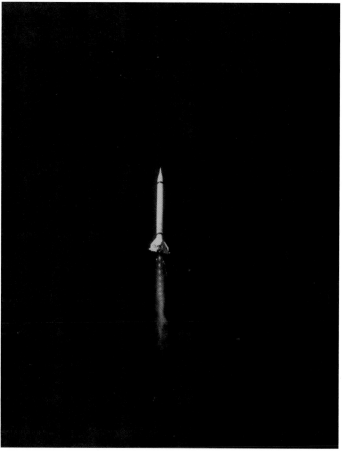

Viking 3 as it begins its climb. The missile can be seen tipping towards the west in response to the engine deflection. *Source: U.S. Navy photograph courtesy of Bill Beggs.*

Viking 3 as it climbed out of sight. *Source: U.S. Navy photograph courtesy of Bill Beggs.*

to shut down. The hoped for altitude of 100 miles would not be reached. *Viking 3* only achieved half of that. Nose separation occurred at 201.3 seconds while the rocket was at an altitude of 47 miles. The impact points of the nose and main body were readily located by optical bearings and aerial search. The nose cone was found 3 miles north and 18.7 miles west of the pad; the main body was 3.7 miles north and 20.2 miles west. The nose was in relatively good condition, but the body exploded on impact and left a crater 5 feet deep and 8 feet across.

Post flight analysis showed the vertical gyro was not aligned to the rocket's vertical axis. The gyroscope precessed away from the axis when it tried to compensate for internal drift of the pitch and yaw amplifiers before launch. The importance of correcting for drift in this manner had not been fully appreciated before this flight. The alterations made to improve the control system had, in fact, done more harm than good. Further exacerbating the guidance problems, large tab corrections had been erroneously made before flight. This made the rocket roll uncontrollably.

Despite the failure of the first three rockets to reach their potential altitudes, a bold plan for *Viking 4* went ahead. Since this was, after all, a Navy project, one of the objectives was to evaluate launching large liquid fuel rockets from aboard a ship. In

USS Norton Sound after its conversion to a missile launcher. Note the *Viking* launcher near the aft end and the helicopter on the forward deck. *Source: U.S. Navy photograph.*

1947, the Navy launched a V-2 from the deck of the aircraft carrier *USS Midway*. Although the missile was only partially successful (it crashed shortly after launch), the exercise provided important operational experience for the Navy. Now it was time to build upon that experience. In February 1948, the NRL submitted a proposal titled "A Navy Shipboard *Neptune* Program," which the Chief of Naval Operations approved. Based on the performance of the first *Viking,* the NRL proposed the fourth rocket be launched from a ship. *Viking 4* was going to sea.

As Navy interest in guided missiles increased after World War II, so did the need for a ship dedicated solely to rocket research. In 1948, the Navy modified the *USS Norton Sound (AV-11)*, a sea plane tender, for this role. Sea plane tenders at the time typically bore the names of bodies of water, particularly sounds. The 540-foot long *Currituck*-class tender was named for the Norton Sound of Alaska. Nome is on the sound's northern shore. Besides providing a vessel where military applications for handling and launching large rockets could be evaluated, the *Norton Sound* proved to be a bonanza for scientists. Prior to its conversion, scientists were limited to collecting data from only one locale, WSPG. With a launch pad aboard a ship, scientists could study upper atmosphere phenomena all over the world.

The Los Angeles Shipbuilding and Dry Dock Company laid the *Norton Sound's* keel on September 7, 1942, at its San Pedro facility. Launched on November 28, 1945, and commissioned on January 8, 1945, the *USS Norton Sound* participated in the Okinawa campaign during World War II. The ship's crew was credited with helping bring down three Japanese aircraft. After the war, the *Norton Sound* shifted from the Pacific Fleet to the Atlantic Fleet, then back again. The Navy selected the tender for conversion to a rocket research ship in late 1947.

The *USS Norton Sound* entered the Philadelphia Naval Shipyard in February 1948 to be outfitted for her new role. This took seven months. Modifications included converting the 200-foot long afterdeck into a launch area with remote control firefighting equipment. The airplane hangar, which was immediately forward of the afterdeck, became a missile assembly shop. An armored blockhouse was constructed on top of the shop. From this vantage point, the firing crew had an excellent view of the afterdeck. Provisions for handling and storing propellants included three 1,350-gallon vacuum-jacketed spheres for liquid oxygen that were installed below deck. Toward the bow, a wooden helipad was added. In October, the ship headed for her homeport, Port Hueneme, California.

Four months later the Navy outfitted the vessel with equipment for handling and launching the *Aerobee* research rocket. This work took place at the Long Beach Naval Shipyard. On its first voyage with the *Aerobee*, the ship steamed to the equator 600 miles off the coast of Peru and fired two rockets. The following year, it launched two more *Aerobee* rockets from the Gulf of Alaska. These rockets carried cosmic radiation and magnetic field experiment packages. Rockets weren't the only thing launched from the *Norton Sound*. It also served as a platform for *Skyhook* high-altitude scientific balloons. Now it would be the launch platform for *Viking 4*. The Navy dubbed the *Viking 4* launch *Operation Reach*.

Viking 4 was not the first large rocket launched from a U.S. Navy vessel. On September 6, 1947, the Navy fired a V-2 from the deck of the *USS Midway*. Although the missile malfunctioned shortly after launch and crashed about six miles away, it provided valuable operational experience for the Navy. Because the deck of a ship was not a stable base to prepare and fire a rocket, this test used an apparatus with two large arms that held the rocket in place until a few seconds before ignition, when they retracted. During those few seconds the rocket stood alone, unsupported, and likely would topple if the ship pitched or rolled. Fortunately, the *Midway* was in calm seas that day, but cooperative weather could not always be counted on if the Navy wanted to regularly fire missiles from ships, especially in a military operation. Overall, the demonstration was considered a success because the *Midway* was able to commence airplane operations immediately after firing the V-2.

Firing a large rocket off the deck of a ship presented numerous challenges. To counteract the threat of having *Viking* topple over if the ship rolled, it was launched from a fixed-rail launch tower that held it in a vertical position until it was safely on its way. What would happen if the ship rolled just as the rocket reached the top of the tower? In such a scenario there was a possibility that the tower would strike the tail of the rocket and send it veering off course. In an extreme case, the missile could hit the launcher and result in damage to both the rocket and ship.

Once the decision was made to fire a *Viking* rocket at sea with a fixed rail launcher, the Naval Aviation Development Center at Johnsville, Pennsylvania, tested the idea with a 1/3rd-scale V-2. They launched the test missile from a platform that simulated the motions of a ship at sea. After this test indicated the concept would work, the Martin Company designed and built the *Viking* shipboard launcher. Engineers at the NRL and Martin Company conducted independent analyses of how the rocket would behave in the launcher. The results between the two were similar, so it looked like the fixed rail launcher would work.

Operation Reach required a new launch stand since the ship did not have a blast pit. The new launch pad had a pyramidal blast deflector like the V-2 pad had. Nozzles in the legs of the stand directed up to 1,000 gallons of water a minute into the jet in case the motor failed to produce sufficient thrust for liftoff. These nozzles were connected to the ship's fire main through valves that could be operated remotely from the blockhouse. Another difference was that the shipboard launcher was fixed in a true vertical relative to the ship's deck. The launch pad at WSPG was tilted a few degrees towards the north to send *Viking* on its intended trajectory. This tilting feature was not needed for shipboard launchings because *Viking 4's* pitch and yaw gyro was oriented 1.5° toward the port beam to deflect the missile's course after liftoff. The launch stand was installed towards the aft of the launch deck, on the ship's centerline at frame 113. It was oriented so the rocket's north fin had a bearing of 45° relative to the ship. The intended trajectory bisected *Viking's* SW quadrant and had a relative bearing of 270°, which took it directly across the *Norton Sound's* port beam.

The launch tower comprised two 24-foot long parallel rails mounted adjacent to the starboard side of the ship. Two sets of two-inch diameter rollers were mounted on the external skin of *Viking 4* in the NE quadrant. One set of rollers was at the aft frame; the other was 10 ½ feet from the rocket's base. These rollers engaged the rails to secure the rocket during the first critical seconds of flight. The forward set of rollers cleared the rails after the rocket climbed 13 feet; the second set as the aft frame cleared the launcher. Thirty pounds of structural reinforcement was added to the tail section skin so *Viking* could withstand loads imparted by the ship's motions while it was in the launcher. The dual rail launcher was installed at the San Francisco Naval Shipyard. Work was also performed there to modify the 60-foot tall servicing structure originally built in Philadelphia to accommodate *Viking*.

Clearance from either rail of the launcher to the skin of the rocket was one inch. Under adverse conditions, once the first pair of rollers cleared the rails, the rocket could rotate about the aft pair, causing it to strike the launcher, so some sort of test was needed to verify its safety limits. Plans were made to fire two dummy *Viking* rockets from the *Norton Sound*. Made using actual tank and aft sections, these duplicated the size and configuration of *Viking*

Dummy *Viking D-1* launch. *Source: U.S. Navy photograph.*

4. The fins were made from plywood covered with fabric. Solid fuel JATO motors that produced a thrust of 5,700 pounds for 3.5 seconds provided just enough power to boost the rockets clear of the launcher and the *Norton Sound*. The JATO motor was canted at an angle of 2.75° from the missile's axis to make sure it cleared the ship. An overall gross weight of 3,180 pounds was calculated to be the right weight for the dummy rockets in order to simulate the same acceleration and velocity in the tower as *Viking 4*. Ballast weights in each rocket not only ensured the proper weight, but they were distributed inside the shell to duplicate the moment of inertia about the pitch axis just like the actual vehicle.

The first dummy rocket, *D-1*, was launched on April 14, 1950, in the Santa Barbara Channel northwest of Port Hueneme. Ironically, the test had been postponed several days because the *Norton Sound* was such a stable ship. The most extreme conditions considered for launch were a 5-degree roll. Therefore, the dummy rocket was to be tested with such a roll. During the first attempt, the ship would not roll more than 2 degrees so the ship returned to port. The next day they tried again.

The ship's commanding officer, Navy Captain John Quinn, shut down the engines and let the ship wallow, but the seas were too calm to get the desired result. He next made some sharp turns while underway at full steam, but still could not get the required roll. Captain Quinn even had the crew run from one side of the ship to the other to make it roll, but couldn't get more than 3 degrees. They returned to Port Hueneme without a launch. On the next attempt, Quinn requested that the destroyer *USS Ozbourn* (DD-846) run circles around the *Norton Sound* at full speed. Surely this would make the *Norton Sound* roll the required five degrees. It didn't. Riding through the destroyer's wake, the roll was less than one degree. Finally, Quinn decided to head to the Santa Barbara Channel, where he knew the seas were generally rough.

Captain Quinn made the right choice, and they encountered rough seas in the Channel. They still didn't get the full five-degree roll, but it at least went past four. Rosen timed the launch so that *D-1* climbed the rails just after a full deflection to starboard, at a time calculated to give the most severe tip-off. The test missile cleared the rails and arced over the starboard side of the ship. After the JATO burned out the rocket continued to pitch into the wind, and it finally hit the water in a more or less horizontal attitude about 300 feet from the *Norton Sound*. This test was so successful that the second test was not needed. Instead, *D-2* would be fired after *Viking 4*, when the *Norton Sound* was on the return leg of its voyage.

Like the first three rockets, *Viking 4* was static fired at WSPG. This test, a 34-second firing of the XLR10-RM-2, took place on March 29, 1950. After a post-firing inspection, the *Viking 4* was shipped by rail to Port Hueneme, accompanied by 20 tons of test and servicing equipment, spare parts, stores, and tools.

Viking 4 carried instruments to investigate cosmic radiation at the earth's geomagnetic equator and high altitude atmospheric pressure at the geographic equator. The 959-pound payload was the heaviest one to date for the *Viking* series. Meeting both requirements dictated a launch site near Christmas Island, in the Pacific Ocean. Ideally, the launch site would be at latitude 0° north and a longitude of 160° west, which is where these meridians intersect. This was the area where the *Norton Sound* previously launched balloons for Princeton University. Scientists could compare the lower altitude cosmic radiation data collected with the balloons to the observations made by *Viking 4*. Experience indicated the weather and sea conditions in this area would be ideal during the month of May.

The *Norton Sound* set sail from Port Hueneme at 10:00 AM on 26 April under the command of Captain Quinn. The following morning, the *Ozbourn* joined the *Norton Sound* as a tracking ship. The *Ozbourn* was equipped with photographic and timing signal equipment to automatically record tracking data from her Mark 25 and Mark 63 radar sets. The vessels were about 250 miles west of San Diego, headed towards the equator when they rendezvoused. During the outbound leg of the voyage, the crew of the *Norton Sound* fired solid-fuel *HVAR* rockets, which left dense smoke trails, from the launching deck for tracking practice. The *Viking* crew finished preparing the rocket and payload for flight.

Moisture and humidity, particularly during the warm tropical nights, could wreak havoc with *Viking's* electrical components, especially the high-voltage circuits in the cosmic radiation package. Because much of the test and calibration work had to be performed in the open, where the ship's steel structure did not interfere with radio signals, the crew built a plywood shelter equipped with fans and electric heaters on the afterdeck for *Viking*. A rubberized fabric

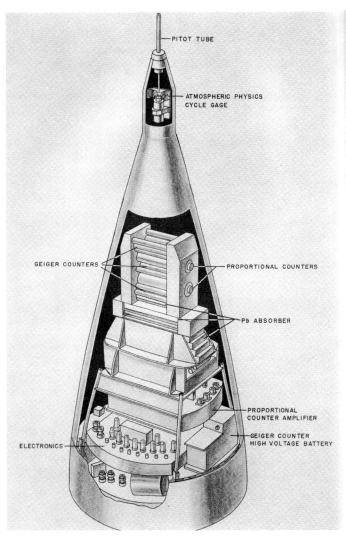

Viking 4 payload. Source: U.S. Navy photograph.

cover was placed over the rocket at night. Hot air from an aircraft engine preheater was ducted under this cover during the early morning hours to evaporate any condensation that had collected during the night.

The two-ship task element arrived in the launch area on 5 May, and the crews began preparations for launch on 7 May. Fueling began at noon on the seventh, with a scheduled launch time of 3:00. There was a solid overcast, so Captain Quinn maneuvered around the area looking for a break in the clouds. At X-minus 45 minutes there was a two-hour hold because of trouble with the magnetic disconnect plug. Electrical contact through this plug was critical before launch because it carried the control and monitoring circuits for the instrumentation. When the countdown resumed, it proceeded to X-minus one minute, when the launch crew could not clear erratic readings on the control and firing panel meters. The launch was postponed, and the crew emptied *Viking's* liquid oxygen and hydrogen peroxide tanks by dumping the propellants overboard. They left the alcohol tank filled. The *Norton Sound* only carried a 7,000-pound supply of the fuel, and *Viking 4* held 4,170 pounds.

Viking 4 being prepared for launch. Source: U.S. Navy photograph courtesy of Bill Beggs.

Inspection of *Viking 4* revealed that during the two-hour delay, water condensed inside the external conduits and pooled around the electrical disconnect plug at the tail. The water shorted out the propulsion system control and monitor circuits. All the efforts taken to protect *Viking* from humidity could not cope with the condensation that occurred during the two-hour delay with liquid oxygen in the rocket. The engineers dried and cleaned the wires, then packed water-resistant grease around them. As a further precaution, they fitted dams made from wax impregnated cloth inside the conduits to direct water away from the wiring.

Then, during preflight tests, problems with electronic noise cropped up in the stabilization system. *Vikings 1* and *2* experienced similar problems. This time, technicians added additional bracing under the gyro mounting platform. They also mounted the batteries that were on the same platform more securely. These remedies altered the mechanical resonant frequency of the platform-battery combination and eliminated the noise problem. The rocket crew also discovered contamination in the hydraulic oil from a decomposing hose. They drained the hydraulic system, refilled it with clean oil, and replaced the hose and filters. Solving these problems took several days, but did not delay the flight.

Viking 4 lifted off on 11 May at 6:00 PM. Rosen timed the launch to occur during the most favorable part of the ship's roll cycle, and the rocket rose from the launch rails cleanly. He timed the roll cycle and found it to take an average of 15 seconds. The ship already had a 1.6-degree list to port, so he timed the launch so the tower was tilted 1.67° to that side. After a slight tip-off transient, the rocket stabilized and gained altitude quickly. The engine fired for 74 seconds, when all the fuel had been consumed. At engine cut-off, *Viking 4* was traveling 5,160 feet per second at an altitude of 24 miles. In an effort to maintain a small zenith angle for the cosmic radiation experiment, the coasting flight roll control system was disabled to make more gas available to the pitch and yaw controls. *Viking* continued to coast upward until it reached a maximum altitude of 105 miles 242 seconds after liftoff.

Telemetry and radar signals were lost at 410 seconds and 428 seconds, respectively, indicating *Viking 4* may have broken up during its descent. Observers reported seeing two splashes directly aft of the *Norton Sound* about 7 ½ minutes after launch. They also clearly saw the vapor trail produced by the descending rocket.

During the return cruise, dummy rocket D-2 was launched. The results were nearly the same as with the first one, and it landed tail first in the ocean a few hundred feet from the *Norton Sound*.

The NRL conducted a study regarding the feasibility of converting *Viking* into a guided missile. The study concluded *Viking* could hit a target 150 miles away with a probable range error of 1,200 feet and an error of 1,500 feet in deflection. Achieving this would require some modification to the rocket guidance system.

Liftoff of *Viking 4* from the *USS Norton Sound. Source: U.S. Navy photograph courtesy of Bill Beggs.*

The NRL report on this study ("Rocket Research Report No. VI: Conversion of Viking into a Guided Missile") did not specify what size or type of warhead might be carried. Instead, the report's authors focused on the guidance system. The NRL proposed using ground stations to send steering commands to *Viking* in a manner reminiscent of the "beam riding" system employed by the Germans with some of their V-2 missiles. JPL was using such a system for the *Corporal* missile, which was then under development. The Navy study proposed using four ground stations to guide the missile. Engine cutoff would be ordered from the ground once the missile reached the desired velocity. This proved to be only a theoretical exercise; no actions were taken to convert *Viking* from a research vehicle into a guided missile.

The existing XLR10-RM-2 engine delivered around 80% of its theoretical specific impulse, or power. In construction of the engine RMI traded efficiency for reliability. RMI had devoted about a year towards improving the efficiency of the 20,000-pound thrust engine, but it was cancelled by BuAir due to a lack of funding. The NRL suggested the project could be restarted and brought to a successful end in six months for a cost of $100,000-200,000. The proposed engine improvements would improve the specific impulse to around 90%, which would significantly boost the potential altitude of *Viking*. Plans were underway for the larger *Viking*, the RTV-N-12a, and it could readily incorporate this engine. In the end, improving the engine proved too expensive compared to the potential benefit, so the engine remained virtually unchanged for the remainder of the *Viking* program.

Viking Fulfilled

Viking 4 was a resounding success, and was the first rocket of the series to exceed 100 miles. However, the *Viking* design team felt their rocket was capable of going higher. To reach greater altitudes, *Viking's* engineers had two alternatives. The first was to increase the specific impulse, or power, of the XLR10-RM-2. Available funding allowed small improvements to the engine, but not the major changes needed to significantly increase the rocket's overall performance. By incorporating these relatively minor improvements in the XLR10-RM-2 an altitude of 135 miles was possible, but that was about all the RTV-N-12 design could achieve.

The second approach, and the one that promised the most benefit, was to increase the propellant load. Simply lengthening *Viking's* tanks was not the way to go, because the increase in weight would have been proportionally greater than the increase in volume. A small increase in length could result in a slight performance increase, but to achieve the significant improvements sought another approach was needed. Instead, the best way to boost potential altitude through increased propellant capacity was to increase the rocket's diameter. By increasing *Viking's* diameter to 45 inches, the propellant load could be increased about 50%, to nearly 12,000 pounds. Plus, Martin's engineering team managed to create an airframe that had the same empty weight as before! This design was designated the RTV-N-12a. Formal work on this version began on July 1, 1950, and its development took nearly two years. Therefore, the next several *Vikings* were of the original RTV-N-12 design.

Viking operations returned to WSPG after the *Viking 4* success. Plans for the next two rockets were very ambitious—the NRL wanted to launch them three weeks apart. *Viking 6* was part of a larger experiment that included observing the annual *Geminid* meteor shower at its peak, so it had to liftoff as scheduled. Rather than try to postpone the *Viking 5* launch until after *Viking 6*, NRL managers opted to launch them close together. *Viking 5* arrived at Orogrande on October 19, 1950. this rocket differed slightly from its predecessor. Modifications applied to *Viking 4* for shipboard launching, namely the rollers and body reinforcement, were not present. The alcohol tank was six inches shorter to allow that

much additional space to be added to the unpressurized instrument section.

Viking 5 carried four groups of instruments to study the upper atmosphere. A pair of 15-foot long whip antennae folded down

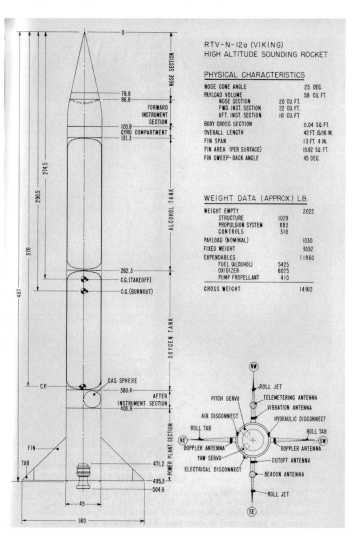

Viking RTV-N-12a schematic. Source: U.S. Navy photograph.

the side of the rocket during launch and extended at altitude. By measuring the propagation of radio signals transmitted through these antennae, scientists studied the properties of the ionosphere. Two cup-like collectors mounted near the nose of the rocket provided measurements of atmospheric conductivity and ion density up to an altitude of 60 miles. Another pair of sensors on the north and south sides of the nose cone measured ion density and energy above 50 miles. *Viking 5* also carried an instrument to study the electrostatic field at the rocket's skin. It comprised a sensor mounted in the unpressurized compartment just aft of the nose cone.

A pair of ground stations in the plane of the rocket trajectory received signals from the ionosphere antennas. One station was 10 miles north of the launch pad; the other was 16 miles north. These stations received the high-frequency reference signal broadcast by *Viking* and two polarizations of the low-frequency signal. By comparing both polarizations with the reference signal, scientists observed how the ionosphere affected radio waves. The NRL ground station, located 7 miles north of the pad, received the rest of the telemetry signals.

Other onboard instruments measured solar X-radiation by photoemission, an ionization chamber, a scintillation counter, and photographic techniques. These included six film packs with various filters mounted on the tail section skin. Two film packs in the nose collected cosmic radiation particles. A pair of movie cameras just behind the nose started at liftoff. Images recorded by these cameras would show which way the rocket was pointing throughout the flight. Information on *Viking's* orientation was critical to the scientists as they tried to interpret data from the other scientific instruments. In addition, the fifth *Viking* carried an array of temperature and pressure sensors. The payload weighed 675 pounds.

In the eight months since *Viking 3*, the Navy built a new hangar in the main base area. It was a buff-colored single-story building with a high roof and a pair of roll-up doors. The central area had enough room for three *Vikings*. Shops, offices, and laboratory facilities lined both sides of the central bay. No doubt the field crew appreciated the brand new, clean, air-conditioned facility as they prepared *Viking 5* for flight.

Inspection revealed a small crack in a weld at the base of the alcohol tank. The field crew repaired the weld and acceptance testing continued. These tests were completed in the hangar on 8 November, and the crew moved the rocket to the launch pad on the tenth. On 14 November the static firing occurred. Although the engine appeared to be firing normally, instruments in the blockhouse indicated it was not producing full thrust. Engine firing was halted after 30 seconds, which was the planned duration. A recorder near the rocket showed the XLR10-RM-2 only generated a thrust of 17,550 pounds. This turned out to be one of the only pieces of data collected during the test. The blockhouse only received data regarding the turbine nozzle-block pressure and alcohol head pressure. Recordings from all the other channels were blank. An on-board timer set to switch the rocket performance channels to the upper atmosphere instruments after engine cutoff malfunctioned and made the change too early.

Because of the lack of comprehensive engine performance data, *Viking's* managers decided to attempt a second static firing that night. Rosen also decided to fire the engine for the full flight duration. Technical problems briefly delayed the test, but at 11:55 PM the engine fired for 71 seconds. It lit up the night sky and was easily visible from the main base area. This time the data channels operated properly. Recorded thrust was 19,340 pounds, which was a little low, but not serious enough to postpone the launch. Besides, *Viking 6* was already in the hangar, so there was some sense of urgency to make the flight.

This flight introduced a number of changes in ground procedures. Previous fueling crews loaded hydrogen peroxide by gravity flow. This required that two crew members hoist a 30-gallon drum of the dangerous liquid onto a platform 13 feet above the ground and let it drain into the rocket. The drum weighed 350 pounds. As a testament to their skill and caution, there were never any mishaps during this cumbersome and time-consuming

Navy headquarters at WSPG. *Source: U.S. Navy photograph.*

procedure. With this flight, the crew used a motor-driven centrifugal pump to transfer peroxide from a storage drum at ground level. Mr. Allen W. Niles, one of the field crew members, designed the new system. Not only was this a safer way to load the highly volatile propellant, but it reduced the time required for this step by 60%.

At the time, the record for altitude by a single stage rocket at WSPG was held by V-2 #17, which reached 114 miles on December 17, 1946. Every member of the *Viking* team wanted to beat that record. Despite its relatively heavy payload, the crew hoped *Viking 5* would be the rocket to do that. Alignment of the fins and fuselage was so good that the fixed-tab corrections were not necessary. Because they weren't needed, the field crew removed the north and south fin tabs, which resulted in a weight savings of seven pounds. The field crew typically ran a pool where they predicted the rocket's altitude. Rosen, who made the official pre-flight predictions, did not participate. For *Viking 5*, most crewmembers were very optimistic and predicted the rocket would break the V-2's record.

Viking 5 lifted off at 10:18 AM on November 21, 1950, and quickly climbed straight into the sky. A slight roll was quickly corrected by the control system. Telemetry indicated the rocket had a slow drift to the west, most likely from a very slight thrust eccentricity. Half a minute into the flight the pitch, yaw, and roll errors were 1.8° north, 1.6° west, and 18° clockwise, respectively. Then, the guidance system corrected the roll error. Forty-one seconds after launch the pitch and yaw errors began decreasing. One minute after liftoff the engine was still firing, and people began to get excited—the altitude record seemed within reach.

The XLR10-RM-2 finally shut down after an amazing 78.9 seconds, longer than any previously recorded thrust duration on a liquid fuel rocket. Surely this *Viking* had to break the record! Everyone eagerly waited for the tracking data as the craft coasted to its apogee. According to the radar tracking station, the peak altitude occurred 248.2 seconds after launch. When the tracking station reported the altitude, the reason for the long engine burn became clear. *Viking 5* reached an altitude of 108 miles. Engine thrust had only been 18,800 pounds; it burned longer because it did not consume propellants fast enough to produce full power.

Movement of *Viking 6* to the launch area using the Barr cart. *Source: U.S. Navy photograph.*

Viking 6 on the launch pad. *Source: U.S. Navy photograph.*

Although the command to separate the nose was broadcast at 402 seconds and the onboard timer operated properly, the explosives failed to detonate. *Viking 5* remained intact until X + 436 seconds, when it was at an altitude of 8 miles. Aerodynamic forces tore the rocket apart. Debris was scattered over a wide area centered at a point 8 miles north and 0.7 miles west of the launch pad.

Despite the lower than hoped for altitude, this flight was a success. It was the highest altitude reached by a *Viking* rocket so far, and the telemetry system performed better than it had on any previous flight. Performance of the upper atmosphere instruments was excellent. Experiments that needed to be recovered—the solar X-ray film densitometers, cosmic radiation film packets, and aspect cameras—yielded mixed results. Three of the film densitometers were recovered in good mechanical shape, but the film itself had been damaged by heat. The aspect cameras were both recovered. Both were mounted in armored boxes. As a result, all 50 feet of film in the north camera magazine was found to be in excellent condition and yielded 2,030 frames covering 363 seconds of the flight. The south camera did not fare quite as well; the film was damaged on impact and had to be cut into 37 pieces that had to be developed individually. The longest piece contained more than 800 frames and covered the first 147 seconds of the flight. The other 36 pieces averaged 32 frames each, but were sufficient to return data for the remainder of the first 360 seconds. Because the

When *Viking 6* ignited, it created a fiery spectacle.
Source: U.S. Navy photograph.

rocket's aspect angle, or orientation, affected the instruments, the film record was crucial for interpreting the telemetry data.

Viking 6 was erected on the pad just six days after the *Viking 5* launch. This rocket was part of a larger effort including *Aerobee* launches, balloons, and ground observation of the annual *Geminid* meteor shower, hence the sense of urgency. The flight was set for the night of 11-12 December, during the peak of the meteor shower. *Viking 6* carried a light load of instruments, so everyone expected to reach an altitude of 125 miles.

Despite the number of high-altitude balloons, *Aerobees*, *WAC Corporals*, *V-2s*, and *Vikings* that had carried instruments into the upper atmosphere, scientists only had a "tentative" profile of atmospheric temperature versus altitude at extreme heights. In 1946, the National Advisory Committee for Aeronautics (NACA) published tables of air temperatures up to an altitude of 75 miles based on the best available data. According to the tables temperature steadily decreased with altitude up to an altitude of six miles; remained at a constant low temperature between six and twenty miles; showed another increase between twenty and thirty-five miles; then dropped again to about fifty miles. Above fifty miles, atmospheric temperature increased steadily. So far rocket-borne instruments showed the same general profile, but the temperatures were lower than those on the NACA tables.

Adding to the conundrum, data collected with rockets did not agree because experimenters often used different techniques and equipment. In an effort to reconcile the differences, atmospheric scientists proposed to launch a series of five rockets and collect other data over a 24-hour period. Through such an approach, the scientists could reconcile the differences and obtain data on day and night time temperatures. They scheduled the experiments from noon on 11 December to noon on the 12th. This 24-hour period was termed T-day.

Four *Aerobee* rockets were to be launched during T-day: three by the Army Signal Corps and one by the Air Force. Air density, which is influenced by temperature, determines the speed of sound. Each Signal Corps *Aerobee* carried grenades that were ejected as the rocket ascended. When each grenade exploded, the flash and sound were recorded on the ground. The time between the flash and the sound could be used to calculate the air density, and therefore, temperature.

Dr. Fred Whipple of the Harvard College Observatory used another approach to determine atmospheric temperature. He collected photographs of meteor tracks to measure atmospheric density between 35 and 60 miles altitude, which could then be used to calculate air temperature. For the first twelve years of his studies, all his photographs were taken in Massachusetts. In 1948, the NRL helped him set up two stations in the Mesilla Valley. Whipple would photograph meteors during T-day. Another group from Stanford University set up an observation station in Alamogordo. To further measure air temperatures, the Army Signal Corps planned to launch a series of high-altitude weather balloons with radiosondes.

Viking 6 was to be launched at midnight. It carried a group of sensors to measure atmospheric pressure throughout the flight. *Viking* would reach an altitude of more than 100 miles, which was higher than the *Aerobee* rockets could reach. Thus, not only would the scientists have data that could be compared to what had been collected by other methods, they would also collect information in regions of the upper atmosphere that had previously been inaccessible.

Optical tracking was one of the most important tools used at WSPG. Using ground-based telescopic cameras, engineers had film records of the orientation and performance of their rockets. Dr. Clyde Tombaugh, best known as the discoverer of Pluto, designed the optical tracking systems at WSPG. The first rockets launched at WSPG carried yellow and black paint patterns in the belief these contrasting colors would be most visible from the ground. After the early V-2 launches, Tombaugh found that black and white was even better. The rockets were generally painted white and had varying portions of their fins painted black. This way, any rolling motions showed up readily on the film records. Flat white worked best—a gloss finish was too reflective, and the resultant glare obscured the outline of the rocket, particularly at the extreme distances involved. Bare metal was even worse.

These considerations would not apply to the sixth *Viking*. Because *Viking 6* was being launched at night, only the engine flame would be visible to the ground cameras. Therefore, the rocket was not painted. This saved 20 pounds, which meant another mile and a half of potential altitude. Leaving the rocket bare also meant the pressure sensors would not be influenced by outgassing from the paint.

A full-duration static test was scheduled for 1 December. Just before firing, oxygen vapor was noticed coming from the roll jets, indicating the turbopump seal had failed, just like *Viking 2*. Because the leak seemed small the countdown proceeded, but when it reached X-0, the igniter did not fire. The field crew installed a new igniter, but it also refused to fire. Technicians checked the circuit and found a short in the igniter relay wiring, which they fixed. At 1:15 in the afternoon the engine fired for 68 seconds.

The next day, the launch crew loaded the rocket with liquid oxygen to see how bad the turbopump seal leak was. Ten minutes after they started filling the tank the magnitude of the problem was obvious. It had to be repaired, but this could not be done with the rocket on the pad. They had to take *Viking 6* back to the hangar, remove the tail section, and replace the pump seal. A similar problem with the first *Viking* took a month to fix; on the second rocket, it took a week to repair the seal. Crew Chief Ed Munnell scheduled his team to work in shifts around the clock. This time the process only took two days, and on Monday, 4 December, *Viking 6* was back on the pad.

T-day arrived at last, but things got off to a rocky start. The first *Aerobee*, fired at 10:00 AM, malfunctioned in the launch tower and only reached an altitude of a few thousand feet. Eleven hours later, the second *Aerobee* launched with no problems. Observers on the ground watched the spectacle as the rocket climbed into the night sky. After the engine quit they waited for the grenades. People on the ground saw the flash from each grenade, followed by the sounds of their explosions a few minutes later. The third *Aerobee* was scheduled for launch at 2:00 AM; the fourth would lift off at noon on the 12th.

So far, the *Viking 6* countdown was proceeding smoothly. At five minutes to midnight, or X-5 minutes, there was a brief hold, just to give everyone a final opportunity to make sure everything was working correctly. *Viking 6* was cleared for flight and the count resumed. Four minutes, fifty-two seconds past midnight, the roar from the XLR10-RM-2 reverberated across the desert, and the pad area became bathed in light from the engine's fiery exhaust. The rocket began its slow climb skyward into the moonless night sky. Observers on the ground tracked the exhaust flame as *Viking* continued to gain altitude. The rocket began a slow drift towards the east, but otherwise seemed to be going well.

Sixty-one and a half seconds after launch, observers at T Station, which was three miles east of the launching pad, saw the flame from the engine appear to go out. Personnel at C Station, three miles south of the pad, noticed the same thing, but for them the engine faded from view at 62 seconds. According to observers at N Station, 6 miles northwest of the launch area, it faded at 62.9 seconds into the flight. At first everyone thought the engine had shut down, but then it seemed to restart after a few seconds. At the same time, the radar return and impact computer seemed to go crazy.

The predicted impact point moved rapidly eastward, and briefly crossed the WSPG boundary. Just as abruptly it moved back within safe limits of the range. At the same time, radar tracking indicated the rocket underwent a rapid deceleration, yet according to telemetry data the engine was working properly. Just as a precaution, the thrust termination command was broadcast to the rocket at 75.5 seconds, but the engine had already shut down at 70 seconds due to fuel exhaustion.

Initial tracking data from C Station indicated a flight time of 336 seconds, which was consistent with the velocity and altitude at 61.5 seconds. This would have resulted in an altitude of 70 miles. Yet, someone who managed to track the missile visually timed the flight with a stopwatch and insisted it lasted 291 seconds. At first, this visual account was discounted. Perhaps he'd started the stopwatch late, or maybe there was something wrong with the watch itself, others reasoned. The rocket impacted in the desert 0.8 mile north and 7.6 miles east of the starting point. It apparently struck the ground in one piece and left a sizable crater. Debris was scattered around the immediate area.

A review of all the available data soon showed the prediction from the C Station data had been wrong. The last received signal from the rocket corresponded to a flight duration of 291.7 seconds. What's more, *Viking 6* had only reached an altitude of 40 miles, which was far below what the rocket should have reached with a thrust duration of 70 seconds. Nobody was sure what had happened, but clearly something had gone seriously wrong. Data from the air pressure sensors only added to the mystery, because they showed extreme fluctuations in pressure along the rocket body. Then, as the various bits of evidence were examined, a clear picture gradually emerged of what went wrong.

The engine had never stopped firing—*Viking 6* went unstable and tumbled under full power! That's why the engine appeared to quit then restart at different times to people on the ground. That also explained the violent deceleration; the rocket began to diverge from the vertical at 58 seconds and reached a horizontal attitude at 64.2 seconds, with its long axis perpendicular to its flight path. Drag forces on the rocket would have equaled 53,000 pounds, causing the extreme deceleration. Once it was horizontal, the rocket rotated in a clockwise direction for a few seconds, then began to cartwheel counterclockwise until the engine shut down at 70 seconds. After that, the missile continued to roll and tumble during most of its coasting flight. Such motions explained the pressure sensor readings. As it reentered the denser regions of the atmosphere, *Viking* regained some stability and streamlined into the ground. The remaining question was why had *Viking* tumbled?

Physical evidence was hard to come by because of the explosion when the airframe hit the ground, but the recovery teams gathered whatever wreckage they could find. Searchers who found fragments of the fins noticed something strange. They recovered pieces of the aluminum skin, but the amount of leading edge strip material was very small compared to other fin parts. This proved to be an important clue. The fin leading edge was a triangular structure with the front fin spar forming its base. Each side of the triangle was made from two sheets of 0.019-inch thick 24ST aluminum, the inner sheet being beaded to the spar and fastened to the outer sheet by rows of spot welds between the beads. The skins were riveted to the machined leading edge strip at the apex of the triangle. *Viking 6* was the first time Martin used aluminum for the leading edge strips as a weight-saving measure. Previous rockets used stainless steel leading edge strips.

Another important clue came from the *Viking 7* fins. They were identical to those used on *Viking 6*. Instrumentation for the seventh *Viking* included temperature sensors on the fins, which were applied using glue that was heat cured. During the curing process, technicians noticed the aluminum skin tended to ripple or buckle in the areas where they applied heat. Suddenly there was a great deal of interest in examining fins from previous rockets.

Fortunately, recovered pieces from previous *Vikings* were kept in the "boneyard," so the investigators could examine fins from earlier rockets. Outer skins on the recovered fins showed signs of buckling over the beads on the inner skins. A temperature sensor on the nose of *Viking 6* registered 502° at 62 seconds. Because this was the only skin temperature measurement they had, the engineers made a reasonable guess and presumed the fin outer skin was at least that hot, perhaps even hotter. At the temperature recorded on the stainless steel nose, 24ST aluminum losses 75% of its strength. In all likelihood, they concluded, the leading edges buckled and possibly ruptured on the north and south fins, followed by the east and west fins shortly afterwards.

Between 47 and 62 seconds the leading edges of the north and south fins began to warp, or suffer a partial failure. This caused the rocket to deviate towards the east. At around 62 seconds, "a major failure of the leading edges occurred, stalling out the fins and causing the rocket to tumble," as described in the post-flight technical report. According to the report, "Until 47 seconds, the stabilization system performance was good; after that time its performance was most unusual."

Despite the disappointing performance of the rocket, the upper atmosphere experiments returned data up to an altitude of 40 miles. Scientists used this data along with the information from the *Aerobee* flights and other experiments to correlate day and night atmospheric temperatures up to that altitude. The *Geminids* arrived as predicted, and the Harvard group photographed 11 meteors on T-night.

Original plans called for *Viking 7* to be the first RTV-N-12a, but development of the new design took longer than expected. Rather than delay the program, the NRL went ahead with a final RTV-N-12 vehicle. The new design would be postponed until rockets 8, 9, and 10. When building *Viking 7*, the Martin Company took advantage of the accumulated experience from the previous rockets.

Obviously, based on the experience with the last flight, they altered the fins. Instead of two thin sheets of material, the flat sides of the new fins incorporated a single sheet of 0.064-inch thick 24ST aluminum. The engineers also added three ribs attached to the topmost spar, and the machined leading edge strip had a larger cross section to better withstand the thermal stresses caused by aerodynamic heating. The flat surfaces were still expected to buckle

slightly, but experiments with a blowtorch showed the overall effect on the trajectory would be negligible. They also altered the steam exhaust valves, which were connected to the roll tabs on the east and west fins. On the sixth rocket the tab on the west fin failed, so this measure was taken to prevent a repeat problem.

Viking 7 carried the same upper air experiments as its predecessor. In addition, it had cosmic radiation film emulsion packets in the nose and solar X-ray film emulsion plates on the aft section. Because this was a day launch it carried the traditional black and white paint pattern, but the nose section was left unpainted so the pressure sensors would not be affected by outgassing. With the lightweight payload (just 394 pounds), Rosen predicted a theoretical maximum altitude of 147 miles under optimum conditions, but his expectation for *Viking 7* was a more modest 124 miles.

The static firing was scheduled for July 31, 1951. During the first vertical pressure test of the fuel tank, Henry Hardin noticed the tank pressure test gauge dropped faster than usual when he opened the bleed line. Typically, when he opened the ¼-inch bleed line, it took several minutes for the test gauge to drop because of the large tank volume. This time, the pressure rapidly dropped about two psi. Hardin repeated the procedure and noted the same result. He suspected something was obstructing the low-pressure alcohol line, probably at the tank outlet. Crew Chief Edward Munnell gave him permission to disconnect the tank and inspect the line.

Viking 7. Note the unpainted nose cone. The nose was not painted so that vapors from the paint at altitude would not affect pressure-sensing instruments. *Source: U.S. Navy photograph.*

View of the pad area taken from the top of the gantry. *Viking 7* is on the launch stand over the blast pit is in the foreground and the blockhouse, which was about 600 feet away, is visible in the background. The tracks for the gantry are clearly visible, and a V-2 launcher can be seen at the end of the tracks. *Source: U.S. Navy photograph courtesy of Bill Beggs.*

Hardin was shocked to find the four-inch diameter tank outlet covered with Mystic tape. During construction, workers placed tape over the tank openings to keep dirt out, but were supposed to remove the tape during final assembly of the components. Somehow, workers at the Martin plant missed this tape cover. Attempting the static firing with the fuel line blocked would have damaged the turbopump and quite possibly the motor. With the tape removed the test proceeded, and the engine fired for 66 seconds with no problems. Thrust was calculated to have been 21,340 pounds.

Immediately after the firing technicians drained the remaining liquid oxygen, alcohol, and hydrogen peroxide from the rocket and weighed the propellants. Everything was carefully measured when it was loaded, so the quantities consumed could easily be determined. Using the remaining propellants as a guide, propulsion chief John Youngquist calculated the precise quantities needed for maximum altitude. His calculations were necessary for optimum performance because each twelve pounds of weight cost about a mile in altitude. Youngquist had to allow for the quantity of liquid oxygen that would boil away while the rocket sat on the pad waiting for launch. Therefore, timing was critical because *Viking* lost 5 pounds of liquid oxygen every second it sat on the pad. If

the launch was delayed, too much liquid oxygen would boil away, imposing two penalties. First, the engine would run out of oxidizer earlier than expected and shut down prematurely. The second penalty came from the fact that there would be excess alcohol and hydrogen peroxide remaining in the tanks, further robbing *Viking* of altitude.

Months earlier the launch was scheduled for the afternoon of 6 August, but Rosen delayed it until 9:30 the following morning due to weather. On launch day, the propellant crew finished loading liquid oxygen ten minutes *ahead* of schedule, which meant Youngquist's calculations would be off. At around X-9 minutes someone noticed a small hydraulic leak, which took about ten minutes to fix. If the count proceeded, by launch time *Viking 7* would be about 100 pounds short of liquid oxygen. While this would only shorten the thrust duration by two seconds, it would cost 18 miles in potential altitude. Youngquist doubted the rocket would reach 115 miles with the quantity of liquid oxygen on board. At the same time, allowing a rocket to stand too long with liquid oxygen on board might create other problems, because the super cold liquid could freeze valves and other components. Oxygen vapor could already be seen coming from the turbine exhaust vent. Rosen faced a dilemma. Should he go ahead with the launch or take time to top off the oxygen tank?

Rosen opted for the latter. The countdown was held at X-8 minutes while the Linde Airproducts truck drove up to the launch

Technicians prepare *Viking 7* for flight. *Source: U.S. Navy photograph courtesy of Bill Beggs.*

Loading hydrogen peroxide was one of the most hazardous parts of preparing a *Viking* for launch. Fueling technicians had to wear hot, heavy protective suits in case some of the highly corrosive and reactive liquid spilled. *Source: U.S. Navy photograph courtesy of Bill Beggs.*

Viking 7 lifts off. Source: U.S. Navy photograph courtesy of Bill Beggs.

pad and the crew added more liquid oxygen. Once they finished the count resumed. *Viking 7* lifted off at 10:59 AM on August 7, 1951. Inside the blockhouse, Rosen started a stopwatch and watched the telemeter scope that showed the combustion chamber pressure. The scope would show when the engine quit. *Viking* needed an engine burn of 71 seconds to beat the V-2 record. Rosen continued to watch the scope. Forty seconds; fifty seconds; sixty seconds; seventy seconds; then the telemeter scope showed the motor had quit. Rosen looked at the stopwatch. Seventy-two seconds!

Actual thrust duration was 71.9 seconds, at which time the loss of oxygen-head pressure initiated shutdown. Telemetry showed the alcohol had been exhausted almost simultaneously, which indicated a nearly optimum propellant load. *Viking 7* was at an altitude of 27.1 miles and a velocity of 5,860 feet per second when the engine quit. The communications link from C Station was connected to a loudspeaker in the blockhouse. C Station had the radar that tracked the rocket and measured its altitude. Herbert Karsch, who manned the radar station, reported *Viking's* progress. "One hundred… one ten…" already this was a record for the *Viking*. "One fifteen… one twenty…" *Viking 7* had established a new altitude record, and everyone in the blockhouse began cheering as Karsch continued his reports. "One twenty… one twenty five…one thirty…" then

Karsch paused. "One thirty-five… that's it, peak." Although the establishment of a new altitude record was never an official flight objective, doing so was a point of pride for every person who worked on *Viking*.

Later, the official altitude was recorded as 136 miles at 265.8 seconds. Throughout the ascent, control of the rocket had been excellent. The maximum pitch error, which came as the rocket passed the speed of sound at 27 seconds, was only 1.4°. The maximum yaw error never exceeded 0.2°. *Viking 7* performed better than expected and was close to its theoretical maximum altitude.

The onboard timer severed the nose section at 430.3 seconds, when the rocket was still at an altitude of 62 miles. This was considerably higher than the desired altitude of 40 miles due to a pair of conditions. First, the timer ran fast and gained five seconds during the flight. Second, the apogee was 12 miles higher than expected. The main body of the rocket landed 49.3 miles north and 3 miles west of the launch pad, which was 16.3 miles longer than expected. Part of the longer range could be explained by an error in the launch angle. For *Viking 7*, the launch table was supposed to be tilted 3° to the north to ensure a proper trajectory. Later examination of photographs of the rocket while still on the pad

Viking 7 climbs skyward. Viking 7 was the most successful rocket of the RTV-N-12 series and reached an altitude of 136 miles. At the time, this was a record for a single stage rocket. Source: U.S. Navy photograph.

showed the angle was accidently set at 4 degrees. The remainder of the range error was probably due to an unexpected increase in the trajectory angle after 50 seconds.

The nose section was recovered, but the film emulsion packs were a complete loss. Each pack comprised a heavy layer of photographic emulsion on a glass plate. As a cosmic radiation particle passed through the emulsion, it left a track that could be studied with a microscope after the emulsion was developed. The earth's magnetic field deflects the majority of cosmic radiation particles; those that get through are usually absorbed or lose energy in the upper atmosphere. Therefore, to study cosmic radiation, scientists need to send their detectors and emulsion plates to great heights. At the time, nobody was sure how much of a health hazard cosmic radiation would present to future space travelers, so there was a great deal of interest in their study. Such packets were being flown aboard high altitude balloons for long-duration exposure, but rockets could climb much higher than balloons. On *Viking 7*, the emulsion plates were placed in armored cassettes that would survive landing. Just as predicted, the cassettes survived, but when

they were opened, the scientists found only a mixture of glass fragments and photographic emulsion.

With the successful *Viking 7* flight, the NRL and Martin Company looked towards the first flight of the RTV-N-12a design. Both versions used the same engine, but that is about the only thing they shared. The RTV-N-12a was a very different rocket than its predecessor. The new design was fatter (45 inches versus 32 inches) and shorter (42 feet compared to 48 feet) than the earlier series. As already mentioned, the new rocket carried nearly 50% more fuel, yet the empty airframe weighed the same. In fact, the empty weight of *Viking 8* was 100 pounds *less* than *Viking 7's*! This meant that 80% of the rocket's weight at launch was propellant.

Glenn L. Martin Company engineers achieved the greatest weight savings by redesigning the fins. RTV-N-12 rockets rested on their fins when on the launch pad, which required the fins to have a very sturdy structure. These were also the attachment points to secure the rocket to the launch pad during static firings. Because of its increased diameter, the RTV-N-12a rocket body was large enough to sit on the pad, and the tie-down points to secure *Viking* during static firing could be incorporated in the aft fuselage. Because the fins no longer had to support the fully fueled rocket or secure the vehicle during static testing they could be built lighter. The redesigned *Viking* had triangular-shaped fins that only had to support themselves. The triangular fins were also smaller—only 10.8 square feet each compared to 15 square feet for those on the earlier rockets, making them even lighter.

Martin personnel even revised the nomenclature for the fins. The four fins were no longer designated by the cardinal points on a compass like they'd been on the first seven rockets; that is, N, E, S, and W for the north, east, south, and west fins, respectively. On the new rocket they were designated NE, SE, SW, and NW.

The new fins had a diamond-shaped cross section. Low spots in the skin were filled in with "Prestite" filler. The skin was also spot welded to the internal ribs. Calculations indicated these fins would heat slower than the trapezoidal ones, and they would only reach a maximum temperature of 475° F. This meant the maximum deflections of the fins due to aerodynamic forces would occur later in the flight. Testing of the fins, which were more flexible than the earlier version, indicated the tabs on the NE and SW fins would not be able to keep unwanted roll movements in check. Because the fins were already finished, external steel caps were applied over the spars. The caps were faired to the rest of the fin with Prestite.

Increasing the diameter of the airframe meant components could be rearranged for easier access. For example, the helical hydrogen peroxide tank could be replaced with a cylindrical one mounted alongside the turbopump, thus improving access to these critical parts. Nearly all of the controls were relocated to an instrument compartment between the tanks and aft section. Only the gyroscopes and their related circuitry were left near the nose.

The post burnout stabilization system never worked very well because there was usually not enough pressure left in the system for the gas jets once the engine was done firing. This system was supposed to stabilize the rocket for the first twenty seconds after burnout. RTV-N-12a rockets were equipped with hydrogen peroxide jets to stabilize the *Viking* throughout the coasting portion of the flight. Small peroxide thrusters were mounted on the NW and SE fins to control roll. (The NE and SW fins had roll tabs on their tips.) Four thrusters at the base of the rocket replaced the nitrogen jets previously used. These stabilized the rocket in the pitch and yaw axes. Each thruster produced a thrust of 20 pounds. The hydrogen peroxide thrusters had their own propellant tank. With the new rocket design, exhaust from the turbine was vented through a nozzle at the base of the rocket to provide an additional 200 to 300 pounds of thrust.

Even the propellant tanks were rearranged. Previously, the alcohol tank was aft of the liquid oxygen tank and was pressurized from a storage bottle. On the RTV-N-12a, the alcohol tank became the forward one and was pressurized using a pair of air scoops on the sides of the fuselage. Valves on the scoops closed once the outside air pressure became too low to pressurize the tank. After that, an onboard pressurization system took over. Compressed air replaced the compressed nitrogen system previously used.

For the original *Viking* launches, the launch pad was tilted three degrees towards the north to help make sure the rockets traveled down range. Now, all rockets would be launched vertically. During the powered portion of the flight, the vertical gyro was tilted according to a timed program. Pickups on the gyroscope ordered the engine to swivel and direct the rocket down the rocket range.

One of the most significant changes, as later events would show, was that only two tie-down points were to be used for static firing. At the Martin plant in Baltimore, this was tested using an assembly that comprised a tail section, gimbal ring, dummy engine, and fifty inches of the liquid oxygen tank. Jacks applied loads at various points, including the engine, rocket support points, liquid oxygen tank, and turbopump attachment fittings. All tests were made to at least 115% of the maximum expected loads. Everything worked well, so the use of two tie-down points was approved for field operations with the actual rockets.

Viking 8 left Baltimore on May 13, 1952, for WSPG. By 30 May it was on the launch pad, being prepared for the static test. A severe sandstorm delayed the beginning of vertical tests until the next day. Finally, the 50-second static firing was scheduled for 6 June. Fueling began at 5:30 that morning. The alcohol tank was filled to 60% of its capacity (3,240 pounds), which was sufficient for the test. The liquid oxygen tank was slightly overfilled with a load of 6,370 pounds. This way, if the test was delayed, the personnel didn't need to worry about having too much oxygen boil away for the full duration. Like the fuel tank, the hydrogen peroxide tank was only partially filled.

When the test began, everything looked fine for the first few seconds. At 3.4 seconds the turbine speed and power plant pressures dropped. Vapor started spewing from the vents and the thrust began to drop. By 4 seconds the engine stabilized at the lower thrust. Munnell and Rosen both noted the changes on the meters on the firing panel. Under the emergency procedures used early in the program, the engine should have been shut down. Now, after ten static tests and seven launches, those procedures had been relaxed to allow some discretion over when to shut down the engine. Rosen made the decision to continue the test. About 8 seconds after ignition people in the blockhouse noted a

deep throbbing in the sound of the engine. By that time, as later examination of data showed, *Viking* was in serious trouble. The engine began "chugging," which induced a 9.5 cycles per second (cps) oscillation in the rocket. Engine thrust had dropped to 14,900 pounds.

Because of previous experience everyone watched for fire, but did not notice the gas venting from the rocket. Peering through the observation ports in the blockhouse, they saw the rocket begin to visibly shake. Suddenly, it broke free of the launch pad. *Viking 8* was airborne! A scant 15.4 seconds had passed since the test began. *Viking 8* headed towards the southeast. Nathan Wagner, head of the cutoff group, was in the blockhouse. "Should we cut it?" he yelled to Rosen, asking permission to send the signal that would shut down the engine.

Concerned with the safety of those around the launch area, including the C Station, Rosen told him to let the rocket continue to fire. He didn't know where *Viking 8* was and did not want to risk a crash near an inhabited site. Better to let the errant rocket continue operating long enough to have it impact in a deserted area. With only a partial propellant load, Rosen knew *Viking 8* would remain within the boundaries of WSPG. Finally, 45 seconds after takeoff, Wagner broadcast the signal. The engine had been firing, albeit at a reduced thrust, for 61 seconds by that time.

Inside the blockhouse everyone waited nervously, until they heard a muffled explosion two minutes after the inadvertent launch. From the blockhouse, one could see a "gray mushroom of smoke" (as described by Rosen) towards the southeast. *Viking 8* crashed to earth 2.4 miles east and 3.0 miles south of the launch pad. It had reached an altitude of 20,000 feet during its brief flight. The rocket broke apart during its descent, so debris was strewn along a NW-SE line. Very few fragments could be found of the tail section because the peroxide tank exploded on impact. The nose section was more or less intact, but the instruments it contained were beyond repair.

The *Viking* engineers were surprised to find out there was a partial film record of the flight. As luck would have it, that morning an Army Sergeant was testing a new lens at one of the theodolite tracking sites. He stopped work when the count neared zero to watch the test. When *Viking 8* unexpectedly lifted off, he quickly turned on the power and traversed his instrument so he could record the flight. He managed to capture the flight from X plus 66 seconds until impact.

Post-flight examination of the launch stand showed the two tie-down fittings were still there, along with parts of the tail section longerons. The longerons failed just above the fittings. Every piece of data was collected and every shred of evidence was examined in an effort to discover what had gone wrong. What emerged was a tale of a series of events that ultimately led to the loss of *Viking 8*. Films of the rocket on the pad clearly showed hydrogen peroxide and liquid oxygen venting from the rocket once the test began. The drop in pressure in these systems led to unstable operation of the engine beginning at 3.4 seconds. A failure of a relay in the power-plant junction box caused the tanks to vent. Apparently there was insufficient clearance between the junction box cover and an adjustment screw on the relay. With the lid probably touching the screw, when the test began, engine vibrations opened the relay, resulting in a loss of voltage to the peroxide and oxygen vent valves.

The new launch stand for the RTV-N-12a rockets incorporated load cells in the legs, which were oriented in the north, east, south, and west directions. These load cells allowed precise measurements of propellant quantities and engine thrust during static tests. While leveling the launch stand, the adjustment stud in the east cell was left with only three threads engaged. This had gone unnoticed because the only way to check the degree of engagement was through a dimensional measurement. When the engine began "chugging," the vibrations caused the threads to fail, probably between 9.4 and 9.8 seconds. With the threads stripped off the east load cell, the rocket began to tip about a line through the north and south legs of the stand. Because the tie-down points were in a NE-SW line, the tip of the nose began to move in an ellipse. Oscillations like this placed severe strain on the tie-down fixtures until the longerons failed due to metal fatigue. A microswitch in the base of the rocket began operating intermittently at 14.35 seconds, indicating separation of the rocket from the stand for the first time. At 15.4 seconds the last activation of the microswitch occurred, indicating *Viking 8* had lifted off.

The NRL and Martin Company introduced a number of changes to prevent a recurrence of this failure on future *Viking* rockets. In the future, four tie-down points would be used instead of two. The safety margins used during the early tests at the factory were clearly insufficient, so the tail structure was strengthened. As an added precaution, Rosen insisted a heavy tie-down structure be used during static firings. The structure attached from the launch stand directly to the gimbal ring on two sides, just below the thrust columns.

The powerplant junction box was redesigned to provide more clearance for the vent valve relay. During a check of the *Viking 9* rocket, the relay could not be mechanically latched with the junction box cover plate in place, which showed the need for this

modification. The load cells were also redesigned to ensure positive engagement and to make them easier to inspect. Finally, rigorous emergency procedures were introduced that required a minimum of judgment by test operators. Events simply happened too fast to be able to assess a situation before potentially catastrophic events occurred. New criteria for cutoff were based on measurements read in the blockhouse during the firing. Upper and lower limits for each parameter were established and marked on the dials. When any reading went outside the established limits, the observer was to command an immediate power cutoff. Operating limits were set within levels that involved any known risks of failure.

Viking 9 arrived at WSPG on October 25, 1952. With this rocket *Viking* launches were relocated to the Navy launch area. Along with the change in launch area and stricter safety procedures, the new design brought other changes to pre-flight testing. Since the RTV-N-12a vehicles had hydrogen peroxide thrusters for post-cutoff stabilization, these were static fired once the rocket was on the pad.

Static firing for *Viking 9* was first set for 5 December, but at X-6 minutes the fire watcher observed hydraulic fluid leaking from the control compartment. The rocket hydraulic reservoir had burst and had to be replaced, which postponed the static test until 8 December. Here, the new safety procedures came into play. During the test, meters in the blockhouse indicated the engine was "hard over" towards the south and the thrust cutoff was ordered after only 3.25 seconds. Subsequent examination of the rocket and launch pad indicated the motor position indicator in the blockhouse was wrong. The rocket was fired again a few hours later, but was shut down at 2.1 seconds, again because of the same "hard-over" indication. Finally, the problem was traced to an intermittent short circuit on the terminal board of a telemetry commutator. On December 9, 1952, the engine fired successfully for 51 seconds.

Preparations for the flight began immediately after the static test. *Viking 9* carried instruments to study solar radiation and film emulsion packs to observe soft X-rays in selected spectral ranges. Dr. Herman Yagoda provided the emulsion packs. Learning from the *Viking 7* experience, this time he coated plastic and cardboard with the photographic emulsion gel. He also dispensed with the armored cassettes, and instead placed his emulsion plates in plastic and cardboard holders secured with cloth tape. *Viking 9* carried six small packs in the aft instrument section with filters that allowed their use to study soft X-rays in space. The instruments in the nose comprised a solar spectrograph; three arrays of photon counters; a pair of 16-mm aspect cameras that faced SW and SE; an indicator that used photocells to record the orientation of the rocket; and emulsion packs to study cosmic radiation. The aspect cameras took photographs of the horizon every 0.2 second. Images recorded by these cameras provided the best source of data on the rocket's orientation needed by scientists to interpret the instrument readings.

The ultraviolet spectrograph contained two cameras and a sunfollower. Each camera observed the solar spectra in different ranges; together they collected data from 450 to 5,200 angstroms. The photon counter arrays were mounted 120° apart in the nose section. One array faced the sun at takeoff. Each array contained

Preparing *Viking 9* for flight. *Source: U.S. Navy photograph courtesy of Bill Beggs.*

fourteen counters. Six counters measured X-radiation beginning at an altitude of 40 miles. The other eight measured ultraviolet radiation up to an altitude of 100 miles. *Viking* also carried two K-25 cameras. With a payload weight of 765 pounds, *Viking 9* was expected to reach an altitude of 186 miles.

Liftoff occurred on December 15, 1952, on the second try. The first attempt took place at 9:16 AM. A morning launch was desired because the sunfollower worked best while the sun was at a low elevation angle. Unfortunately, when the firing switch was thrown the turbopump did not turn on, so no propellants reached the combustion chamber. Inspection of the rocket showed the line to the steam generator was blocked by frozen peroxide. Technicians cleared the line and steam generator, then wrapped the line with insulation. After two more brief holds to correct minor problems, *Viking 9* lifted off at 2:38 PM.

Ground based instruments used to observe the flight and obtain trajectory data included seven Askania theodolites, three Mitchell theodolites, four tracking telescopes, three Bowen-Knapp cameras, five IGOR cameras, three SCR-584 S-band radars, one *Nike* radar, and six Doppler stations. A new installation, the *Nike* radar provided better velocity data than could be obtained with the SCR-584 units. This required that *Viking 9* carry a *Nike* beacon. (*Nike* was an Army surface to air missile undergoing development at that time. It is described in another chapter.)

Weighing 14,615 pounds at launch, *Viking 9* climbed very slowly, almost ponderously, at first. The XLR10-RM-2 produced a thrust of 21,170 pounds. Powered flight lasted 98.6 seconds, which was 8.6 seconds less than expected. Due to the shortened thrust duration *Viking 9* only reached an altitude of 135 miles. Postflight analysis found there had been a 9% error in propellant loading. The mixture ratio of fuel to oxidizer was assumed to be 0.867, but the average flight mixture ratio was 0.93. This resulted in a surplus of 500-600 pounds of liquid oxygen when all the fuel was consumed.

Viking 10 carried a radio propagation experiment with antennae that folded along the side of the airframe during boost like the one launched on *Viking 5*. Studying the signals received from these antennas provided information on the physical properties of the ionosphere. In addition, the nose section contained a radio-frequency mass spectrometer to measure positive ion composition of the atmosphere above 100 miles. The rocket also contained a series of pressure sensors to measure atmospheric pressure and high altitude winds. A pair of sensors inside the fuselage measured air pressure in the forward instrument section and the motor compartment. There were two synchronized 16-mm gun cameras in the forward instrument section to measure sky illumination. They were equipped with a rotating Polaroid filter disc. A K-25 aerial camera in the aft instrument section photographed the earth

Viking 9, the first successful rocket of the RTV-N-12a series, lifts off. Because the rocket was so heavy, the liftoff was much slower than with earlier *Vikings*. *Source: U.S. Navy photograph courtesy of Bill Beggs.*

Viking 10 on the launch pad. *Source: U.S. Navy photograph courtesy of Bill Beggs.*

Hydrogen peroxide loading into *Viking 10* prior to launch. *Source: U.S. Navy photograph courtesy of Bill Beggs.*

through a 90° prism. It was loaded with infrared film. Another gun camera was located at the base of the rocket to obtain a motion picture of the earth.

After undergoing preflight checks and an uneventful 51-second static test, *Viking 10* stood ready on the launch pad on June 30, 1953. Almost immediately following ignition, the motor exploded and the bottom of the rocket burst into flame. Hank Hardin, who manned the launch console, immediately threw the firing switch to the cutoff position. Robert Schlechter, who had replaced Munnell as the crew chief, ordered the carbon dioxide fire extinguishing and water spray systems to be turned on. The fire quickly subsided to a small flicker in the east quadrant, but this was only inches from the hydrogen peroxide tank. *Viking 10* remained upright on the pad.

Peering through the blockhouse window, Rosen saw the fire persisted, despite the thousands of gallons of water being sprayed on the rocket. The spray was directed too low to reach the fire, and he feared the peroxide tank would detonate at any second. Whitish vapor rolled up from the blast pit as the load of liquid oxygen spilled from the shattered rocket. For ten minutes the fire in the east quadrant continued, fed by leaking alcohol. Fire Chief Ernest Boyd dashed into the blockhouse almost half an hour after the initial explosion.

Inside the blockhouse, everyone feared the continuing fire would either ignite the peroxide or weaken the structure to the point where the rocket collapsed. Either event would result in a massive explosion. Finally Paul Smith, the *Viking* Operations Manager, volunteered to go outside the blockhouse and direct a fire hose on the flame. Chief Boyd offered to accompany him. They raced from the blockhouse, dragged a fire hose onto the pad, and began spraying water on the rocket. The fire, which had been burning for half an hour, went out almost immediately.

An hour after the explosion another problem surfaced. The explosion shattered an alcohol line in the after compartment and

the fuel dribbled out of the tank. This is what had been feeding the fire. The problem was, the vent valves were closed and the draining propellant was drawing a vacuum in the top of the tank. There was no electrical control over the rocket, so Hardin could not close the valves from the blockhouse. Dimples began to appear around the top of the tank as the leak continued. If the process continued the tank would collapse, bringing the entire rocket down in a heap of twisted metal. A collapse would also likely trigger an explosion as the remaining alcohol spilled out.

Surveying the situation with Rosen, Schlechter came up with a solution; have someone shoot a hole into the top of the tank to relieve the vacuum. Joe Pitts came running out of the blockhouse with a carbine slung over his shoulder. (No explanation has ever been given for why someone had a rifle in the blockhouse.) Rosen, Schlechter, Smith, and Pitts took up positions behind a concrete barricade about 50 yards from the rocket. Smith directed Pitts to aim for a spot about eight inches below the top of the tank. He took aim and fired. A small hole appeared in the tank, where Smith had directed. Almost immediately the dimples in the tank began to disappear.

With yet another crisis met and overcome, the next step was to drain the alcohol tank. At first, a small amount spilled on the side of the rocket and immediately burst into flame. Everyone scattered as the firemen quickly put out the fire. After that draining continued. Finally, about three hours after the explosion all of the fuel was

Fire! When the launch button was pushed for *Viking 10* the engine exploded. *Source: U.S. Navy photograph courtesy of Bill Beggs.*

out of *Viking 10*. Now the crew could move the gantry back into position around the rocket and secure it to the launch pad. By the end of the day, the explosives had been removed from the nose and the hydrogen peroxide tank was emptied. What remained of *Viking 10* had been saved.

Rosen ruefully examined the blackened, charred remains of the rocket. He decided to salvage what he could of *Viking 10* and have the Martin Company rebuild it. The next day, the nose section was removed and the rocket (or at least what was left of it) was taken down from the pad and returned to the Navy hangar. A visual inspection indicated the damage had been limited to the motor section, aft instrument compartment, and control compartment. The tanks, nose, gyro compartment, and forward instrument section were still in good shape. Even the turbine assembly and valves could be saved. On 18 July the Navy shipped the rocket back to Baltimore to be rebuilt.

Detailed analysis revealed the liquid oxygen propellant valve had failed, which resulted in a nearly maximum flow-rate prior to ignition. About 0.62 second after alcohol began flowing into the combustion chamber, the propellants ignited with a powerful explosion that blew apart the combustion chamber and ruptured the liquid oxygen line. This, in turn, triggered a second explosion and the resultant fire. One way to prevent this from happening

again was to completely redesign the propellant system to ensure absolute control over the engine starting sequence, but this was too costly. Instead, Martin and RMI opted to establish stricter quality control standards on power plant components and to create more consistent procedures for engine testing and servicing.

Viking 10 was the last of the series under the initial contract. To continue the research program, the NRL awarded Martin a second contract for four more rockets. Since *Viking 9*, a great deal of work had gone on to improve the guidance system. When it looked like the rebuilt *Viking 10* would be finished around the same time as *Viking 11*, the NRL decided to incorporate the most up to date guidance system in the earlier rocket, rather than simply reconstruct what it had. This simplified preparations and saved money, because the same ground equipment could support both rockets and only one type of spare parts had to be kept in stock. NRL managers also decided to launch the two rockets as close together as possible. Such a move would save money because the crew would launch two rockets during a single trip to WSPG.

It took eight months to repair *Viking 10* and ship it back to WSPG. On May 7, 1954, it was fueled with 5,530 pounds of alcohol, 6,188 pounds of liquid oxygen, and 385 pounds of hydrogen peroxide. These quantities were based on the results of the 52.7-second static test on 26 April. Since the last launch

The fire-blackened remains of *Viking 10*. Upon close examination, project managers found the damage was not as bad as it could have been, so they decided to rebuild *Viking 10*. *Source: U.S. Navy photograph.*

From the nose down – view of *Viking 10* from the top of the gantry structure. *Source: U.S. Navy photograph courtesy of Bill Beggs.*

Rebuilt and incorporating the latest design improvements, *Viking 10* successfully flew on May 7, 1954. *Source: U.S. Navy photograph.*

camera faced south-southwest. The camera was installed in the nose section, about 12 feet from the tip. It was fitted with a right-angle prism protected by a small fairing so the camera body did not protrude from the rocket's skin. Through such an arrangement, as the rocket ascended, the earth was in the camera's field of view. The camera pointed 24° upward so the rocket body would not appear in any photographs.

This time performance of the engine was excellent and the propellant mixture ratio was correct. The engine produced a thrust of 21,400 pounds and burned for 104.7 seconds. *Viking 11* reached an altitude of 158.4 miles. Throughout the ascent, the stabilization system kept the pitch and roll to only a few degrees. At 331.8 seconds the control jets introduced a slight roll. That way, when the nose separated from the rocket 19 seconds later, the camera was pointing toward the earth.

Previously, the engineers encased the cameras in metal housings to protect them from impact when they landed. Frequently, these housings cracked open and exposed the film. This time, the camera was modified so the film wound into a steel cassette that would survive the landing. As it turned out, the impact of the nose section was unusually gentle. The only damage to the camera was a chipped prism and a slightly bent shaft, and it was

attempt, the water nozzles at the launch pad had been cleaned and adjusted to improve their effectiveness in case of another accident. The countdown proceeded smoothly, and at 10:00 AM MST, *Viking 10* lifted off.

Engine cutoff occurred at 100.6 seconds. The rocket, which started out weighing 14,750 pounds, now weighed just 3,655 pounds. It was traveling at 5,720 feet per second at cutoff. Its motor silent, *Viking 10* coasted to a peak altitude of 135.9 miles, which was 19% below expectations. Once again, there had been a disparity between the flight mixture ratio and the bulk ratio at loading. More than 500 pounds of liquid oxygen remained in the tank. Despite the lower than expected altitude, the instruments performed well and the quantity and quality of data returned rivaled that obtained from any previous research rocket flight.

A little more than two weeks later, on May 24, 1954, *Viking 11* was launched. At launch *Viking 11* weighed 15,005 pounds, making it the heaviest rocket of the entire series. After lifting vertically from the platform, the gyros ordered it to begin its tilt towards the north. This rocket carried a newly designed instrument section. It was self sufficient, with its own 15-channel telemetry system; Doppler and beacon equipment; and antennas. Instruments in the nose section measured heat transfer during atmospheric reentry.

In addition, *Viking 11* carried a K-25 camera programmed to obtain high altitude photographs of the earth. At launch, the

At 15,005 pounds, *Viking 11* was the heaviest one of the program launched. In spite of its weight it reached 158 miles, the highest altitude reached during the entire *Viking* series, which was a new altitude record for single-stage rockets. *Source: U.S. Navy photograph courtesy of Bill Beggs.*

Viking 12, the last of the program to be launched at WSPG. Source: U.S. Navy photograph courtesy Bill Betts.

still in operating condition when found. After replacing the shaft, the scientists pronounced the camera able to fly again.

The K-25 was electrically operated to take a picture every six seconds starting at an altitude of 55 miles and continuing for 312 seconds. The camera received pulses from a timer. Since this signal was also broadcast via telemetry, the precise point in the flight where each photograph was taken was known. From the time record and trajectory, the altitude of the rocket at any pulse could be determined. Unfortunately, due to a wiring mistake, the camera did not work as planned. Only 39 pictures from 65 pulses were recorded, so photo interpretation techniques had to be used to calculate the altitude for each image. This was not as accurate as determining the altitude when the altitude and time pulse could be correlated. Eventually, though, the interpreters were able to correlate images and pulses to obtain precise data. Overall, the quality of the pictures surpassed anything previously obtained.

Like its predecessor, *Viking 12* carried heat transfer instrumentation and a K-25 camera to obtain high altitude photographs of the earth. This time the camera pointed slightly downward so the horizon would be in the center of the picture at peak altitude. At launch it faced to the west. Because of the orientation the prism was not needed. Prior to launch, photo technicians milled the edges of the film to ensure its smooth

passage through the camera.

Viking 12 lifted off on February 4, 1955. Powered flight lasted 102 seconds, and the engine generated a thrust of 20,500 pounds. The rocket coasted to an altitude of 144 miles. The nose separated from the body as planned, but this time the landing impact was particularly severe. Fortunately the steel film cassette survived, even though the camera was completely smashed. When developed, the photos were even better than those obtained on the previous flight.

The photographs covered portions of Mexico and the southwestern United States from WSPG to the Pacific Ocean. Details included railroads, the curvature of the earth, the Gulf of California, the Pacific Ocean, snow-covered mountains, and even smog over Los Angeles. Coverage encompassed nearly the entire state of California.

By the time *Viking 12* flew, the U.S. Navy was working on *Project Vanguard*. Throughout the early 1950s experts had discussed how to launch an artificial satellite of the earth. The Army and Navy each championed different ways to accomplish the task. The Army proposed using a launch vehicle based on the tried and true *Redstone* missile. Their calculations showed a *Redstone* equipped with several solid-fuel upper states could do the job.

The Navy suggested building a satellite launch vehicle based on the *Viking* and *Aerobee* rockets. The NRL named this project *Vanguard*. Initial *Vanguard* studies looked at using the RTV-N-12a for a first stage; an *Aerobee* for the second stage; and a solid-fuel third stage that provided the final "kick" to put a small satellite in orbit. On July 28, 1955, White House Press Secretary James C. Hagerty announced the United States would launch a satellite during the upcoming International Geophysical Year (IGY.) The IGY was set for July 1, 1957-December 31, 1958. Both the Army and Navy submitted their respective satellite proposals for consideration by the White House.

Viking 12 lifts off. Source: U.S. Navy photograph courtesy of Bill Beggs.

Viking 12 in flight. Source: U.S. Navy photograph.

President Eisenhower did not wish to use a converted military missile to launch the first American satellite, so he opted for *Vanguard*. At the time, Eisenhower wanted to establish a precedent to allow satellites to overfly other nations without diplomatic protests, particularly from the Soviet Union. Establishing such a precedent was critical to America's long-range defense plans, because ultimately reconnaissance satellites would be the only way to peer behind the Iron Curtain. The President felt using a rocket with no weapon connection to launch a scientific satellite

Recovery of Viking 12 from the desert. Source: U.S. Navy photograph courtesy of Bill Beggs.

Viking 13, otherwise known as Vanguard TV-0, prior to launch. Source: U.S. Navy photograph courtesy of Bill Beggs.

would be less provocative to the Soviets and would establish the precedent he needed. The White House and the National Academy of Sciences also wanted to avoid charges that the United States was using the IGY to further military research.

The Glenn L. Martin Company received the contract to build the *Vanguard* rocket. As the design progressed, the Martin engineers realized the XLR10-RM-2 was not powerful enough, so they switched to the General Electric X-405 engine, which generated a 27,000-pound thrust. The X-405 burned kerosene and liquid oxygen. *Vanguard's* first stage was 45 inches in diameter, just like the second *Viking* series. Similarly, the *Aerobee* did not have the necessary performance for the second stage. *Vanguard's* second stage was built upon *Aerobee* technology—it burned a hypergolic combination of white inhibited fuming nitric acid (IWFNA) and unsymmetrical dimethylhydrazine (UDMH.) Like *Aerobee*, these propellants were pressure-fed to the combustion chamber. Aerojet, the California-based company that built *Aerobee*, also built *Vanguard's* second stage. The third stage, which was built by the Grand Central Rocket Company, looked like the easiest section, but it wasn't. Designers had a difficult time finding the right propellant combination that gave the desired thrust, burn time, and overall performance. Overall, the *Vanguard* rocket barely had enough power to reach orbit, which drove a need to miniaturize components and minimize structural weights.

Martin proposed using the two remaining *Viking* rockets as the first *Vanguard* test vehicles. These launchings took place at Cape Canaveral, Florida. The first flight, TV-0, which was actually the 13th *Viking*, was launched on December 8, 1956. TV-0 tested the range instrumentation system and provided valuable experience for the Florida-based launch crew. *Vanguard* TV-1 was a two-stage rocket that comprised a *Viking* with a solid-fuel upper stage. This stage was the prototype for what would become the *Vanguard* solid-fuel third stage. TV-1 flew on May 1, 1957. This was the last launch of a *Viking* rocket.

Night launch of *Vanguard TV-0*. Source: U.S. Navy photograph courtesy of Bill Beggs.

10

Aerobee

The *Aerobee* proved to be one of the most enduring rocket programs ever conducted at White Sands. Between the first launch in 1947 and the last flight in 1985, 1,037 *Aerobee* rockets flew. Over the course of the nearly 40-year program, the rocket went through many changes and improvements, but all *Aerobee* vehicles could trace their ancestry to the *WAC Corporal*. The Applied Physics Laboratory (APL) of Johns Hopkins University led the development of the *Aerobee*. In early 1946, the Rocket Sonde Research Branch of the Naval Research Laboratory (NRL) identified a need to develop a rocket for upper atmosphere research.

As the Rocket Sonde Research Branch pursued this idea, two separate approaches emerged that resulted in two different rockets. One rocket was relatively large and could carry a 500-pound payload to 100 miles. This became the *Viking*, which was described in an earlier chapter. The other rocket was much smaller. It was capable of lofting a 150-pound payload to 200,000 feet. This became the *Aerobee*. While the *Viking* could carry significantly more than the *Aerobee*, it was also significantly more expensive: roughly $500,000 versus $20,000. Therefore, it would be possible to launch more *Aerobee* rockets because they cost less. Based on these cost figures, it should be possible to launch 25 *Aerobee* rockets for the cost of a single Viking. With a payload capacity of 150 pounds per rocket, 25 *Aerobees* were capable of lofting 3,750 pounds of instruments. What the *Aerobee* lacked in payload capacity it could make up for with the sheer number of rockets launched.

The Applied Physics Laboratory was created in 1942 when the Navy asked Johns Hopkins University to work on the proximity fuse. Later in the war, the Navy had the APL work on ways to defend ships against missile attacks. After the war, the APL continued working on rockets for the Navy under the aegis of *Project Bumblebee*. Knowing of the NRL interest in upper atmosphere research, Merle A. Tuve and Henry H. Porter, both of the APL, suggested to James A. Van Allen that he survey the rockets available for scientific research within the United States. An important event during Van Allen's survey was the visit to APL by Rolf Sabersky of Aerojet Engineering Corp., the manufacturers

(along with Douglas Aircraft Co.) of the *WAC Corporal*, in early January 1946.

Van Allen submitted his report to Tuve on 15 January in a memo entitled "Liquid Powered Sounding Rockets for High Atmospheric Studies." In his report, Van Allen concluded that no fully satisfactory sounding rockets existed. Van Allen noted that neither the Army nor the Navy had "any existing long range program for the principal purpose of providing vehicles for upper atmospheric research." He then went on to recommend that APL act as an agent for the Navy Bureau of Ordnance in the development of new scientific sounding rockets. These sounding rockets were to be based on the *WAC Corporal* design. With only a 25-pound payload capacity, the *WAC Corporal* was deemed too small for the program Van Allen had in mind.

On the heels of Van Allen's report, APL requested that Aerojet prepare a detailed proposal for the delivery of 20 sounding rockets capable of carrying 150 pounds to 200,000 feet. Aerojet was to deliver these rockets at a rate of 3 per month, beginning in July 1946. Following a conference at APL on 2 February, Aerojet submitted a letter proposal on 22 February bearing the lengthy title "Proposal to Develop Sounding Rockets Capable of Attaining Altitudes in Excess of 600,000 Feet [182,880 m] and Carry a Payload from 300 to 1,500 Pounds [136 to 680 kg], This to Include Liquid Rocket Motor and Fuel Development and Also to Develop Efficient High Thrust Launching Rockets."

On March 1, 1946, Van Allen recommended that the Navy Bureau of Ordnance negotiate a contract with Aerojet for the

The *Aerobee* research rocket. *Source: U.S. Army photograph.*

procurement of 20 liquid-propellant sounding rockets, 15 of which would go to APL and 5 to NRL. The contract, which was valued at $370,000, was formally awarded to Aerojet on 17 May for 20 XASR-1 sounding rockets. Van Allen named the new rocket the *Aerobee*. This was derived from Aerojet (the *Aero* part) and Bumblebee (the *bee* part of the name.) The rocket performance stipulated was the delivery of 150 pounds of payload to over 300,000 feet; obviously, the *Aerobee* would have to be considerably larger than the *WAC Corporal*. At APL, which was assigned the task of technical direction by the Navy, Van Allen took charge of the *Aerobee* program.

The industrial team that built the *WAC Corporal* built the *Aerobee*. Aerojet Engineering was the prime contractor, while Douglas Aircraft Co. performed aerodynamic engineering and some manufacturing. The original *Aerobee* was about 19 feet long and weighed roughly 1,600 pounds at launch. It consumed the same propellants as the *WAC Corporal* (a mixture of aniline and furfuryl alcohol for the fuel and red fuming nitric acid as the oxidizer). The regeneratively cooled engine produced a thrust of 2,600 pounds. A 6-foot long solid-propellant booster accelerated the vehicle to about 1,000 feet per second before dropping off. Like the *WAC Corporal*, the *Aerobee* was launched from a tower. In the case of the *Aerobee*, the tower was 140 feet tall and provided 90 feet of guided travel.

Aerojet and the Nigg Engineering Corporation designed the tower. Work began under the authority of a letter of intent; BuOrd didn't award the formal contract for $40,000 until August 14, 1947. As originally designed, it had a 3° tilt towards the north to direct the rocket uprange. Like the *WAC Corporal*, the *Aerobee* was unguided. Construction on the tower began in May. Then, on 19 June, LTC Turner ordered the work stopped. He was concerned that the trajectories of unguided rockets were unpredictable and presented too high a risk of venturing beyond the range. His concerns were understandable—less than a month earlier, an errant V-2 had impacted in a cemetery overlooking Juarez, Mexico.

Turner's directive delayed the program, but it forced the development of better ways to control the flight of the *Aerobee*. Van Allen developed a comprehensive range safety plan for the *Aerobee* firings. He proposed that the tower be modified so it could be tilted to compensate for low altitude winds. A capability to adjust the tower up to 7° would compensate for at least 75% of the situations that occurred at WSPG. If surface winds were rapidly variable, or would require the tower to be tilted beyond what was available, then the launch would be postponed. Van Allen also proposed that the rockets be equipped with a radio cutoff device that would sever the fuel lines if a flight was headed off the range. The trajectory would be observed using a simple system of guide wires that would give a visible sky screen. These wires would be placed east and south of the launch pad. If an observer saw the rocket was deviating from the trajectory prescribed by the guide wires he could order thrust termination. As a final measure, Van Allen suggested a series of flights using live boosters and dummy *Aerobee* upper stages be conducted to demonstrate the reliability of the cutoff receiver and the overall stability of the rockets.

During a meeting in late June, Van Allen presented his safety program to a group of military and civilian rocket experts at WSPG. Major General Hughes, the Assistant Chief of Army Ordnance for Research and Development, was one of the participants in the meeting. He approved the plan and allowed construction on the launch tower to resume.

The first *Aerobee* test took place at White Sands on September 25, 1947, when a dummy *Aerobee* was launched with a live booster to check out stage separation. Similar tests followed on 2 adn 31 October. Then, on November 24, 1947, the first full-scale *Aerobee* was launched with a cosmic radiation payload. Unfortunately, this rocket only achieved an altitude of 34.7 miles, far below expectations. A burst diaphragm that had been brazed into the nozzle of the second stage caused a tip-off at staging and sent it veering off course. Because the trajectory violated range safety rules the engine termination command was sent after 35 seconds. Ordinarily the engine would have fired for 44.8 seconds. Terminating the thrust early at least kept the rocket within the boundaries of WSPG. The next flight took place on March 5, 1948. Once again the rocket carried a cosmic radiation package. Everything worked this time, and the rocket climbed more than 73 miles.

The fourth *Aerobee*, launched on 26 July, held a set of aerial reconnaissance cameras in its nose. It reached a peak altitude of 70 miles. As later reported by Van Allen, it returned "...a large number of high-quality aerial photographs of large areas of the earth's surface and of cloud formations in the lower atmosphere...."

In March 1949, the Navy sent the *Aerobee* to sea aboard the *USS Norton Sound*. (For a description of the *Norton Sound* and its conversion from a seaplane tender to a rocket launch ship, see Chapter 8.) The *Norton Sound* was equipped with a 70-foot tall launch tower that was half the height of the one at WSPG. The tower was also hinged at the base so it could rest flat on the deck when not in use. It was also placed in the horizontal position for loading the rocket. Once the rocket was in place the tower was erected to the vertical position. The first three sea launches took place at the geomagnetic equator, a few hundred miles off the coast or Peru. Nine months later, in January 1950, two *Aerobee* rockets were launched in the North Pacific and the Gulf of Alaska. During one of these cruises, the propellant valve on one of the rockets malfunctioned during prelaunch preparations. About ten minutes before the scheduled launch, the sustainer motor ignited and the *Aerobee* blasted off without its booster. Thanks to quick action by the radar operators, the errant rocket was tracked to an altitude of 19 miles.

Aerojet designated the original *Aerobee* the XASR-1; the Navy referred to it as the RTV-N-8. The Air Force decided to purchase *Aerobee* rockets for its own research efforts. Rather than launch them from WSPG, the Air Force launched their *Aerobee* rockets from Holloman Air Force Base. Air Force rocket programs began at Holloman with the *North American Test Instrument Vehicle*, or *NATIV*, in 1948, and the project was terminated the following year. The *Aerobee* rockets launched from Holloman used a new launch pad not far from the tower and blockhouse that had been built for

NATIV. Air Force *Aerobee* rockets were designated the RTV-A-1, and differed from the Navy rockets in that they used high pressure helium rather than compressed air to force propellants into the combustion chamber. The Navy adopted the helium pressure system and designated their rockets RTV-N-10.

The first *Aerobee* flight from Holloman took place on December 2, 1949. This rocket, which carried instruments to measure solar radiation and cameras to photograph the earth, reached an altitude of 60 miles. Less than two weeks later, on 15 December, the second Air Force *Aerobee* blasted off. The sustainer failed to ignite, and the rocket crashed in the desert a short distance from the launch tower after climbing less than a thousand feet into the air. At about this same time, the Air Force spearheaded a program to upgrade the sustainer engine thrust from 2,600 pounds to 4,000 pounds. These became known as the RTV-A-1a and RTV-N-10a rockets.

Dr. James P. Henry of the Air Force Aero Medical Laboratory began rocket flights with monkeys aboard V-2s at WSPG in 1948. Henry launched four monkeys and two mice aboard V-2s. None of the hapless passengers survived. One of the rockets exploded shortly after launch, while the parachutes failed on the others. By the time of the last biological payload aboard a V-2 the program was winding down. With the supply of V-2 rockets nearing an end Dr. Henry switched to the *Aerobee*. Aeromedical *Aerobee* #1, which was the twelfth RTV-A-1, carried a Capuchin monkey in its nose on April 18, 1951. Because of the hazardous nature of the propellants, technicians who fueled the rocket had to wear bulky and heavy asbestos suits. On the day of the first aeromedical flight

Master Sergeant Charles Gilford was in charge of the fueling crew. He stayed on task for seven hours, wearing the protective suit the entire time. Gilford reportedly lost eight pounds from wearing the suit for so long. One of the technicians who worked with Gilford, Airman Jack Marshall, adorned the helmet of his suit with electronic tubes, a 1,000-watt light bulb, and a coil of copper wire. Marshall also attached plugs and a switch panel to the faceplate of his helmet. The switch panel listed the names of the planets. He set the switch to Mars "in honor of the space rat."

The *Aerobee* lifted off flawlessly. Unfortunately, the results were the same as the V-2 flights; physiological data on the primate's reactions were successfully recorded, but the parachute failed. The first live recovery finally occurred on September 20, 1951, with the second aeromedical *Aerobee*. After carrying a Rhesus monkey and 11 mice to 236,000 feet, the rocket's parachute deployed properly and all animals landed alive. Then things went wrong.

Recovery crews took several hours to find the nose cone. Rhesus monkeys do not tolerate heat very well, and the desert sun proved too intense for the monkey. It died of heat prostration about two hours after recovery. Two of the mice also succumbed to the midday sun. The final biological *Aerobee* carried two Capuchin monkeys named Pat and Mike and two mice, Mildred and Albert, on May 21, 1952. The parachute worked properly after the rocket reached 36 miles. This time, the capsule was recovered quickly and all four passengers were in good shape.

The Air Force launched the first 4,000-pound thrust *Aerobee* on 17 October 1951. It reached an altitude of 71 miles, which was

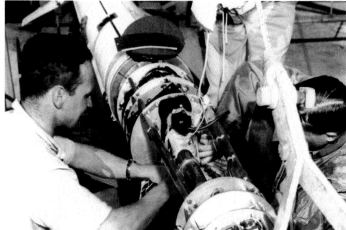

Placing *Albert V* in the nose section of Aeromedical *Aerobee #2. Source: U.S. Air Force photograph.*

Recovery of *Albert V.* The Rhesus monkey was alive when the rocket was found, but died of heat prostration before the recovery team could reach the main base. *Source: U.S. Air Force photograph.*

a significant improvement over the earlier versions. The 4,000-pound thrust rocket became the "standard" *Aerobee*. Interestingly, the Air Force sponsored the higher thrust motor in an effort to dispense with the solid fuel booster, but only one launch attempt was made with this single stage configuration and it failed.

In 1952, the Air Force and Navy teamed with Aerojet to further improve the *Aerobee* design. The general plan was to keep the basic design and the 4,000-pound thrust engine, but to improve overall performance by improving the rocket's mass ratio. Originally, the *Aerobee* tank sections were made from type 19-9DL steel. The improved rockets had tanks made from type 410 stainless steel. Magnesium was used for most of the rest of the airframe.

Contracts for the improved *Aerobee* were awarded by the Air Force in 1952, and in 1953 by the Navy. There ended up being two versions of this rocket. The *Air Force Hi* could loft a 150-pound payload to 145 miles. The *Navy Hi* had slightly longer tanks and could reach an altitude of 170 miles with the 150-pound payload. The Navy rocket achieved greater performance because its tanks were slightly longer. Collectively, both versions were designated the *Aerobee Hi* and were designed specifically to meet the needs of scientists, who used them as high altitude observatories.

Serious aerodynamic questions emerged during the design phase of the *Aerobee Hi* program. With a greater "fineness ratio"—that is, the ratio of length to diameter—and higher burnout altitude, stability could be a problem. Wind tunnel tests and theoretical studies showed the rocket *should* be stable at burnout, but there were still lingering questions. Two additional changes were made to assure stability. To eliminate possible disturbances to the flight path by uneven burning as the rocket exhausted its fuel, a propellant shutoff valve was added to ensure a clean shutdown. The Navy also developed slightly larger fins, which were incorporated on both versions.

There were still concerns regarding the stability of the new design, so the NRL devised a special test rocket; a standard *Aerobee* with extended tanks. The performance of this rocket was between that of the standard version and the *Aerobee Hi* because it used the heavier tank. It flew successfully, thus validating the design.

The Air Force *Aerobee Hi* test program comprised five flights. These rockets did not carry any scientific instruments. The first flew on April 21, 1955. This was the 55th *Aerobee* launched by the Air Force. It carried an overweight payload of 215 pounds and reached an altitude of 123 miles. This was just one mile less than the pre-flight prediction. The second rocket (Air Force 57) was launched on 23 June. It only reached 40 miles, far short of what it was supposed to. Fortunately, the body of the rocket was recovered so the cause of the failure could be determined. The throat of the thrust chamber had burned through at 32 seconds, causing an eccentric thrust. Further analysis showed this was due to too high a content of NO_2 in the oxidizer.

For the next flight, the NO_2 content was limited to 6.5% to prevent another nozzle burn through. This rocket also used the larger Navy-designed fins, thus eliminating the need for ballast carried on the first two rounds. Again, the *Aerobee Hi* did not live up to expectations; it reached an altitude of 105 miles. Preflight predictions were that it would climb 135 miles. No definitive cause could be found, but the most likely cause was excessive drag caused by fin warpage due to insufficient thermal protection on the leading edges. The fourth *Aerobee Hi* in the Air Force program (AF-75) blasted off on December 13, 1956. Extra thermal insulation had been added to the leading edges of the fins. Peak altitude was 120 miles; still short of predictions, but better than its predecessor. Telemetry showed the engine had burned three seconds longer than normal, but at a slightly lower thrust, which resulted in the lower altitude.

Since the problems encountered on the last three flights seemed to be peculiar to each rocket and did not indicate a design flaw, the last test round carried a scientific payload. AF-78, the fifth *Aerobee Hi* test round, blasted off from Holloman Air Force Base on June 18, 1957, with a load of instruments to study the ionosphere. This rocket reached 106 miles. A week later AF-79 performed even better; it climbed to 125 miles.

Adding to the Air Force's confidence that there was not a problem with the basic *Aerobee Hi* design, the Navy test program

Aerobee staging. This particular image is of a later variant, the *Aerobee 150*, but the process remained practically unchanged throughout the 37 years this type of rocket was in use. *Source: National Aeronautics and Space Administration.*

with their rockets was underway at the same time. The Navy's *Aerobee Hi* program, covered under contract Nonr-1265 (00), called for the Aerojet General Corporation (as the company was then known) to produce 14 rockets. The Navy design began with the type 410 stainless steel tanks developed for the Air Force *Hi* rockets. To meet the performance requirements under contract Nonr-1265 (00), the tanks had to be lengthened slightly to provide more propellant.

Seeking every possible way to boost the performance of the standard *Aerobee*, Aerojet began a program to improve the thrust chamber. They tried building a lighter, more compact version of the chamber that could burn RFNA containing 22% NO_2. The oxidizer used up until then contained 6.5% NO_2. Increasing the concentration of nitrogen dioxide in the oxidizer increased its density and improved the performance of the motor. Unfortunately, during the test program there were repeated combustion chamber burn-throughs, so both the 22% RFNA oxidizer and lightweight combustion chamber were abandoned. Aerojet returned to the 6.5% mixture previously used, and introduced yet another combustion chamber design that was between the old and new designs. This thrust chamber was lighter than the one used on the standard *Aerobee,* but not as light as the troublesome version created for the *Aerobee Hi.* It had a double acid inlet to improve pressure distribution in the injector. While testing the new engine, Aerojet engineers discovered that the water content in the acid played a critical role in its performance. Their results led to new specifications for low water content acid, which improved the performance of the *Aerobee* engines.

Another way to improve the mass ratio and overall performance of the *Navy Hi* was to use a hot-gas pressurization system, rather than the compressed helium system, to force propellants to the combustion chamber. The hot gas system used a small solid-propellant gas generator. Hot gases from the generator mixed with helium from a small container to produce the necessary pressure. This system was lighter than the single, large helium pressure tank

then in use. The first Navy *Aerobee Hi* (NRL-37) used this system on August 25, 1955. The *Aerobee* failed to ignite, and the rocket crashed in the desert a short distance from the tower. NRL-38 also used the hot-gas system. It suffered a "hard start" when the sustainer ignited, and it exploded just after leaving the tower.

Scientists around the world had agreed to an "International Geophysical Year" commencing in 1957. The NRL wanted to use the *Aerobee Hi* as a tool to learn about the upper atmosphere, so rather than take the time necessary to perfect the hot-gas system, they opted to return to helium pressurization. Another difference between the Air Force and Navy *Aerobee Hi* designs was that the latter used a pressure regulator from the *Nike* antiaircraft missile. This regulator was superior to the ones previously used and had the further advantage of costing considerably less. Problems continued to plague the Navy test rockets, even with a return to the cold-gas system. The next rocket, NRL-39, failed when the *Aerobee* engine did not ignite due to a failure in the range safety circuits. It crashed in the desert after reaching an altitude of only a few thousand feet.

The next two rockets, launched on May 8, and June 4, 1956, performed better, but still did not live up to expectations because of combustion chamber burn-throughs. These rockets used the 22% RFNA mixture. With a return to the 6.5% mixture performance and reliability both improved. The final Navy model of the *Aerobee Hi* was the RV-N-13b version, and it was used extensively during the IGY.

In 1959, the newly created National Aeronautics and Space Administration (NASA) adopted the *Aerobee Hi* and gave it the designation *Aerobee 150.* The *Aerobee* went through numerous changes, resulting in a family of sounding rockets, but the basic design remained virtually the same. Additional launch sites included Wallops Island, Virginia, Fort Churchill, Canada, and the U.S. Navy ship *USS Norton Sound.* On January 17, 1985, the final *Aerobee 150* lifted off from White Sands Missile Range. It carried a 571-pound ultraviolet light experiment to an altitude of 105 miles. It was the 1,037[th] *Aerobee* launch.

Aerobee Hi research rocket. *Source: U.S. Air Force photograph.*

Typical *Aerobee Hi* Schedule

X-6 months	Begin Instrumentation design
X-5 months	Instrumentation layout and design complete
X-4 months	Wiring diagram complete
X-3 ½ months	Electrical work
X-2 ½ months	Shop work complete; begin assembly of payload
X-2 months	Rocket complete; NRL prechecks
X-7 weeks	NRL interference tests
X-6 ½ weeks	Photographs
X-5 ½ weeks	Equipment leaves NRL
X-4 weeks	Rocket arrives at WSPG; equipment arrives at WSPG
X-3 weeks	NRL personnel arrive at WSPG; rocket hydrostatic tests
X-18 days	Rocket gas-leak tests
X-15 days	Begin installation of instrumentation
X-13 days	Mix fuel and fill oxidizer cart
X-7 days	Prepare tower for rocket; horizontal interference test
X-6 days	Weigh and measure rocket for center of gravity
X-5 days	Erect rocket in tower; test high-pressure helium tank
X-2 days	Vertical interference tests
X-1 day	Begin flight preparations; weather prediction for launch time
X-6 hours	Lower nose cone over payload
X-5 ½ hours	Navy firing crew and fireman arrive in launch area
X-5 hours	Weather prediction for launch; begin aniline (fuel) fill
X-4 ½ hours	Begin acid (oxidizer) fill
X-3 hours	Final telemetry check; connect pull-away device
X-2 ½ hours	Final check of emergency cutoff circuit
X-90 minutes	All range stations manned; final check
X-75 minutes	Install booster igniter; all personnel to blockhouse
X-60 minutes	Begin pressurization
X-30 minutes	Set roadblocks; set tower tilt
X-12 minutes	Beacon filament on
X-6 minutes	Telemetry on external power
X-5 minutes	Final tower tilt adjustment
X-4 minutes	Pressurization complete; telemetry on
X-3 minutes	Instrumentation on internal power
X-2 minutes	Beacon on internal power
X-35 seconds	Telemetry recorders on
X-10 seconds	Arm firing circuit
X-0	Launch

ASP research rocket. WSPG was the launch site for a variety of research rockets. Besides the *Aerobee*, a variety of solid-fuel rockets carried payloads on sub-orbital trajectories over New Mexico. This is the *Atmospheric Sounding Projectile*, or *ASP*. The Navy developed the *ASP* as a low-cost vehicle to carry instruments into the radioactive clouds from nuclear detonations. Cooper Development Corporation produced the rocket, which was first flown at WSPG on February 3, 1956. Testing began at Point Mugu, California, but was moved to WSPG to take advantage of the range's tracking and instrumentation capabilities. The ASP proved to be very versatile, and could carry a 25-pound payload to 200,000 feet. In the 1960s, the *ASP* was combined with the *Nike* booster to create a two-stage sounding rocket. *Source: U.S. Army photograph.*

11

Loki

Named for the Norse god of trouble and mischief, the *Loki* was a high-speed antiaircraft rocket. In terms of the number of rockets launched, it was one of the largest projects conducted at WSPG during the 1950s. *Loki* was an attempt to counter the threat of high performance aircraft of the era. In the years immediately after World War II, advances in aircraft design threatened to render the Army's inventory of antiaircraft guns obsolete. Existing antiaircraft guns did not have the range, muzzle velocity, or flexibility to counter supersonic airplanes flying at high altitudes. In its report of May 29, 1946, which became a "policy document" for the War Department, the War Department Equipment Board (popularly known as the "Stilwell Board," after its chairman, General Joseph W. Stilwell) recommended the Army continue to develop conventional guns, but should focus most of its effort on the "development of a new propulsive power."

During World War II Germany attempted to develop a small, relatively low-cost rocket to defend against Allied bombers. Engineers at Peenemünde developed an unguided, fin stabilized rocket called the *Taifun* (Typhoon). The *Taifun* was about six feet tall and used prepackaged hypergolic propellants, so it could be maintained in a ready state at all times. Had it been deployed, salvos of *Taifun* missiles could have been fired to break up bomber formations. Although considerable effort was spent on this project—in the last year of the war more than 1,400 were launched—the *Taifun* never reached combat.

American Army leaders wondered if the idea might be resurrected and developed into a successful weapon system. Mr. Klaus Scheuflin, one of the key persons in the development of the *Taifun* at Peenemünde, was offered a contract to work in the United States under the aegis of Project Paperclip in 1946. Three other engineers from the German group at Fort Bliss were also assigned to the project. Mr. Scheuflin prepared a feasibility study for a free-flight liquid fuel rocket and proposed a development program. This study was informally discussed by the Army Field Force Board #4 at Fort Bliss, and a plan was formulated for submission to higher headquarters.

In December 1947, the Department of the Army approved plans for the development of an antiaircraft rocket weapon, the *Loki*. It was to have a horizontal range of 27,000 yards, a vertical range of 20,000 yards, and be capable of intercepting targets roughly the size of a B-29 bomber flying at 1,000 miles per hour. Dispersion could not exceed plus or minus 4 mils for 66% of the rounds. ("Mils" is an artillery term used for angular measurement. One mil is the angle formed by a one meter displacement at a distance of one kilometer. A full circle equals 6,400 mils.) Further requirements for the weapon included a time of flight not to exceed 30 seconds to reach maximum altitude. It was to be fired from a launcher that held 64 missiles. Ground crews had to be able to load the launcher in 60 seconds.

Army Ordnance awarded the contract for *Loki* to the Eclipse-Pioneer Division of the Bendix Aviation Corporation. The contract directed Bendix to provide the complete *Loki* system, exclusive of fire control. As specified, the *Loki* used liquid propellants. Bendix studied two versions. One weighed 245 pounds and used a proximity fuse to detonate the warhead when it approached the target. The other was an order of magnitude smaller and weighed just 24 pounds. This missile had an impact detonating warhead that exploded when it hit the target. Army officials opted for the smaller rocket after weighing the relative effort and expense required by a battery to bring down various size aircraft. It was also felt the smaller missile would be less expensive and faster to develop.

The design consisted of an unpowered dart-like warhead and a liquid-fuel booster. At the end of the boost phase, drag would be greater on the booster than on the warhead, which caused the two to separate. Its job done, the booster would fall to earth while the warhead continued on its way. The missile reached a speed of approximately 4,570 feet per second by the time the booster burned out, which was at an altitude of 3,000 feet. Four small fins were attached to the base of the booster. Dispersion due to thrust malalignment was a possibility for *Loki*, so the rocket was given a rotation of 17 revolutions per second by the booster. (*Malalignment* is the term used to describe thrust eccentricities that might occur due to uneven burning of the propellant.) The warhead reached an altitude of 84,000 feet in just 30 seconds, and even at that point it was still traveling over 1,800 feet per second.

Traveling at such high speeds, *Loki* needed a particularly fast acting fuze. On February 29, 1952, the Army amended the contract with Bendix to include the development of an electronic fuze. The fuze was a point-detonating type consisting of an arming mechanism, detonation device, and self-destruction device. The warhead armed itself when the missile was approximately 300 feet from the launcher. The self destruction device detonated the warhead after 32.5 seconds if it had not hit its target. The fuze was to detonate the warhead 0.85 millisecond after hitting the target. Even with such a fast acting fuze, the warhead would still penetrate the target by about three feet before exploding.

Developing the fuze presented several challenges. At first, Bendix proposed using a piezoelectric, or "lucky" crystal in the nose. When crushed, this type of crystal generates an electrical current. If the temperature of the lucky element reaches 250° F, it loses its voltage generating capability. A problem arose when it was discovered the skin of the *Loki* could reach 400° due to friction with the air. One of the contractors, the Erie Resistor Corporation, determined the internal temperature of the warhead was "dangerously" close to 250°. Thermal insulation seemed to be the answer.

Early in the project Bendix engineers presented a set of arguments in favor of liquid fuels. Among other considerations, at that time solid propellants could not deliver as much power per pound of weight as liquids; a characteristic known as *specific impulse*. Since these missiles would have to be ready to fire with little or no warning they needed to use hypergolic (self-igniting) propellants that could be stored at room temperature. Bendix

selected a white fuming nitric acid (WFNA)/aniline propellant combination. WFNA is nearly pure nitric acid. It contains less than 2% water and less than 0.2% dissolved nitrogen dioxide. Nitric acid is relatively easy to store compared to other oxidizers and produces a high impulse per unit volume, but it is highly corrosive and has to be handled with extreme care. Because aniline ignites spontaneously on contact with nitric acid *Loki* did not need an ignition system. Similar propulsion systems had been thoroughly tested by the JPL for their liquid fuel JATO units and the *WAC Corporal*. Like the *Taifun*, *Loki* burned a solid fuel in a gas generator to produce the pressure needed to force the propellants into the combustion chamber.

Creating a liquid-fuel booster for *Loki* proved to be more difficult than anticipated, and the missile team at Bendix soon found they were falling behind schedule. *Loki* was actually unstable during the initial portion of the boost phase, but the motor burned out before the rocket began tumbling. If the hypergolic propellants did not ignite quick enough, the excess fuel and oxidizer in the combustion chamber could actually lead to a loss of control. Bendix studied how the chemical properties of the propellants themselves affected the ignition lag. They also performed an extensive study of propellant mixing as a function of injector design.

As the testing progressed, it was discovered that the WFNA had some undesirable decomposition characteristics. Fuel flow characteristics at low temperatures also proved problematic. Because of these problems, Bendix considered switching to an aromatic amine fuel with RFNA as an oxidizer. Company engineers also had to conduct a fairly extensive program on the corrosion resistance of rocket metal parts to the combustion gases produced by WFNA and aniline. Studies of the rocket chamber and nozzle materials showed that 4130 steel was superior to cast aluminum.

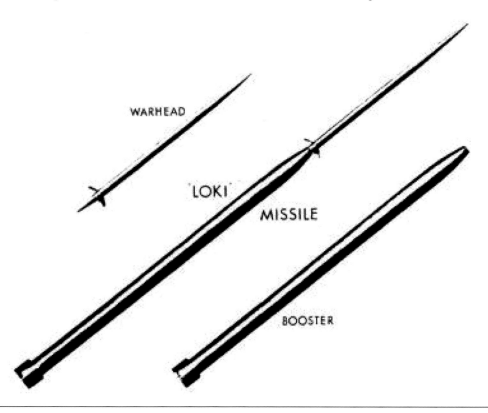

Schematic of the major components of the *Loki* antiaircraft missile. Once the solid-fuel booster burned out, the unpowered dart-like warhead continued on its own. The *Loki* was unguided, and was intended to be fired in volleys. *Source: U.S. Army photograph.*

In the course of this study they tested various coatings to protect the rockets.

Shortly after Bendix submitted their report that gave the advantages of liquid propellants over solids JPL issued a set of counterarguments. The JPL report, which was dated October 1, 1947, pointed out that solid propellant rockets were generally cheaper than equivalent liquid fuel ones; that a solid fuel system can be serviced and operated in the field by relatively unskilled crews after brief instruction; and the densities of solid fuels are between 20-55% greater than the average densities of liquid propellants. The JPL report also raised concerns about the movement of liquid propellants in their tank during sharp maneuvers and the effect it would have on rocket stability.

In view of the advantages claimed by JPL and the mounting problems encountered by Bendix in the development of a liquid fuel booster, the Ballistic Research Laboratories (BRL) at Aberdeen Proving Ground, Maryland, began a study of *Loki* performance with a solid fuel booster. The BRL selected one of the GALCIT polysulfide rubber/perchlorate propellants for the study. Their study indicated the solid propellant version of *Loki* would perform as well as, and probably better than, the liquid fuel version. Rather than halt work on the liquid booster at that time, the Army decided to let Bendix and JPL continue work in parallel on each type of booster to see which one proved superior.

JPL, assisted by Army Ordnance personnel, began test firings of their *Loki* design at WSPG on June 22, 1951. Rounds 2 through 6 flew three days later; Rounds 7 through 11 were launched on 13 July. Over the course of the next five months, the JPL launched 23 more *Loki* rockets at WSPG. By February 1952, the solid-fuel booster had proven itself clearly superior to the liquid-fuel version,

The *Loki* antiaircraft missile. *Source: U.S. Army photograph.*

so the Army directed Bendix to discontinue their work on the latter for an operational missile, but allowed liquid propellant research to continue. (This was the contract amendment that tasked Bendix to develop the electronic fuze. The amendment also stipulated that Bendix design and build an interim launcher and two test launchers for the solid-fuel rockets.) JPL received contract DA-04-495-ORD-18 for $2 million to develop the solid fuel version of *Loki*.

The three major components (booster, warhead, and fuze) made up the complete *Loki*, which was designated "Rocket, HEAA, 76 mm, T-220." *Loki* ended up being a long and slender missile; the booster was just 3 inches in diameter and 63 inches long. The warhead was even smaller, with a diameter of 1 3/8 inch and a weight of 5.9 pounds. It carried about two pounds of high explosive. Overall length of the rocket at launch was 103 inches. The propellant was a polysulfide-perchlorate mixture.

With the missile configuration settled, the next question was the launcher. Bendix considered several different launcher designs, including:

1. a single-tube repeater type where missiles were brought into firing position by a belt;
2. a magazine type with loaded magazines fed into the breech by trucks;
3. a revolver type with six magazines that could be rotated into position; and
4. a radial loader that automatically picked up loaded magazines, aligned them, fired the missiles, then repeated the cycle until six magazines were fired.

Launcher development started at a relatively modest level, and began with a design for an 81-round magazine for the liquid-fuel missiles. In October 1950 the basic concept for the launcher had been settled and detailed design began. By this time, the engineering team realized the launcher had to be completely automatic and operated by remote control. In its "final" configuration, the launcher incorporated a 64-round magazine. Rocket Launcher, Antiaircraft, T-128 Model I, was in the advanced design stage in February 1952 when the decision was made to drop the liquid-fuel version of *Loki*. The launcher had been designed for the liquid-fuel missile, so further work was needed to adapt it to the solid-fuel *Loki*.

The major changes to the launcher included reducing the number of rounds in the magazine from 64 to 46. The magazine also had to be lengthened because the solid-fuel *Loki* was longer and slightly fatter than its liquid-fuel counterpart. The redesigned launcher was named the Rocket Launcher, Antiaircraft, T128, Model II. On July 10, 1952, the Army amended the Bendix contract once more to include the design and construction of a four-tube launcher. This latest amendment also covered the delivery of 820 fuzes and new tubes for the *Loki* interim launcher.

To hasten development of the launcher, it was built on the existing 90mm antiaircraft gun M2 mount. Adapting this piece of World War II hardware created its own series of problems, which the Bendix engineers overcame. In May 1953 Bendix submitted a report that indicated the first order of importance was to demonstrate the loading operation, followed by the launcher's operation in elevation and azimuth. They expected to demonstrate the loading process with Launcher #1 on or before July 15, 1953. The traverse and elevation tests were set on or before 31 August.

Launcher #1 was demonstrated at the Bendix plant in Teterboro, New Jersey, for Army officials on 28 October, then was shipped to WSPG for field testing. Launcher #2 was undergoing assembly at that time. Field testing continued throughout the rest of 1953 and 1954. In January 1955 an unforeseen problem delayed the field test program—the launcher was hit by lightning. It took four months to repair the damage. By the time of this problem there had been more than 2,500 *Loki* launches.

During 1952, 302 *Loki*s were fired at WSPG. For the calendar year 1953 the total was 1,157 firings. Nearly the same number of *Loki* rockets (1,125) flew in 1954. Often these were salvo launched from the 46-round magazines. During single firings the launcher worked fine, but during salvo firings, there were frequently malfunctions. After adjustments to the missile retainers launcher performance improved significantly. One test, or "firing event," called for six salvo firings of 46 missiles. Unlike previous tests, this time all were successful. *Loki* missiles could also be ripple fired.

In the 1960s, the Air Force developed a meteorological rocket that was very similar to the *Loki-Dart* called the *Owl*. Source: U.S. Air Force photograph.

For each of the "firing events," which often involved hundreds of rockets, WSPG provided range facilities, data collection, and data reduction. Launches to compile ballistic firing tables constituted a major portion of the effort. Time, range, and trajectory data for rockets fired at various quadrant elevations was necessary for the fire control system.

Between April 1955, when the launcher was repaired, and September 1955 there were 902 *Loki* launches. Prior tests with multiple magazine launches resulted in blast damage to the T-128 launcher, so a protective blast deflector was added during the repairs. Even with this blast deflector in place the launcher failed to perform satisfactorily, especially during multiple-magazine tests. The problem had to do with the terrific heat generated by the solid-fuel rocket motor's exhaust. The heat caused the firing tubes to expand, which affected the missile dispersion pattern. This problem was never solved. By the time of these tests the *Nike Ajax* guided missile rendered the *Loki* obsolete. As an unguided projectile, the *Loki* would have had very limited effectiveness against a target that could maneuver. The *Loki* antiaircraft missile program was terminated in September 1955.

Termination of the antiaircraft missile project did not spell the end of the *Loki*. In March 1955 the Navy identified the need for a simple, relatively inexpensive way to measure winds between 100,000 and 150,000 feet. The Office of Naval Research (ONR) decided the best way to accomplish this would be with a rocket that would carry a radar target rapidly to the desired altitude and eject it into the wind stream. *Loki*, which could reach an altitude of 180,000 feet, met this need. In this role it was referred to as the *Loki-WASP*, or just simply *WASP*. WASP was an acronym for Weather Atmospheric Sounding Projectile.

NRL first replaced the explosive in the warhead with bundles of light metal strips called window, or chaff. The chaff was ejected from the base of the warhead by a piston that could be set to function from 20 to 130 seconds after launch. The expelled chaff would fall at a rate of 400 feet per minute at 110,000 feet. The *WASP* carried 14 ounces of chaff. Ground-based radar could track the chaff as the winds carried it along. The NRL also developed a metalized parachute that could be tracked with radar.

The Navy built a launch tube that could be attached to a standard 5-inch deck gun. This launcher comprised an extruded aluminum tube with internal helical guide rails to impart the necessary spin on the rocket. Having such a launcher meant the *Loki-WASP* could be fired from virtually any Navy ship. Mounting the launcher to the top of the gun barrel prevented the use of the mount as a gun battery. The NRL, working with Cooper Development Corporation, also developed bore-riders that attached to the fins of the rocket so it could be fired directly from a 5-inch gun. A three-man crew of Gunner's Mates or technicians could launch a *WASP*.

In flight tests at WSPG, the chaff was tracked for as long as 27 minutes above 102,000 feet. This was unusual; experience showed reliable wind measurements could only be obtained within the first 5 to 7 minutes after ejection due to dispersion. The metalized silk parachute offered several advantages over the chaff. The most obvious advantage was the lack of dispersion of the target. It could also be tracked all the way to the ocean surface within the limits of the tracking ship and its radar capability. Through testing, it was discovered that the wind results from the metalized parachutes compared favorably to data collected using balloons. On June 1, 1956, a metalized parachute was tracked from 97,000 to 24,000 feet over WSPG. That same day a chaff round was tracked from 117,000 feet down to 102,000 feet.

The metalized fabric parachutes were five feet in diameter and weighed five ounces. General Textile Mills in Carbondale, PA, manufactured the parachutes. The NRL also tested a 0.5-mm thick metalized Mylar parachute, but in the preliminary tests they did not perform well. Radar failed to detect the Mylar chute on the first test. There was a radar return on the second flight, but it later appeared this was only part of the Mylar parachute.

The *Loki-Dart* became one of the most widely used meteorological sounding rockets of all time, and well over 10,000 were launched. Throughout its service life, the basic design underwent numerous modifications and upgrades. The final versions, the *Super Loki* and *Viper III,* remained in use until 2001.

The *Super Loki-Dart* meteorological rocket used a larger booster than the original version. Rockets of this type continued in use into the 21st Century. *Source: National Aeronautics and Space Administration.*

12

Corporal

As the culmination of the ORDCIT project, the *Corporal* was the first large American-designed ballistic missile. While its capacity of carrying a 1,500-pound warhead across a range of 75 miles was less than that of the German V-2, the *Corporal* represented a considerable improvement in many technical areas over the earlier missile.

When von Kármán first mapped out the ORDCIT rocket program the United States was at war. Therefore, he set a very fast pace for missile development. The original program called for, as part of its third phase, a study of ramjet propulsion with an eye towards creating a missile that weighed around 10,000 pounds with a 75-mile range. Soon after phase 3 began, the JPL group concluded the course of research that would produce the quickest results was to build a missile that used a liquid-fuel rocket motor for propulsion.

The ORDCIT group settled on using the familiar acid-aniline propellant mixture and designed their missile around a 20,000-pound thrust motor. To reach the desired range, the missile would have a thrust duration of 60 seconds. In his initial planning, Dr. von Kármán scheduled flight tests of this prototype missile to begin on March 1, 1945. The flight test program would comprise ten rockets. Because their first rockets were named *Private*, they selected the name *Corporal* for this new missile. The prototype missile would be the XF30L20,000, or *Corporal E*. In mid-1944, the ORDCIT group spawned the Jet Propulsion Laboratory (JPL). Building a liquid fuel rocket engine that produced 20,000 pounds thrust represented an order of magnitude increase over anything previously built in the United States. Such a motor would require considerable testing before it was ready for a flight vehicle, so the JPL group decided to test it at the recently established Muroc Test Station. Von Kármán's original schedule proved too optimistic, and by the time the Second World War ended the *Corporal E* had yet to fly.

The end of World War II did not halt work on *Corporal E*, but it did have the effect of slowing the project's pace. A less stringent schedule was developed that allowed lessons learned with the *WAC Corporal* series of rockets to be incorporated into the *Corporal E*. By the end of 1945, JPL engineers were testing the 20,000-pound

thrust motor at the Muroc Station. This motor was essentially a scaled-up version of the motor built for the *WAC Corporal*, which delivered a thrust of 1,500 pounds. The *Corporal E* consumed a propellant mixture similar to that used on the *WAC Corporal*; that is, the fuel was a mixture of aniline and furfuryl alcohol, and the oxidizer was Red Fuming Nitric Acid (RFNA).

There were two different motors built for the *WAC Corporal* rockets. The first motor built for the *WAC Corporal A* rockets comprised a relatively thin-walled steel combustion chamber with a helical rib machined around its outer surface. A cylindrical outer jacket fit snugly over the machined rib, forming a helical channel around the combustion chamber. Fuel circulated through this channel before reaching the injectors to cool the motor. The motor for the *WAC Corporal A* weighed 50 pounds. *WAC Corporal B* rockets used an improved, lighter motor. Half-round steel stampings were spot-welded to the combustion chamber to form a helical channel around its exterior. This eliminated the need for the cylindrical outer jacket and reduced the motor weight to 12 pounds.

Producing these lightweight motors presented many challenges. At first, several large metal stamping companies rejected the design as impossible to build. A relatively small firm, the Alloy Diecraft Company, agreed to try and eventually succeeded. The biggest problem was that following the contours of the combustion chamber required the stamped material to elongate by 34%. Deep-drawing steel was not available, so SAE 1010 and 1020 carbon steel had to be used, which only has a practical elongation of 20%. This was solved by redesigning the die so that the material only had to elongate by 16%.

Copper brazing was used on the first two lightweight motors to join the helical cooling channels to the combustion chamber, but this proved unsatisfactory. Solar Aircraft Company of San Diego perfected a process of electrical-resistance seam welding of the components. The new motors passed a 650 psi hydrostatic pressure test.

The first combustion chambers built for the *Corporal* missile copied the *WAC Corporal A* design and weighed 650 pounds. These motors were made from mild steel. As the motor for the

WAC Corporal B evolved, this design was used to create the so-called lightweight *Corporal* motor. Four lightweight motors were built: one of 18-8 stainless steel; one from 1909DL stainless steel; and two of mild steel. All four motors failed during testing. The regions where the inner and outer shells were joined was poorly cooled and the motors burned through. Since the internal pressure loads were carried by the inner shell, this had to be relatively thick, which resulted in high wall temperature and loss of strength. JPL designers tried modifying the heavyweight motor using elements of the lightweight design, but these engines did not work either. Therefore, the first *Corporal* test rockets used the 650-pound motors.

On May 23, 1945, the Army Ordnance Department asked that all agencies working on guided missiles provide a status report of their work. At that time, JPL was considering three slightly different variations of the *Corporal*. The first, the *Corporal E*, used compressed air to force propellants into the combustion chamber. Fabrication of the first few missiles of this design was already underway. *Corporal F* used a turbopump propellant system. It was in an early stage of engineering design, and work had started on only a few components. *Corporal G* would have used a chemical gas generator to feed propellants to the combustion chamber. It never progressed beyond the paper study stage.

Corporal was a command guided missile, that is, commands were sent to it from the ground to correct its trajectory while it was in flight. This was different than the majority of the V-2s launched during World War II. All the V-2s were assumed to follow the same path during powered flight. Therefore, hitting the desired target became a function of precisely aligning the missile before launch and controlling the cut-off velocity to achieve the correct range. In practice, the German missiles exhibited considerable dispersion. Small variations in fin alignment, thrust asymmetries, errors in placing the missile, and atmospheric effects contributed to missile dispersion. At a range of 150 miles, even a 1% error would place the missile a mile and a half off target.

The *Corporal's* trajectory could be divided into three parts: vertical ascent; powered flight at a decreasing elevation angle; and coasting flight as a ballistic projectile along a parabolic path. Control over the first two phases of the flight was critical for accuracy. This required a system for maintaining control about all three axes during these portions of the trajectory. The two basic means of controlling the missile were to maintain the yaw axis along a fixed azimuth, establish a predetermined trajectory and set the pitch angle as a function of time, or to control the pitch and yaw by radio signal from a ground station. Both techniques required the roll be controlled by on-board means. As previously described, the V-2 utilized the first technique.

In the end, von Kármán opted for a combination of the two means. Ground-based radar would be used to accurately map the actual flight path on two plotting boards. One of the plotting boards showed the trajectory in the horizontal plane, while the other displayed the flight in the vertical plane. The radar was based on the World War II SCR-585 unit. In its modified form for the *Corporal* it was designated AN/MPQ-12. Additionally, there were ten telemetry channels to report on conditions inside the rocket.

This data was presented on a series of graphic recorders. This meant the operator had two sources of data throughout the flight. The plotting boards showed the mean trajectory, and the second displayed fluctuations around this trajectory. The operator could use this information to send control signals to the rocket.

During the early portion of the flight, the missile would not be traveling fast enough for the control surfaces on the fins to be effective. For the initial ascent, the missile was controlled by four carbon vanes in the engine exhaust, similar to the technique used on the V-2. Once the missile reached sufficient airspeed, the external vanes located along the trailing edges of each fin stabilized it.

The first *Corporal* test missile, the XF30L20,000 *Corporal E*, was launched on May 22, 1947. JPL designed the airframe, which was built by the Douglas Aircraft Company. The motor was built at JPL; Sperry Gyroscope Company provided the guidance system; Army Ordnance furnished a DOVAP transponder; and the Signal Corps Electronic Laboratory provided the radar tracking beacon. This was the first American-designed and fabricated surface to surface missile. At the beginning of the flight, the missile was 12° off due north, but after 30 seconds of flight the on-board guidance system corrected this to 6°. After 160 seconds, a control signal was sent to deflect the missile to the left and it responded as planned. Missile 1 reached an altitude of 129,000 feet and a range of 62.5 miles. This was within two miles of the target. This flight proved highly successful and exceeded everyone's expectations.

Corporal E #2, fired on July 17, 1947, was not as successful. As recorded in the JPL report on the flight:

"...after the closing of the firing circuit, a starting delay of about 8 to 10 seconds was observed. The rocket motor then started, but insufficient thrust was developed, and the test vehicle stood burning in the launcher or about 90 seconds. At the end of that time, sufficient fuel had been exhausted to equalize weight of the vehicle to thrust. Corporal E then rose in a short trajectory, tilted over, and impacted a few hundred yards east of the launching area."

In actuality, the missile only reached an altitude of about 50 feet before it toppled over and fell to the ground. After that, it was thrust along the ground for about 100 yards. After studying the telemetry data, the JPL team concluded the most likely cause for the failure was a malfunction of the main air regulator. Unfortunately, since not all parts of the air regulation system could be found, a more detailed explanation could not be determined.

The third missile, launched on 4 November, started well and flew as expected until 43 seconds after liftoff, when the motor suddenly quit. Early in the flight the rocket veered off course and looked like it would head outside WSPG if allowed to continue. Control signals were transmitted to the rocket to direct it back within the safe limits of the range. Telemetry records showed wild fluctuations in the combustion chamber pressure after 10 seconds of flight. Rather than the expected 60 mile range, this rocket only reached 14 miles.

Work had continued on a lighter-weight engine for the *Corporal*. This resulted in a radically new design, an axially cooled steel motor that weighed just 125 pounds. Rather than using the previous practice of wrapping a fuel conduit around the combustion chamber, this new engine comprised a series of 44 longitudinal channels bundled together. This gave the combustion chamber interior a "corrugated" appearance. A smooth, un-corrugated shell that encased the chamber carried the pressure load of the engine. Both shells were made from type 1020 mild steel. This engine required a new injector design. The new injector had 52 pairs of impinging jets for the fuel and oxidizer. This axially cooled engine worked well and was incorporated in the fourth *Corporal E*.

Other design changes in Round 4 included a modification of the jet vanes; the use of pneumatic pistons in the control system instead of a rotary air motor and gear box; and replacement of the tapered boat-tail with a cylindrical aft end. This was the first of seven redesigned "production" missiles produced by Douglas Aircraft. A new launcher was used for this missile. Previous *Corporal Es* rested on their fins on the launch pad. The new launcher had four struts that supported the missile before launch, taking the load off the fins. These struts secured the rocket just ahead of the aft section. Once it rose four inches, the arms would fall away from the missile body. After 19 months' work, on June 7, 1949, *Corporal E* #4 stood ready for launch.

Almost immediately after it took off the missile veered to the west. At about 15 seconds it began to roll, then at 23 seconds Range Safety ordered thrust shutoff. Round #4 reached an altitude of 66,000 feet and traversed a range of 14 miles. Telemetry showed the control system performance was radically different than what had been expected.

In an effort to diagnose the problem, JPL engineers static fired an engine mounted in an aft body section just like that of Round #4 at Muroc. They were surprised to learn the jet-vane hinge moment was four times greater than expected. The engineers also discovered the exhaust flame entered the control mixer, burned away some of the pneumatic tubing, and softened the springs on the control system mixer bar. Obviously a new jet-vane holder and protective flame shield would have to be added to subsequent missiles. They also concluded vibrations adversely affected the mechanical autopilot.

In September 1949 Dr. Louis G. Dunn, Director of the JPL, and some of his staff traveled to Washington, D.C., to meet with (then) Colonel Holgar N. Toftoy of the Missiles and Rockets Branch, Office of the Chief of Ordnance. Colonel Toftoy expressed his disappointment in the progress being made on guided missile programs in general up to that time. At this meeting, all Army surface-to-surface missile programs were reviewed with an eye to determine the best approach to meet an operational capability by mid-1954 for a mid-range missile carrying a 1,500-pound warhead. Because the General Electric *Hermes* missiles were not as far along in their development as the JPL missile, it was decided to transform the *Corporal E* into an interim guided missile system. In view of increasing world tensions, Toftoy directed the JPL to develop a new guidance system for the *Corporal* as a "crash program." He went on to state that a Circular Probability Error (CPE) of ½ mile would be acceptable. To expedite the process,

Colonel Toftoy further directed that existing components and techniques should be used whenever possible.

Several months after the meeting, Army Ordnance officials requested that the Defense Department elevate the *Corporal E* to a weapon development program. Not convinced of the missile's merits, senior managers at the Department of Defense turned down the request. This kept the *Corporal E* at the same priority level as other Army missile programs and slowed its development. Toftoy and other Army Ordnance officers did what they could to help the program. On January 18, 1950, Toftoy sent a letter to the JPL that called for an accelerated program to develop the *Corporal* into a weapon system. The outbreak of hostilities in Korea six months later added further urgency to this directive.

Initial warhead and fuze development were carried out by the Picatinny Arsenal in New Jersey. In 1950, Picatinny began work on General Purpose (GP) high explosive and Cluster Fragmentation (CF) warheads for the missile. Having conventional warheads available would give field commanders more options for using the missile.

During the 12 months following the ill-fated flight of Round #4 another series of design improvements were made to the *Corporal E*. An electro-pneumatic control system designed by the JPL replaced the all-pneumatic system previously used. The nose cone, which would carry the warhead, was emptied for this missile. Telemetry gear and other equipment previously carried in the nose cone was moved to the stowage compartment just aft of the nose. Round #5 carried a Doppler transponder and AN/DPW-1 radar beacon that had been modified for the *Hermes A-1* program. Because so many changes were made to the design, Round #5 was static fired at WSPG in June 1950. Vibrations caused an aniline fuel line in the aft section to break and caused a fire that briefly engulfed the entire missile. The fire was quickly extinguished and the missile was saved. As repairs were made, special precautions were taken to make sure all connections were secure.

Round #5 lifted off on July 11, 1950. A disconnect coupling, designed to bleed excess pressure from the compressed air tank, malfunctioned. This reduced the propellant flow rates into the combustion chamber, which reduced overall performance of the missile. *Corporal E* #5 achieved a range of 51.2 miles, which was only 3.45 miles short of expectations. The JPL guidance system, or autopilot, comprised an electronic automatic pilot that drove air-operated servo motors, an overriding radar control for the climbing leg of the trajectory, Doppler cutoff, and an integrating accelerometer for the descending portion of the trajectory. Despite the failure of the coupling the engine and guidance system worked well, so the flight was considered a success.

Round #5 marked the end of *Corporal* test-vehicle development and the beginning of an accelerated program to transform the missile into a tactical weapon. Army leaders in Washington decided the *Corporal* would be a precision weapon capable of striking small targets.

The disconnect coupling failed again on Round #6, which was fired on November 2, 1950. This missile impacted 35.9 miles from the launch pad, which was approximately 34 miles short. Later static tests of the *Corporal E* propulsion system demonstrated the dome loader regulator also failed, which caused an over-rich fuel mixture. It was also deemed likely that Round #5 suffered this type of failure too. As reported in the JPL report:

"In Round 6, the radar beacon was used to provide azimuth overriding guidance, which operated satisfactorily until the flight beacon transmitter failed at 36 seconds. The azimuth error was 126 feet east at impact. The Doppler beacon was provided to initiate shutoff of the flow propellants to the rocket motor when the missile had achieved a velocity calculated to carry it to the target in ballistic trajectory. However, the missile did not reach a velocity sufficient to effect shutoff of the propellants at the predetermined velocity. Furthermore, the Doppler beacon itself failed at 24 seconds."

The telemetry equipment also failed. Extreme vibration probably caused all the electrical equipment on the missile to fail.

The Army awarded contract DA-04-495-ORD-21 to Douglas Aircraft for an additional 20 missiles on October 9, 1950. These missiles, which were the first of the operational *Corporal* type, were slated for further testing of the tactical guidance and control system by JPL. The expected accuracy for the new missiles was plus or minus 100 feet in azimuth and plus or minus 500 feet in range. During December, *Corporal* became the first American missile approved to deliver an atomic warhead, the XW-7. Soon after the Army awarded JPL with a contract to develop *Corporal* into a complete weapon system.

On January 16, 1951, Round #7 reached a range of 63.85 miles; five miles short of the target. This was the first round to have in-flight propellant shutoff. Structurally, this was the first *Corporal* to employ a 19-cell air tank. The body shroud that covered the 19-cell arrangement gave the missile its distinctive polygon fuselage appearance. The disconnect coupling that had given trouble on the previous pair of flights was redesigned.

This missile carried a new engine cut-off system. Since range was a function of cut-off velocity, precise control over shutting down the engine was necessary for target accuracy. The German V-2 reduced errors in final velocity by first throttling back the thrust. *Corporal E* Round #7 had a quick-shutoff valve capable of operating in a few milliseconds. Unfortunately, problems continued to plague the control system. A failed connection between the central power supply and autopilot allowed the vehicle to start rolling 40 seconds into the flight. Errors in the data transmitted from the ground radar accounted for nearly half of the range shortage.

Round #8, which flew on 22 March, also landed a few miles short of the target. Nearly four months later, Round #9 overshot the target by 20 miles because the Doppler transponder failed and

Placing one of the early *Corporal* missiles on the pad at the Army launch area. The *Corporal* used the same gantry structure as the V-2 and other missiles. *Source: U.S. Army photograph courtesy of Bill Beggs.*

Early *Corporal* ready for launch. The *Corporal* pad was placed over the blast pit at the Army launch area. *Source: U.S. Army photograph courtesy of Bill Beggs.*

Corporal missile liftoff. *Source: U.S. Army photograph courtesy of Bill Beggs.*

The *Corporal* climbs out of sight, headed towards its downrange target. *Source: U.S. Army photograph courtesy of Bill Beggs.*

the missile did not respond to the propellant shutoff signal. The tenth rocket did not fly.

All the accumulated experience of the *Corporal E* program was applied to the next missile. Round #11 comprised the basic configuration of the eventual tactical missile. The most visible change was in the fin shape. *Corporal* now sported four delta-shape fins, which gave the rocket a more streamlined appearance. The new fins improved stability and ease of control over the original design.

Round #11 also had a newly designed nose cone that could accommodate a 1,500-pound warhead. Once again, there were problems with the guidance system. Shortly after liftoff, the power supply frequency regulator failed and the rocket followed a nearly vertical trajectory. As it climbed it drifted slightly to the west, over the Organ Mountains towards Las Cruces. Range Safety cut off the propellant supply and the missile impacted about 15 miles west of the launch pad, between WSPG Headquarters and the City of Las Cruces. This rocket flew on October 10, 1951, and ended the *Corporal E* testing and development program.

Even before the *Corporal E* test program was over the Army ordered the missile into production. During the summer of 1951 several companies were invited to submit bids for the *Corporal* production contract. The Department of the Army recommended an industrial program calling for the procurement of 200 missiles,

spare parts, and manuals on March 15, 1951. Once the Secretary of Defense approved the program final bids were solicited from several companies. The Firestone Tire and Rubber Company received the production contract. A letter order for $6,888,796.00 went to Firestone on July 17, 1951. When funds became available for the 1952 Fiscal Year, contract DA-04-495-ORD-159 for $13,695,592.00 replaced the letter order. Gilfillan Brothers, Inc. received the contract for the ground guidance equipment. In June 1952 Firestone received a supplemental contract for an additional 120 missiles, bringing the total production to 320.

Ground handling and launching equipment represented another major segment of the *Corporal* missile system. As a tactical weapon, the missile had to be fully field mobile. Firing tests prior to December 31, 1950, used existing facilities at WSPG, including the gantry crane and non-portable launcher developed during the *Corporal E* program. One of the first contracts for the design and development of tactical ground support equipment went to the International Derrick and Equipment Company (IDECO) in Torrence, California. IDECO was expected to submit their preliminary study results and designs by March 1951, with prototype equipment delivered during the third quarter of that year.

JPL engineers were not satisfied with IDECO's plans for the erector and launcher, so the construction phase of the contract was cancelled. Le Tourneau succeeded IDECO in attempting to design a vehicle for transporting and erecting *Corporal* on its launcher. In particular, the Le Tourneau design for an electric motor driven erector proved easy to control, and was accepted as the initial prototype. Working with Firestone, Le Tourneau redesigned the Type I erector. The Le Tourneau design for a launcher was another matter, and JPL went on to design their own. Firestone received the contract to produce these pieces of equipment and then to redesign them based on evaluations during firing tests.

Some provision had to be made to service the missile once it was in the vertical position, and the Army tried to adapt commercially available equipment. Stemm Brothers, Inc produced a piece of equipment known as the *Hi-tender* for work in apple orchards. This would work as a servicing platform. The *Hi-tender* was redesigned and mounted on a five-ton truck chassis. One of these modified *Hi-tender* platforms collapsed and fell about 15 feet while being used at WSPG. Fortunately the men in the operator's cage only suffered slight injuries, but the accident revealed the *Hi-tender* was not suitable for this purpose. Another piece of commercial equipment, a Miller Orchard Spray unit, was modified to service the erected missile.

Initially, rockets produced by Firestone were shipped to the JPL, where they were dismantled, inspected, reassembled, and tested. They were then shipped to WSPG. The first Firestone-manufactured *Corporal* was fired at White Sands on August 7, 1952. Throughout 1952 there were 29 *Corporal* flights, including the missiles fabricated by Douglas Aircraft for the JPL development program. Organizationally, these firings were conducted differently than the previous ones. For the initial series of *Corporal E* firings, the JPL research staff personally supervised each launch. Such an arrangement was not practical, as the pace of firings picked up, so a Field Operations and Test Section (FOTS) was created in August 1951 to coordinate JPL activities at WSPG. FOTS personnel became permanent residents at White Sands in early 1952.

FOTS-supervised launches included evaluation of tactical field equipment. The complete suite of new tactical equipment included a missile erector truck, portable launcher, and separate vehicles for servicing, propellants, and compressed air. The first full scale field test using tactical field equipment took place in September 1952.

Planning for the Engineer-User (E-U) Program began in the spring of 1952. As described by JPL personnel:

> "*Past conventions have usually dictated that any new weapon development be given engineering tests by that arm of the Army which has had responsibility for the particular weapon program. These tests have then been followed by tests of the weapon under operational conditions, as conducted by the using arm of the eservice. This practice was somewhat altered insofar as the Corporal was concerned. In the interests of saving time, money, and manpower, a joint team of Army Ordnance Corps and Field Forces personnel was formed as an Engineer-User Team for the Corporal missile.*"

Creating an E-U team with Ordnance Corps and Field Forces personnel combined engineering and operational personnel, which was another first for the *Corporal* program. The advantage of such an approach was that engineering personnel could see the missile being used by operational personnel and gain insight into the *Corporal's* faults and areas for improvement. From January 30, 1953, to January 22, 1954, there were 14 E-U launches. These flights revealed the azimuth control met military specifications, but the range accuracy left a lot to be desired. Of the 14 E-U flights, equipment malfunctions occurred about 54% of the time.

Missiles were fired at ranges of 30, 50, and 70 statute miles. Most of the range problems were due to difficulties with the propellant cut-off valve. E-U round #2, fired on February 26,

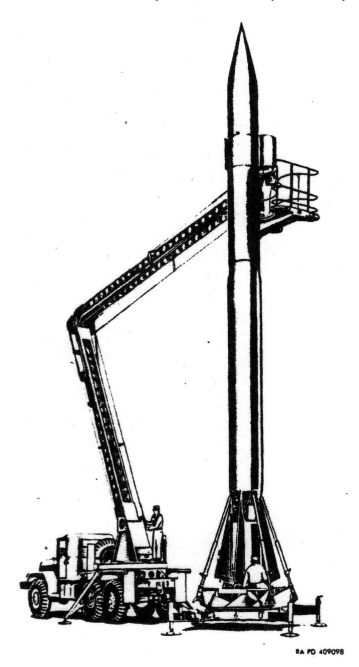

A commercial orchard spray unit was modified to become a mobile servicing platform for the *Corporal*. *Source: Development of the Corporal: The Embryo of the Army Missile Program.*

RA PD 409098

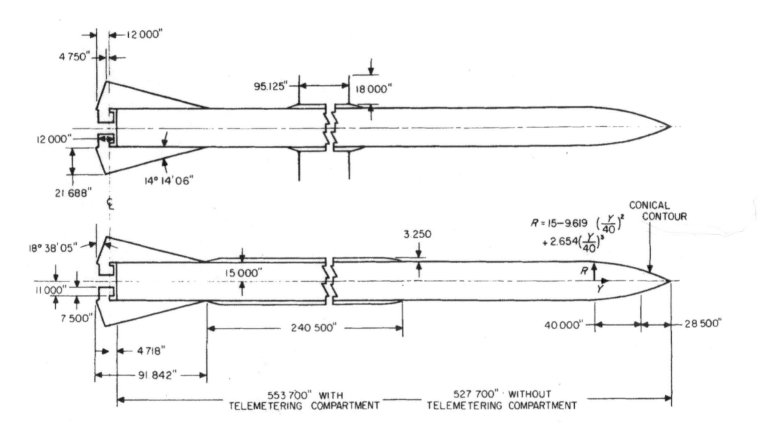

$$R = 15 - 9.619 \left(\frac{Y}{40}\right)^2 + 2.654 \left(\frac{Y}{40}\right)^3$$

Dimensions of the *Corporal* missile. *Source: Development of the Corporal: The Embryo of the Army Missile Program.*

1953, even overshot the target by more than 52 miles when the missile did not respond to the fuel cut-off signal. Another finding from the E-U program was that rain caused many components to malfunction, and the missiles could not be fired until their interiors had thoroughly dried. In general, most of the problems with the *Corporal* were due to the fact that it was a research vehicle that had been converted to an operational weapon.

In January 1954, *Operation Bondoque* was conducted to determine the tactical suitability of the complete Type I *Corporal* system. Personnel from JPL, Army Ordnance, and the prime contractors participated. By the spring, it became evident that the introduction of the *Corporal* to the Army Field Forces posed more problems than anticipated. To alleviate this situation, JPL was asked to assume a greater degree of overall program coordination. During the summer, representatives from the Army Field Forces, Ordnance, *Corporal* contractors, and JPL established a set of operating procedures. In addition, the *Corporal* Technical Consultants Office, which included one representative each from JPL, Firestone, and Gilfillan, was established at Fort Bliss. JPL began a bi-weekly *Corporal News Bulletin* to keep all agencies involved in the program up to date.

Troops were already training for the *Corporal* system, and three Field Artillery Missile Battalions had been formed. On February 5, 1953, the first *Corporal* launch by an all-military crew

Field equipment test at WSPG. The *Corporal* launch pad included four retractable arms that held the missile until it lifted off. *Source: U.S. Army photograph courtesy of Bill Beggs.*

took place. In late 1953, the Army activated the 246th, 247th, and 259th Field Artillery Missile Battalions at Fort Bliss. Each Battalion comprised two Batteries; a Firing Battery and a Headquarters and Service Battery. These units were still receiving items of basic equipment as late as mid-1954, when field firing operations began at WSPG.

The field firing operations took place at a different site than previous launches. In October 1953, Fort Bliss established the Red Canyon Range Camp in the northeast corner of WSPG. The camp was opened as a temporary facility to conduct *Nike Ajax* air defense missile training and annual service firings. The 259th performed four successful *Corporal* firings from the Red Canyon Range Camp in December 1954. The following month, the unit was deployed to Europe with the full array of *Corporal* field equipment. The 96th Ordnance Direct Support Company accompanied them.

In the meantime, E-U firings at WSPG continued. The E-U team and JPL personnel launched E-U rounds 15 and 16 in May 1954. From August through November, the Chief of Ordnance asked the E-U team to perform climactic tests with the *Corporal*. One phase included extreme cold and heat tests, from 60 degrees below zero to 180 degrees above. Missiles were also subjected to temperature variation and humidity tests. In general, the *Corporal* did not do well in these tests because the systems were too delicate.

Another weakness in the *Corporal* system was that the missile's radio guidance system could be jammed. The system relied upon the fixed-frequency DOVAP instrumentation system used at WSPG. DOVAP measurements provided information on the missile's position in space, velocity, and acceleration. The operating frequencies of this system were well known, so there was fear an enemy could jam the signals.

Early on, the *Corporal* espoused a process of continuous improvement, where lessons learned during tests led to design changes in subsequent missiles. These changes eventually led to the Type II *Corporal*. Firestone received contract DA-04-495-ORD-437 in January 1953 for the production of 465 Type II missiles in January 1953. Most of the changes between the Type I and Type II missiles were in the guidance system. A new Doppler unit that

used a tunable missile transponder with an input frequency range of 450 to 480 megacycles replaced the DOVAP-based unit. Minor improvements were also made to the radar link to provide better tactical operation. The launcher, erector, and servicing platform were also redesigned for the Type II missiles.

Propulsion received attention as well. A new oxidizer mixture of stabilized fuming nitric acid (SFNA), a mixture comprising 82.9% nitric acid, 14% nitrogen dioxide, 2.5% water, and 0.6% hydrogen fluoride was combined with a fuel of aniline, furfuryl alcohol, and hydrazine. SFNA did not decompose as rapidly under certain conditions as the original RFNA oxidizer. When stored in sealed containers at the desired upper temperature limit of 160° F, RFNA developed excessively high pressures due to the decomposition of the acid. The addition of hydrogen fluoride made the oxidizer more stable.

What is considered as the first Type II round was flown on October 8, 1953. Actually, this was a Type I *Corporal* airframe with the improved Type II guidance system. This missile impacted 234 meters short and 116 meters right of the aiming point, which was well within the tactical circular probability of error (CPE). Slightly more than a year later, on October 28, 1954, the first missile manufactured by Firestone under the ORD-437 contract flew. During the year between the prototype and first Type II production round, most of the missiles flown were Type I rounds with the upgraded electronics. Gilfillan manufactured the components for these missiles. Previously, Firestone had contracted directly with various manufacturers for electronic equipment.

Type II missiles began replacing Type I types among deliveries from Firestone's Los Angeles plant. Although the Type II *Corporals* were entering the testing program, there were still a number of Type I models on hand. These were used by JPL, the Army Field Forces, and Chemical Warfare Service as test vehicles for the Type II program. A few missiles tested the feasibility of radical design changes for future production runs and/or further system development. Among the changes tested was the use of an air-driven alternator as a substitute for the chemical batteries then in use.

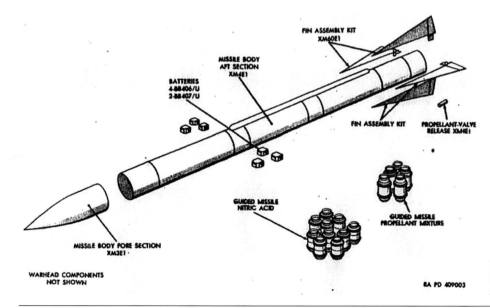

Major subassemblies of the *Corporal*. Source: *Development of the Corporal: The Embryo of the Army Missile Program.*

JPL fired 57 Type II missiles between the first ORD-437 round and the end of calendar year 1955. The E-U team also conducted firings during this period—21 Type II *Corporals* between February and December 1955. Throughout these firings, the *Corporal* Type II showed a significant improvement in accuracy. The typical CPE was 350 meters, which was much better than the Type I missiles. In 1956, the Army began to quickly replace Type I missiles with the Type II model. The Type II *Corporal* (Guided Missile Artillery, M2 [XM2E1]) was classified as the standard type by the Army. By March 1956, the Army had a total of 12 *Corporal* battalions equipped with Type II equipment, 6 of which were based in Europe.

Further improvements in the guidance system let to the Type IIa version, which was deployed to field troops in 1957. The air-turbine alternator previously tested at WSPG was incorporated in the Type IIb, which was deployed in 1958. The air-turbine replaced the chemical batteries previously used, which had proven unreliable. Quick-disconnect fins that shortened the time required to prepare a round for firing were also incorporated in the Type IIb design. These missiles were designated M2A1.

A Type III was test flown in 1957. With a completely redesigned guidance system, it was expected this would demonstrate increases in reliability, accuracy, tactical usability, and maintainability. The biggest changes occurred in the ground portion of the guidance system. Type II missiles with the Type III guidance equipment did show significant improvements in accuracy. The Chief of Ordnance even directed that the Type III *Corporal* be developed as a "shelf item" that could be put into production without delay should the program be approved. Despite such promise, this missile never progressed beyond experimental status. Throughout much of the 1950s, JPL worked on large solid-fuel rocked motors suitable for field artillery use. Their work eventually led to the *Sergeant*. Development of this missile looked so promising that on May 23, 1957, the Army cancelled the *Corporal* Type III program.

Although its range gave Army ground forces greater reach and added depth to the battlefield, the *Corporal* had several shortcomings as a field artillery weapon. For one thing, the missile units were large. A *Corporal* Battalion was made up of 250 personnel and required 35 vehicles, including the relatively large transporter/erector. *Corporal* was not a quick-response weapon that could be called upon for rapid interdiction and fire support in a highly mobile combat environment. Once a firing battery occupied a site, it usually took around nine hours before the first missile was ready for launch. *Corporal* was better suited for preplanned strikes against fixed installations like major headquarters, logistical bases, and marshalling areas well behind the front lines. Another problem area was the liquid propellants were highly toxic and required considerable care to handle.

Solid propellants, on the other hand, promised such advantages as simplicity of operation, ease of handling in the field, and lower cost. In the late 1940s solid propellant rocket technology was not as developed as liquid-fuel systems, so the Ordnance Department opted for the *Corporal*. From the beginning, Corporal was intended as an interim weapon that would be used until something better came along. Therefore, work continued on large solid-fuel rockets that would be suitable for field artillery use.

Advances made in the development of large solid-fuel motors ultimately spelled the end for the *Corporal* as a tactical weapon. The Army deployed the solid-fuel *Sergeant* in 1962. The following year, the first *Sergeant*-equipped units were sent to Germany. *Sergeant* proved much easier to handle in the field than *Corporal* and was better suited as a field artillery missile. For example, it only took an hour to prepare and launch a *Sergeant*. This missile also employed a self-contained inertial guidance system that was not susceptible to jamming like the command guidance system used on *Corporal*. With a range of 25-75 miles, the *Sergeant's* capabilities were similar to the *Corporal*. As the Army activated units equipped with the newer missile the *Corporals* were withdrawn from service. The drawdown of *Corporal* battalions was quick—the first European *Corporal* battalion was inactivated on March 31, 1963, and the last unit was inactivated on June 25, 1964. Less than a week later, the Army reclassified the *Corporal* as obsolete.

This was not the end of the *Corporal's* military career. In the mid-1950s the British Government agreed to purchase 113 *Corporal* missiles for the Royal Artillery. In 1957, the 27th Guided Weapons Regimental Royal Artillery became the first British unit to receive the *Corporal*. The 27th Regimental kept its *Corporal* missiles until 1966.

Corporal, the Army's first tactical ballistic missile. *Source: U.S. Army photograph courtesy of Bill Beggs.*

Although the *Corporal's* active service life was relatively brief and no missiles were ever launched in anger, it deserves an important place in the history of American rocketry. *Corporal*, which began as an experimental test vehicle, was the first American designed ballistic missile. At the time of its development, the 20,000-pound thrust motor that propelled *Corporal* was the largest liquid fuel rocket built in America. In addition, *Corporal* was the first missile certified to carry an atomic warhead. With this capability, for the years it was deployed, *Corporal* played an important role in America's ability to deter potential aggressors in Europe.

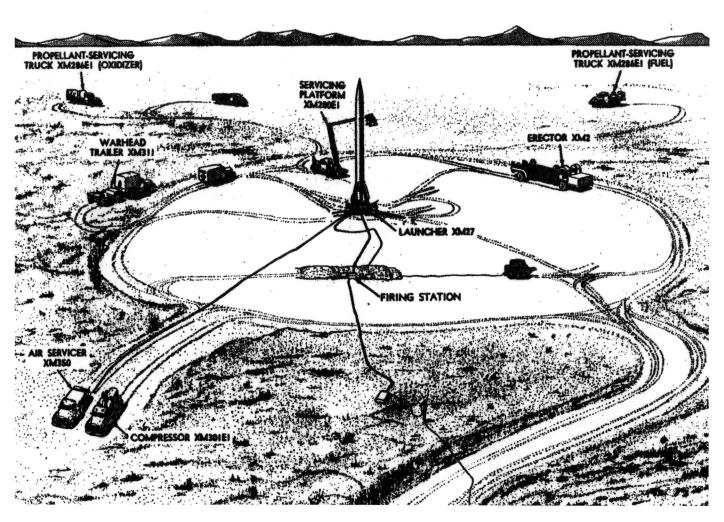

Typical layout of a *Corporal* firing position. *Source: Development of the Corporal: The Embryo of the Army Missile Program.*

13

Nike Missiles

The *Nike Ajax* was one of the iconic images of the Cold War. At a time when many Americans feared a surprise aerial attack by the Soviet Union, hundreds of these missiles stood ready for launch around dozens of major cities in the country. Like many missiles tested at WSPG, the *Nike* had its origins in World War II.

Influenced by intelligence reports of German rocket developments, in February 1944 the Army Ground Forces requested the Ordnance Department develop a "direction-controlled, major caliber, antiaircraft rocket torpedo." The Ordnance Department decided that the current state of the art was not sufficiently advanced for the design of a specific missile. Rather, senior leaders decided the development of an antiaircraft weapon should be incorporated into the general guided missile studies then underway.

The damage being inflicted on German and Japanese cities clearly demonstrated the need for effective air defenses. Even with a system of antiaircraft artillery, radar, and interceptor aircraft, Germany could not halt the Allied air offensive. The situation for Japan, which lacked a means to counter the B-29 *Superfortress*, was even worse. Looking to the future, Army leaders realized the problem of providing an adequate air defense system would become even more complex, and that new, more capable antiaircraft weapons would be needed. This was around the time that jet aircraft were entering combat. Operating at higher speeds than most piston-engined airplanes, jets presented a considerable challenge to existing air defense artillery. Aircraft then on the drawing boards would be even faster and would fly even higher, beyond the capabilities of conventional antiaircraft guns. Based on studies conducted over the late winter and early spring of 1944, the Ordnance Technical Committee recommended that the Ordnance Department embark on a program to procure test missiles and required ground equipment.

Approval for the development of antiaircraft missiles was given to the Chief of Ordnance on January 26, 1945, by the Army Service Forces. A few days later, the Chief of Ordnance asked that the Bell Telephone Laboratories (BTL) conduct a formal study to determine the technical characteristics of an antiaircraft guided missile. Simultaneously, the Army Air Force requested that BTL conduct a similar study for winged missiles. BTL could not conduct two studies at the same time, so it was decided that a contract would go to BTL for a comprehensive study without limitation on whether the missile should have wings or not. On this basis, the Ordnance Department and Army Air Force jointly sponsored the contract and agreed to share its results.

The Western Electric Company, BTL's parent organization, received a contract on February 8, 1945, for Bell Telephone to perform a complete paper study of the problem. This project was named *Nike*, after the winged Greek goddess of victory. Under the terms of the contract, BTL was to explore the feasibility of constructing an antiaircraft missile system that could engage a B-29 size target flying 600 miles per hour at altitudes from 20,000 to 60,000 feet. The effective horizontal range of the missile was around 12 miles. BTL completed the initial study by the middle of May 1945, and it resulted in a document titled "AAGM Report," dated 15 July. (AAGM is an acronym for "Antiaircraft Guided Missile.") The report writers concluded there was a good likelihood that an effective surface to air guided missile could be built by extending radar and computer techniques developed during the war, and by exploring the (then) relatively unknown realm of supersonic flight.

Nike was to be a complete weapon system, not just a missile vehicle. Throughout the study BTL scientists followed two precepts. First, they decided *Nike* should be based on existing hardware and technologies as much as possible. In other words, it should not depend upon some hoped for major breakthrough for success. Such a pragmatic approach would expedite development. The second paradigm was that the missile itself should be as simple as possible, and the most complex elements of the system would remain on the ground.

After studying the state of rocket development in the United States and allied countries, the BTL personnel recommended that:

"A supersonic rocket missile should be vertically launched under the thrust of a solid-fuel booster which was then to be dropped; thence, self-propelled by a liquid-fuel motor, the missile should be guided to a predicted intercept point in space and detonated by remote control commands; these commands should

be transmitted by radio signals determined by a ground-based computer associated with radar which would track both the target and the missile in flight."

The Western Electric contract was amended on September 21, 1945, to cover the research, design, development, and engineering work required to develop the *Nike* antiaircraft missile and necessary ground equipment. BTL selected Douglas Aircraft Company as the major subcontractor for the missile. Douglas in turn contracted with Aerojet Engineering and the Jet Propulsion Laboratory (JPL) for work on the missile propulsion system. BTL retained control over the design and construction of the radars, computer, and missile control system.

Created on July 27, 1945, the first schedule for the project called for a development period of four years, with field testing to commence in 1949. Like many other projects this schedule proved overly optimistic, and it had to be revised numerous times. The missile was proposed to be about 19 feet long with an overall weight of 1,000 pounds; 300 pounds of which was fuel and oxidizer. Four large triangular fins were at the aft of the fuselage, with four smaller, movable surfaces near the nose for steering. *Nike* was to be fired vertically, and boosted to supersonic speed in about two seconds by a high-thrust solid-fuel booster. The original booster design used eight solid fuel motors with a combined thrust of 93,000 pounds. The booster motors were relatively short, which gave the *Nike* a somewhat squat appearance at liftoff.

At the end of the boost phase the booster assembly dropped away, and the missile continued under the power of the liquid-fuel sustainer. Performance calculations were built around a 3,000-pound thrust regeneratively cooled engine that burned an aniline/furfuryl alcohol fuel mixture and an oxidizer of Red Fuming Nitric Acid (RFNA). High-pressure air forced the propellants into the combustion chamber. The sustainer had a thrust duration of 24.3 seconds. By the time the sustainer shut down, *Nike* would be

The *Nike-46* used a cluster of solid-fuel motors for a booster, giving it a short, squat appearance. *Source: U.S. Army photograph.*

traveling at 2,500 feet per second. The missile then coasted, or "zoomed," to intercept its target. If the missile continued to climb, it would still be traveling at 1,150 feet per second at 96,000 feet. The initial acceleration with the solid-fuel booster was expected to be 25 g, with a peak of 35 g when the sustainer finished.

A three-axis stabilization system was planned to control *Nike* in the pitch, yaw, and roll axes. Ground equipment included two radars: one to track the target and one to track the missile. Information from the radar units was fed to a computer that calculated the optimum trajectory to intercept the hostile aircraft. Course corrections were then transmitted to the missile to guide it to its target. When the missile was in the proper location a ground command detonated the fragmentation warhead.

Flight-testing began in 1946 with a series of uncontrolled vertical flights using dummy upper stages. Initially the missile lots were identified by year, so the first series of 14 missiles was designated model *Nike-46*. These firings tested launch methods, booster propulsion, stage separation, and flight stability. At that time the realm of supersonic flight was largely unexplored, so collecting aerodynamic data was particularly important. The first four *Nike-46* missiles had wooden dummies to represent the second stage. These were ballasted with lead so they weighed 1,000 pounds to simulate an operable missile. The dummy missiles comprised production-type fins attached to fuselages made from laminated mahogany.

The first *Nike-46*, designated missile 46-A, was launched on February 24, 1946. The booster was a cluster of four Aerojet solid-fuel rockets that delivered 22,000 pounds' thrust each for two seconds apiece. Originally, the engineers studied a booster made up of eight T10E1 rockets with 11,000 pounds' thrust each, but this design was rejected at the end of March 1946 when larger Aerojet motors became available. Aerojet was to deliver 56 booster motors, which were assembled in clusters of 4 by Douglas Aircraft. The propellant mixture for these motors was 73% potassium perchlorate, 26.85% Paraplex P-10, and 0.15% tertiary butyl hydrogen peroxide. Missile 46-A reached an altitude of 30,600 feet. The booster separated cleanly after two seconds, just as planned, and the second stage coasted to its peak altitude. The next two flights were similarly successful and reached altitudes of 43,300 and 42,150 feet each.

On October 8, 1946, missile 46-1, which was the first vehicle with a powered second stage, reached a peak altitude of 140,000 feet. The second stage motor, Aerojet model 21-AL-2600, delivered a thrust of 2,600 pounds. Missile 46-2 reached 110,000 feet, but strayed some 17 miles from the launch pad. The eighth powered *Nike-46* landed even further away. These flights demonstrated the need to be able to destroy the missiles in flight in case of a runaway round. Round 2 (missile 46-2) was deemed partially successful; the next five failed due to booster problems. Rounds three, four, and five had problems with booster separation, which affected the operation of the sustainer motor. The boosters on rounds six and seven exploded on the launcher.

Changes were made to the booster on missile 46-8 to prevent another explosion, but the rocket veered towards the southwest. When last seen, the missile was still climbing and was about two miles away. Its peak altitude was estimated at 102,000 feet, about 16 miles from the pad. The second stage was never found, but based on the early trajectory engineers estimated it impacted about 25 miles away. The last *Nike-46* firing took place on January 28, 1947. In actuality, this was missile 46-4. When the firing signal was given there was a flash and burst of smoke from the missile, but it failed to move. Subsequent inspection showed only one of the propellant grains had burned, and that was at a greatly reduced pressure, so the motor did not generate enough thrust for liftoff. Two *Nike-46* rounds, one dummy and one of the powered models, were not flown. These were held for later tests.

The single-motor booster from the Navy's *Terrier* program was adapted for the *Nike*. Source: *U.S. Army photograph*.

Instrumentation was meager at best. In every case, the tracking beacon was silenced at or near the end of boost, frustrating the planned tracking tests. Ground tracking cameras returned photographic records of the flights, but evaluation of the film records had to be performed by hand and was painfully slow. On-board instrumentation included accelerometers, fuel regulator pressure gauges, aerodynamic pressure sensors, and a heliograph. The heliograph provided a record of the relative position of the sun and horizon. Such records were especially important to reconstruct the attitude and orientation of the missile during its flight. Data from these instruments was recorded on movie film. The film magazines were protected by armored casings and shock-absorbing packing. Retrieval of this information was dependent upon recovery of the missile wreckage after impact.

Problems encountered during the *Nike-46* tests led to changes in the missile design. Previously, the booster motors used a single grain of Aeroplex K-6 propellant; for *Nike-47*, this was replaced with two grains of Aeroplex K-14. The new propellant burned slightly slower, so the thrust was reduced from 22,000 pounds to 18,000 pounds per motor, but the thrust duration was increased from 2 seconds to about 2.5 seconds. Internal changes in the motors gave better support to the propellant grains so they would burn more evenly. The booster motor nozzles were canted so the line of thrust of each motor passed through the center of gravity of the missile. Guide rails were also installed between the missile and booster. Some of the failed *Nike-46* rounds showed indications of sideways movement of the boosters. Hopefully the guide rails would prevent this from happening in the future. The *Nike* boat-tail was also redesigned to place the booster thrust directly against the base of the missile body.

Like the *Nike-46* tests, the *Nike-47* series began with inert upper stage flights. Five of these rockets were launched in September and October 1947. The dummy upper stages were made with steel bodies and standard missile aft sections and fins. The altitudes achieved by these test vehicles varied from 29,300 to 34,000 feet. While the boosters separated cleanly and individual motors appeared to perform well, the missiles went off course.

Precise inspection of the spent booster motor casings showed there were slight variations in the canted nozzles. The variances were enough to create thrust eccentricities that made the missiles deviate from the desired trajectory. Correcting such a problem would have required the development of whole new manufacturing processes, so the decision was made to return to straight nozzles for the remainder of the *Nike-47* missiles.

There were four more *Nike-47* flights; for these the upper stages were powered. Aerojet had refined the 21-AL-2600 acid-aniline motor, and the improved motor weighed 10 pounds less than the *Nike-46* units. The motors delivered the same performance as the earlier ones—a sea-level thrust of 2,600 pounds for 21 seconds. In the new power plant system, a single inertial-actuated starter valve/feed regulator replaced the two components used on *Nike-46*. Two of the *Nike-47* missiles reached altitudes between 115,000 and 120,000 feet; on the other two, premature detonation of the range safety destruct packages kept them from reaching their peak altitudes.

The booster continued to be a problem, so in 1948 Douglas Aircraft tried a radical approach. The Johns Hopkins University Applied Physics Laboratory (APL) was working on a ramjet powered antiaircraft guided missile for the Navy under *Project Bumblebee*. APL contracted with the Alleghany Ballistics Laboratory for the solid-fuel booster that would propel the ramjet missile to a high enough speed to operate. Alleghany Ballistics Laboratory was a Navy-owned facility in West Virginia operated by the Hercules Powder Company. It was on the site of a former ammunition factory, and was one of the leading centers for solid-fuel rocket motor development. This led to the Alleghany JATO T39 2.6DS-51,000 unit, which was about 120 inches long and 17 inches in diameter. This motor produced an average thrust of 51,100 pounds with a thrust duration of 2.6 seconds. In March 1948, designs were completed to adapt the Alleghany motor as a single-unit booster for *Nike*.

The resulting vehicle was considerably longer than previous *Nikes*, in part because a space had to be provided between the booster and upper stage to avoid obstruction of the latter's exhaust. The connecting structure was in the form of a sleeve and ring attached to the front end of the booster by means of three struts that left an ample vent area for the flame from the *Nike* motor. A conical steel cap with a graphite tip was placed over the top of the motor to protect it from the hot exhaust. Four large fins of a modified diamond shape were mounted near the aft end of the booster to stabilize the missile.

One advantage the Alleghany motor had over the previous Aerojet units was that it used a cast double-base propellant that was nearly smokeless when it burned. The Aerojet motors produced a dense smoke, which would clearly show a potential enemy where the missile was launched. Using a single motor rather than a cluster of four had advantages in the areas of cost, handling, and assembly. Therefore, further development work on the Aerojet boosters was

Nike launch. Source: U.S. Army photograph.

stopped, but they continued to be used in the testing program until the inventory on hand was depleted. This led to a situation where the 1948 series of tests included two distinctly different booster configurations.

Missile testing during the year served two functions. The new booster had to be qualified and control system testing began. The first *Nike-48* was destroyed when its booster exploded shortly after launch. The next missile was far more successful—it reached an altitude of 122,000 feet. During its flight it stabilized two times out of five commands before losing hydraulic pressure. *Nike-48-22*, which was missile round 20, could only be stabilized during the first command period. Round 21 failed to roll stabilize during any portion of its flight, but missile 22 responded to all commands except when the program interval was too short. As firings continued the complexity of the control tests increased.

The first flight with the Alleghany Ballistics Laboratory booster took place on June 17, 1948, using a *Nike-47* dummy upper stage. This was the beginning of the *Nike* 48-0 flight tests. The 48-0 series tested the single motor booster design. On the first flight the booster fins failed 2.3 seconds after launch, when the missile was traveling at a speed of 1,600 feet per second and had reached an altitude of 1,800 feet. Modifications were made to strengthen the fins on subsequent rounds. The next four flights were with powered *Nike-47* design upper stages. Three were launched vertically; the fourth one, which flew on July 13, 1948, was launched at an elevation of 40°. On three of the four tests the thrust duration of the *Nike* motor was shorter than expected. The first time this happened, it was later presumed the aniline tank had not been completely filled.

Another possible explanation was that lateral accelerations dislodged the fuel tank outlet. On the third powered round the engine cut off 5½ seconds early. Uncovering the tank outlet seemed the only way to explain this problem. Burning time was two seconds short on the 40° firing, but because of the nature of the trajectory it was expected that some propellants would be left in the tanks. Because problems with the tank outlets seemed a possible cause in all three cases the outlets were redesigned.

Radar development was underway throughout 1948, and the hardware underwent numerous changes from what had been initially proposed. Both the target and missile had to be tracked separately. The original plan was to have two antennae about 12 feet apart on a common rotating platform. By the end of the year this was abandoned in favor of having two identical radar mounts placed 50 to 100 feet apart. Construction of computer components also began in 1948. The computer built upon gun directors developed during World War II. It processed tracking information from the target and missile radars to calculate an intercept trajectory for the *Nike*. Once the circuit design was frozen component construction progressed quickly.

Missile testing continued throughout the summer and fall of 1948, with 26 firings in all. These were divided into three test series, based on their design and test purposes: the 48-0, which has already been described; and the 48-1 and 48-2 models. These, in turn, led to *Nike* models 484 and 490, which constituted the final missile configuration. *Nike* 48-1 missiles tested roll stabilization and steering controls, and the 48-2 tested new aerodynamic designs.

Trajectory calculations showed Nike's range could be increased if the fin area was reduced by one-third, so fins for the 48-2 missiles were smaller than those previously used. Further performance gains could be realized if the fin thickness was reduced from 6% to 2½%. Other changes incorporated in the 48-2 version included lengthening the fuselage by 20 inches to accommodate a larger warhead; changing the shape of the aft body section from a tapered boat-tail to a cylinder; and adding a fairing along the body to cover external plumbing and wiring. Wind tunnel tests with models of the 48-2 uncovered stability and roll control problems with the new design. This led to several changes, including a return to the original fin area. Other changes based on the wind tunnel tests included decreasing the distance between the control fins and main fins, and replacing the single large external conduit with four smaller ones. This modified version became the *Nike 484*.

Flight tests with the *Nike 484* began with three firings in May 1949. After these flights an austerity program was imposed on the project, so there were no further launches until January 1950. During the first quarter of the new year there were sixteen flights. They covered the complex steering tests originally planned as Phase 4 of the program. As could be expected with any new vehicle problems cropped up in the tests. Roll control proved to be a particularly thorny problem, and several different solutions

A *Nike* missile ready for launch from the single rail launcher. *Source: U.S. Army photograph courtesy of Bill Beggs.*

were tried before satisfactory results were achieved. Because the missiles were heavily instrumented and there were very thorough telemetry records these problems could be tracked down and corrected. During this series of tests predetermined pitch and yaw acceleration commands were transmitted to the missile from the ground using the radar to missile communications circuit for the first time.

Progress continued to be made with the radar and computer components of the system. In November 1949 the missile tracking portion of the radar system was delivered to WSPG. The complete radar system comprised an antenna trailer, radar control van, modified M2 optical tracker, and 400-cycle generator. This was set up at tracking station site C, which was three miles south of the launch pad. Testing began in December with a Martin B-26 *Marauder* bomber equipped with a beacon and receiver. As the aircraft flew simulated guidance commands were transmitted from the ground. For comparison purposes, the same aircraft was tracked using two optical theodolites at the Doña Ana Camp. Testing of individual computer components was underway at the same time.

The launcher underwent many changes, too. When the booster design changed, the *Nike* launcher progressed from a 4-rail arrangement used for the cluster booster configuration to a single rail (or monorail) version. The original monorail launcher weighed 5,000 pounds. Because the *Nike* was supposed to be a portable system a program was initiated to create a lighter version. Through the use of aluminum alloys and other design changes a lightweight experimental launcher was built that weighed only 2,050 pounds. This launcher could be transported by air, and could be unloaded and assembled in ten minutes by an eight-man crew. In the end, the lightweight launcher cost significantly more than the standard model so it was only used for a few test firings.

Testing with the *Nike 484* configuration continued into 1950. In March of that year the eighth *Nike* Planning Conference was convened at WSPG. At the conference it was decided to use the remaining *484* missiles (there were 6) to prove proper roll and steering control at high altitudes. The next series of missiles bore the designation *Nike 490*. The initial batch of 16 missiles, designated the *Nike 490A*, were assigned to a precise performance test program that was to be completed before the official *Nike* system trials.

On July 24, 1950, a meeting convened in Washington, D.C., with representatives from the Army, Navy, and Air Force. Participants at the meeting received a presentation of the design objectives and equipment plans for the *Nike* tactical system. Briefly, they learned the tactical system had been designed to provide, at the earliest possible date, an effective defense against maneuvering bomber aircraft traveling at speeds of 650 knots at an altitude of up to 60,000 feet. The effective range of the system was to be 25 nautical miles. Such a system would be effective against presently known bomber type aircraft and those predicted for the near future. In keeping with existing antiaircraft artillery organizational doctrine, the fire unit for this guided missile system was to be the Battery, with several Batteries constituting a Battalion.

The three major elements of the *Nike* system comprised the missile, tracking radars, and computer. These formed a "closed loop" control system. The radars tracked the target and missile separately. Radar data was provided to the computer, which calculated the flight path through a predicted intercept point, and the missile radar was then used to send course corrections to the missile. The only difference between the target and missile tracking radars was that the latter included communications circuits to send corrective signals to the *Nike*.

Based on observations made during the *Nike 484* tests, the *490* model introduced a number of changes. In an effort to increase the range of the missile as well as lighten and simplify the booster-missile support sleeve, the sustainer motor was started after stage separation. Components inside the missile were rearranged to place the center of gravity closer to the dynamic balance point, or center of pressure, to improve aerodynamic response during supersonic flight. Some of the electronic components were repackaged to simplify pre-flight adjustment. The fins once again received attention; a new type of composite construction was tried to ease production and save nearly 50 pounds of weight. Two of the missiles carried bladder-type propellant tanks in an effort to obtain complete expulsion of the fuel and oxidizer.

These modifications brought mixed results. For example, while the delayed start of the sustainer motor yielded satisfactory results from a structural perspective, nine of the first ten missiles with this modification exhibited shortened thrust duration. It was found that the RFNA propellant line burst diaphragm functioned at booster ignition, and some of the oxidizer leaked out before the second stage ignited. The two missiles with the bladder-type propellant tanks failed because they could not withstand the negative accelerations that occurred at booster burnout. Changes in the hydraulic control valves and fins resulted in roll and control oscillations. Even though these problems were not completely solved, the 1950 firing program was brought to a close after ten launches. The missiles had exhibited satisfactory launch, boost, separation, and sustainer ignition. The radar tracking and command link performed well.

Six *Nike 490A* missiles remained. The first three months of 1951 were devoted to eliminating the problems that had been identified in the earlier missiles. Three of these rounds were equipped with experimental acid-gasoline engines. Readily available, gasoline would be a better tactical choice than aniline for a fuel if such a motor could be made to work satisfactorily. Results from the six remaining *Nike 490A* vehicles (rounds 60 through 65), which flew between April 12 and July 14, 1941, were disappointing. Test objectives were successfully achieved on only two of the six rounds. Round 63, the first one with the acid-gasoline engine, exploded at ignition, so the remainder of the *490A* missiles used the acid-aniline propellant mixture. The other failures in the series were attributed to control system problems.

On October 16, 1951, the first *Nike 490B* flew. Round 66 incorporated all the experience gained from the *490A* series. Modifications had been made to the control circuit on this missile to prevent a recurrence of the problems that plagued the *490A* vehicles. The modifications worked and the missile flew successfully. Now all that remained was the supreme test—the *Nike* missile had to intercept and shoot down a drone aircraft.

Nike moved into its next phase, the R & D System Tests. The series, which comprised 23 flights, began with the firing of Round 67 on November 15, 1951. This marked the first firing of a *Nike* missile with all its ground control equipment. Round 67 was completely successful; the missile was directed at a ground radar reflector target 15 miles north of the launch pad. Firing at a ground target was the most cautious procedure; for the first time the Computer/Target Radar/Missile control loop was closed. A 16-foot tall, two-panel corner reflector was erected on a slight rise of ground. The surveyed coordinates of the target location were entered into the computer so that the function of the missile tracking and guidance system could be verified. Ground clutter was likely to interfere with the radar once the missile reached the end of its trajectory, so steering orders were zeroed two seconds before impact. The missile passed within 50 feet of the target. On the next

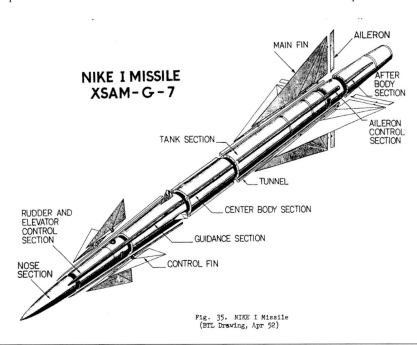

NIKE I MISSILE
XSAM-G-7

AILERON
MAIN FIN
AFTER BODY SECTION
AILERON CONTROL SECTION
TANK SECTION
TUNNEL
CENTER BODY SECTION
RUDDER AND ELEVATOR CONTROL SECTION
GUIDANCE SECTION
NOSE SECTION
CONTROL FIN

Fig. 35. NIKE I Missile
(BTL Drawing, Apr 52)

Nike missile cutaway showing major subassemblies.
Source: U.S. Army photograph.

QB-17G target drone. Source: U.S. Army photograph.

flight the radar beacon was lost at 12.75 seconds; the safety system destroyed the missile at 18.25 seconds.

Round 69 was the first attempt at intercepting an aerial target, and it was highly successful. On November 27, 1951, this missile shot down a QB-17G target drone flying at an altitude of 29,000 feet over WSPG. The time of flight was 37.5 seconds. Of the 23 flights in the R & D System Test series 20 were launched against aerial targets. Seven of the twenty were considered "successful." The fourth successful missile, Round 77 on February 5, 1952, scored the first direct hit on a drone at an altitude of 24,300 feet. However, *Nike* did not need to hit the target to score a kill; all that was needed was a close detonation of the fragmentation warhead.

Another four missiles were "partially successful." Of these, one of them detonated close enough to the drone to score a "C" kill. A "C" kill was defined as sufficient damage to prevent the plane or its crew from completing the mission. After landing, engineers found the *Nike* warhead produced 168 holes in the QB-17G. Dummies aboard the aircraft simulated the crew. Several of the simulated crew members were considered wounded or killed. After sustaining such damage, it would be highly unlikely that a manned aircraft would be able to continue to its target.

Nike carried three separate warheads located in the missile nose, mid-section, and tail. When detonated, they created a spherical pattern of thirty-grain fragments. All three warheads were detonated simultaneously through a primacord harness running the length of the missile. Using three separate bombs produced an adequate spray pattern. The nose warhead weighed 12 pounds. The barrel-shaped mid and aft warheads each weighed 150 pounds. Fragmentation material in the mid and aft warheads comprised a double layer wrapping of rectangular steel wire that had been scored at intervals to produce about 30,000 30-grain fragments. The dome-shaped nose warhead contained a section of 20-grain steel pellets set in resin.

Responding to the threats posed by Soviet bombers armed with atomic weapons and Communist aggression in Korea,

Nike production had been placed on a "crash program" basis in mid-1950. The result of this was that design and fabrication of prototype tactical missiles began in early 1951, even before the R & D System Tests were finished. The first tactical missile, *Model 1249*, was launched on February 25, 1952, two months before the last R & D flight. Just three months after the last R & D System Test flight, the first production line missile (No. 1249B-1001) roared off the launcher at WSPG. Envisioning further missile developments, *Nike* became known as the *Nike I*.

Beginning production while development was still going on created many problems. For example, drawings would be incomplete and inadequate as a basis for any procurement contracts. With the introduction of developmental changes, components already ordered would have to be scrapped and new ones ordered. Expeditors faced problems securing raw materials in time to meet production timetables. The lack of field experience meant there was no way to estimate spare parts and maintenance requirements. Spare parts estimates were based on mortality experiences with other complex electronic items. With *Nike* being pursued on a "crash" basis, there was no way to properly predict program costs.

The Navy was also working on antiaircraft missiles, and one of them—the *Terrier*—showed a great deal of promise. Like *Nike*, *Terrier* was a two-stage missile. In fact, *Nike's* booster was based on the one developed for *Terrier*. Because it looked as though the Navy missile would be operational first, during 1951 Army officials proposed using *Terrier* as an interim weapon system until *Nike* became available. There were significant differences between the two. *Terrier* was a "beam-riding" missile that followed the radar beam that tracked the target. (The radar beam came from the ground, not the missile.) If the *Terrier* deviated from the center of the beam, its guidance system corrected its flight path. *Nike* relied on command guidance from the ground to intercept its target and used two radars: one to track the missile and one to track the target. The Army began work on a suitable ground control system for a land-based version of *Terrier*, but before the work progressed very far the *Terrier* schedule had slipped, and it looked like *Nike* would be ready first after all.

The *Model 1249* missile used an engine based on the acid-gasoline motor tested with the first *Nike 490A* in 1951. After the explosion in the *490A*, further flights of the acid-gasoline engine were suspended until more static tests could be made. The *1249's* engine was uncooled. Both the combustion chamber and nozzle throat were ceramic lined for protection. Initially, the engine burned a mixture of JP-3 jet fuel and White Fuming Nitric Acid (WFNA). Based on propellant studies and tests conducted in late 1952 the fuel was changed from JP-3 to JP-4. The improved motor was incorporated in the first *Model 1249* missile launch in February 1952. As the missile matured, the propellants were changed to an oxidizer of Inhibited Red Fuming Nitric Acid (IRFNA) and a fuel mixture of Unsymmetrical Dimethyl Hydrazine (UDMH) and JP-4. This combination was subsequently used for operational missiles.

Like other *Nike* system components, the *Model 1249* booster underwent an evolutionary process. During the R & D tests three different types of boosters were used: the heavyweight 3-DS-47,000 X201A3; the lightweight 2.5-DS-59,000 X216A2; and the lightweight 3-fin 2.5-DS-59,000 XM5. Alleghany Ballistics Laboratory produced all three motors. The X201A3 delivered an average thrust of 47,000 pounds for 3 seconds, while the X216A2 and XM5 both produced 59,000 pounds for 2.5 seconds. For flight stabilization, three fins with an 86-inch circular span were mounted around the aft end of the booster. When assembled, the *Model 1249* booster-missile combination was 31 ½ feet long and weighed 2,325 pounds. The XM-5 became the M-5, and was the basis for the final *Nike* booster.

Between January and May 1953, BTL conducted a series of 49 contractor evaluation tests at WSPG. These tests included the prototype ground equipment set that had been assembled in Whippany, New Jersey. Originally, Army officials planned to move the ground equipment to WSPG by air transport, but the aircraft

were needed to ship materiel overseas. (The Korean War was still going on.) With this mode of travel ruled out, it was decided to ship the equipment to WSPG via truck convoy. It took 10 days to complete the 2,610-mile journey; the convoy left on 25 October and arrived on November 4, 1952. This afforded an opportunity for a thorough road test of the vehicles and guidance equipment. Upon arrival at WSPG, initial testing showed no trace of damage to the guidance equipment from the road trip.

The contractor tests demonstrated that the *Nike* system would perform according to contract specifications in a field environment. The first flight (Round 301P) was fired on January 27, 1953; the last one on 12 May. Of the 49 rounds fired, 21 (43%) were completely successful; 11 (22.5%) achieved a "qualified" intercept; and 17 (34.5%) failed to reach intercept. Telemetry revealed that at least 14, and possibly 18, of the "qualified" and unsuccessful firings were due to a design error in the roll amount gyroscope. This error was not discovered until after the contractor tests were completed. Six missiles were fired in a "rapid fire" test. All six were fired in 5 minutes, 50 seconds.

The last twelve firings were made from an alternate site, located so that normal missile fight paths to the intercept point would pass directly over the missile tracking radar. These tests proved the automatic circuitry that directed the missile around the radar. Moving to an alternate site provided experience taking down and setting up the ground guidance and control equipment. The two-mile move was completed with a 15-man crew in about 20 hours. In all, the contractor tests were responsible for the introduction of 4,000 changes to the missile in less than four months.

The first prototype *Nike* Battery equipment, along with the prototype Assembly Area equipment set, was delivered to the Army Ordnance Corps at WSPG on May 15, 1953. This did not signal the end of the contractor's R & D efforts. Not all design problems surfaced in the short time between development and production. Some problems in the system only showed up during more extensive testing or crew training. BTL personnel continued

Nike testing included firing multiple missiles in rapid fire exercises. *Source: U.S. Army photograph* courtesy of Bill Beggs.

Aerial view of the Red Canyon Range Camp, ca. 1955. *Source: U.S. Army photograph.*

to correct these shortcomings and improve system performance well into 1955, when the *Nike I* guided missile system was classified as a "standard type" by the Army.

When BTL turned over the prototype equipment set to the Army, *Nike* moved into the Engineering-User Test Program. This program combined Army engineering tests and the user, or service tests, which are normally conducted separately. Combining the tests conserved time and equipment. BTL allocated 1,000 Model 1249B missiles for the Engineering-User tests. E-U flight tests began in June 1953.

The Army activated the first anti-aircraft guided missile unit in the fall of 1953. With the activation of this unit, the Army implemented a "Package Training Program" for the cadre of newly activated *Nike* Batteries to use tactical equipment under actual firing conditions against Radio Controlled Aerial Targets, or RCATs. The 36th Antiaircraft Missile Battalion was the first unit to participate in this program. The Army Air Defense Artillery School at Fort Bliss was responsible for *Nike* crew training. Fort Bliss did not have range facilities for such a large-scale program, and the Army launch area at WSPG wasn't suitable either. To meet the need for *Nike* missile training, Fort Bliss established the Red Canyon Range Camp (RCRC) near the northeast corner of WSPG.

Construction at RCRC began in September. The entrance to the Range Camp was off of U.S. Highway 380, about 16 miles west of Carrizozo, NM. Located in the eastern foothills of the Oscura Mountains, the camp headquarters was situated in a flat area below the Chupadera Mesa. A missile assembly area was situated several miles southwest of the main camp. This is where the *Nike* missiles were assembled, fueled, and prepared for firing from the launch area that was a few miles further to the southwest.

Soldiers from the 495th Antiaircraft Artillery Missile Battalion at Fort Bliss were dispatched to RCRC to help build with construction. Initially, conditions were very primitive. Troops lived in squad tents erected over wooden frames. Army cots and a single pot-bellied stove were the only furnishings in each tent. Even the camp headquarters operated out of a tent. Water was a problem. Eventually a single well was drilled, but the water contained so much alkali that it was not drinkable, nor could it be used for washing. Lye soap wasn't powerful enough to deal with the mineral content of the well water. The water from this well was used to flush the toilets (once they were built—the first troops at

Red Canyon Range Camp headquarters shortly after it opened. *Source: U.S. Army photograph.*

Post Exchange (PX) at the Red Canyon Range Camp. *Source: U.S. Army photograph.*

Red Canyon Range Camp mess hall. *Source: U.S. Army photograph.*

RCRC used field latrines) and charge the fire hydrants (another amenity that was added later). For drinking, cooking, and bathing, water had to be trucked in every day from Carrizozo. Colonel Daniel A. O'Conner was appointed the first commander of RCRC on October 28, 1953.

The 36th Antiaircraft Missile Battalion was the first tactical unit to participate in the Package Training Program. Batteries received most of their training at Fort Bliss. When the units completed the basic required training, they moved to RCRC for further training that culminated in the firing of at least one successful missile out of three. Once this was accomplished the units were declared operational.

At first, RCRC was planned as a temporary facility for two years or less, until the planned completion of McGregor Range at Fort Bliss. This proved overly optimistic, and RCRC remained in use for nearly six years. Late in 1954 the Army began conducting Annual Service Practice (ASP) firings at RCRC. *Nike* battery crews rotated back to RCRC, where they performed live firings against RCATs to maintain proficiency. Facilities were added, including a mess hall, barracks and administrative buildings, motor pool, dispensary, recreation and service club, fire department, shower house, latrines (with flush toilets), theater, and a small post exchange (PX.) On April 4, 1955, Lieutenant Colonel John J. McCarthy assumed command of RCRC. He enjoyed the assignment so much that he remained until August 10, 1959, when air defense missile firings moved to McGregor Range on Fort Bliss and the RCRC closed. The number of personnel at the camp numbered about 500, and the mess hall served as many as 1,500 meals a day.

Operation Understanding was one of the most important functions performed at RCRC. This was a special Army program to educate community leaders about the *Nike* missile system. The *Nike* system depended upon the construction of firing sites around major cities. Local citizens sometimes opposed the sites. For example, in 1957 the proposed location of a site at the Los

Angeles International Airport brought strong opposition from the local community. One of their concerns was having booster casings impacting in residential areas. Of course, what they failed to recognize was that the only way these missiles would be fired would be if the United States were under aerial attack by hostile bombers that likely carried atomic bombs. After the mayor and other civic leaders visited RCRC as part of Operation Understanding their opposition evaporated.

Visitors to RCRC under Operation Understanding included mayors and city officials, civil defense leaders, church, civic, educational and industrial leaders, and newspapermen. Occasionally, a governor or senator made the trip. They were all flown in military aircraft but paid their own expenses. The missiles were fired at RCATS as the visitors watched from ridges to the east. Of course, one area that was not on the tour was "Booster Alley," the portion of the desert west of the launch area where most of the boosters impacted. This area was littered with boosters that stuck in the ground like arrows after being shot straight up into the air.

One of the best known, and most beloved, residents of RCRC was a wild burro named *Nike* that became the camp mascot after it was caught. The burro even had his own "formal" uniform; a red blanket with his name and "RCRC" emblazoned on it. Camp personnel tried to have him wear it when there were special visitors present, but *Nike* didn't like having it put on him. Whenever he sensed someone was going to put the dreaded blanket on him *Nike* went into hiding. *Nike* pretty much had the run of the camp, and frequently crashed parties and other gatherings. *Nike's* favorite spot was the PX, where soldiers would give him beer. He became so obnoxious that if a soldier did not share his libation, the burro would often nip at him. On a few occasions *Nike* poked his head into the chapel and brayed along with the hymns.

One of the most beloved "characters" at the Red Canyon Range Camp was a wild burro nicknamed *Nike*, shown here shortly after his capture. *Source: U.S. Army photograph.*

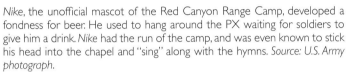

Brigadier General William L. Bell.
Source: U.S. Army photograph.

Nike, the unofficial mascot of the Red Canyon Range Camp, developed a fondness for beer. He used to hang around the PX waiting for soldiers to give him a drink. *Nike* had the run of the camp, and was even known to stick his head into the chapel and "sing" along with the hymns. *Source: U.S. Army photograph.*

The chapel was a particular source of pride at the Red Canyon Range Camp. It was built by the soldiers in their off hours using whatever material they could find. The frame for the building was fabricated from surplus pieces of railroad track salvaged from the Southern Pacific line. Steel bracing came from the doors of the old Lincoln County jail. The bells in the steeple were booster nozzles recovered from Booster Alley. Booster shipping crates provided a supply of lumber. The soldiers quarried red rock from a nearby hillside. The only official cash expenditure for the chapel was $200, which the men donated for roofing shingles.

Brigadier General William L. Bell assumed command of WSPG on August 1, 1954. Born in Norfolk, Virginia, on June 5, 1904, he attended John Marshall High School at Richmond and Hampden-Sidney College at Farmville, Virginia, prior to entering the United States Military Academy at West Point. He graduated with a Bachelor of Arts degree and commissioned as a Second Lieutenant on June 13, 1929. Lieutenant Bell was then assigned to the 29th Infantry Division, Fort Benning, Georgia, where he completed the Company Officers Course at the Infantry School.

He was detailed to the Ordnance Corps on July 1, 1932, and attended the Massachusetts Institute of Technology, where he received a Bachelor of Science degree in Mechanical Engineering. He then attended the Ordnance School at Aberdeen Proving Ground, Maryland. On March 5, 1936, he was permanently transferred to the Ordnance Corps.

By the time the United States entered World War II he'd reached the rank of Major. His early postings with the Ordnance Corps included Picatinny Arsenal, Watertown Arsenal, Springfield Armory, Aberdeen Proving Ground, and as an instructor in Ordnance and Gunnery at the United States Military Academy.

During the early stages of World War II, Major Bell was responsible for the establishment of numerous small arms

Missile assembly area at Red Canyon Range Camp. *Source: U.S. Army photograph.*

By placing missiles on sliding rails they could be rapidly loaded onto the launch rail. *Source: U.S. Army photograph* courtesy of Bill Beggs.

plants throughout the United States. He served as a member of the Ordnance Department Board in 1942 and 1943, and had assignments in the Ammunition Branch of the Industrial Division, and the Ammunition Division of the Industrial Service, both in the Office of the Chief of Ordnance. Later in the war he spent 15 months in the China-Burma-India Theater as Theater Ordnance Officer.

Upon his return to the United States, Bell was assigned to the Atomic Energy Commission and was promoted to Colonel (Permanent) on March 17, 1952. Following his assignment with the Atomic Energy Commission he assumed command of Picatinny Arsenal in Dover, New Jersey, and received promotion to Brigadier General on January 21, 1954.

General Bell became Commanding General of White Sands Proving Ground, succeeding General Eddy, who had retired on July 21, 1954. Colonel Homer Thomas filled in as interim commander of WSPG during the period between General Eddy's retirement and General Bell's arrival. Brigadier General Bell was transferred to the Office of the Chief of Ordnance on January 31, 1956, as Assistant Chief of Research and Development. He was promoted to Major General on March 16, 1956, but died unexpectedly three days later of a cerebral hemorrhage.

More than 3,000 missiles blasted off from the Red Canyon Camp during the six years it was in operation. Even though they were surplus, it was relatively expensive to convert B-17 bombers into QB-17G target drones. Therefore, most of the missiles were launched against Q-18 and Q-19 RCAT drones. These drones were small propeller driven airplanes that carried radar reflectors to create the illusion of a larger aircraft to the target radar. They were launched by a small contingent at the nearby Oscura Range Camp.

In 1959, the Army completed the McGregor Range at Fort Bliss and RCRC closed. All the buildings except for the chapel were removed, leaving only the concrete pads they stood on and the entrance gate behind. The chapel was later sold and removed by a civilian contractor. *Nike*, the camp mascot, was given to a local rancher.

By the time this happened, the *Nike I* had become the *Nike Ajax* and was deployed throughout the United States. The first *Nike* battery was deployed at Fort Meade, Maryland, on May 30, 1954. The following year, there was a renewed sense of urgency to deploy the *Nike Ajax* when the Soviet Union revealed their jet-powered *Bison* bomber. At the Soviet Aviation Day celebration in July 1955, the Soviets flew what appeared to be 60 *Bison* bombers past the reviewing stand. What Western observers didn't know was that the Soviets only had ten of the strategic bombers—Communist leaders had them circle around and repeat the fly-by six times. This led to an inflated estimation of the Soviet bomber fleet and concerns over the "bomber gap."

The first tactical version of the missile was designated the *Nike I XSAM-A-7* (Experimental Surface to Air Missile – Army – design number 7.) In July 1955 it became the *Nike I* Antiaircraft Guided Missile System. During the mid-1950s, *Nike* batteries were installed in defensive "rings" around major cities and industrial areas. The New York Defense Area was one of the largest in the country, with 20 *Nike I* installations. By June 30, 1958, there were 222 *Nike I* sites in the continental United States and 24 in Europe. Ultimately, *Nike Ajax* batteries were also deployed by NATO members Germany, France, Denmark, Italy, Belgium, Norway, Netherlands, Greece, and Turkey. Asian allies Japan, South Korea, and Taiwan also had *Nike Ajax* missile units. Although it represented a tremendous advance in guided missile technology, *Nike* was somewhat limited in its capabilities. *Nike* could only track one target at a time, and there was no effective way to coordinate launchings between batteries.

Nike Ajax batteries comprised two separate locations. The Integrated Fire Control Area contained the radar and computer systems. This was usually situated on a hilltop where the radars

The *Nike B*, which became the *Nike Hercules*, was a nuclear-capable antiaircraft missile capable of knocking bomber formations out of the sky. *Source: U.S. Army photograph courtesy of Bill Beggs.*

Nike Hercules launch. *Source: U.S. Army photograph.*

would have a clear view. Missiles were stored in underground magazines at the Firing Area. Elevators brought them to the surface, where crewmembers pushed them by hand across twin steel rails to one of four launchers. The Control and Launch Areas were generally 1,000-6,000 yards apart. One of the quirks of the equipment was that the two sites had to be a minimum of 1,000 yards apart.

Army planners feared the Soviets would attack with large formations of bombers and overwhelm the *Nike's* capabilities. In the early 1950s, they looked at the possibility of equipping the *Nike* with an atomic warhead that could knock whole formations out of the sky. *Nike I* was too small to make that practical, so BTL recommended building a larger missile that could carry an XW-7 atomic warhead. The Chief of Ordnance approved an engineering study of the new missile in August 1952. In December, the Deputy Chief of Plans and Research approved plans for the larger missile.

Two months later, the Army asked BTL to submit a detailed proposal for a *"Nike B"* missile. Soon after that, the Joint Chiefs of Staff approved the *Nike B* and gave it a 1A priority. On July 16, 1953, the Secretary of the Army formally established the project. Western Electric was the prime contractor for the overall system. Subcontracts went to BTL for the radar and guidance systems and Douglas Aircraft Company for the missile.

In its first configuration, the *Nike B* quadrupled the *Nike I* components; that is, the booster comprised a cluster of four M-5 motors and the sustainer utilized four of the acid-aniline liquid engines. The first test firing of a *Nike B* took place on March 11, 1955, at WSPG. From the start, the liquid fuel upper stage proved problematic. For one thing, it was so complex, with the plumbing for four separate combustion chambers, that reliability suffered. Then, on September 30, 1955, one exploded during a static test. The explosion killed one worker and injured five others. After this incident it was decided to develop a solid-fuel upper stage for *Nike B*.

Overall reliability continued to be a problem, and out of the first 20 firings, 12 had to be terminated early. One of the successful flights occurred on October 31, 1956, slightly more than 19 months after the first launch, when the *Nike B* intercepted a drone aircraft for the first time. Another major milestone came on March 13, 1957, with the first flight of the solid fuel sustainer. By that time, both *Nike* missiles had received new names. On November 15, 1956, the *Nike I* became the *Nike Ajax* and the *Nike B* became the *Nike Hercules*.

Nike Hercules extended the reach of its predecessor. It had a maximum range of 90 miles; a speed of 2,700 miles per hour; and could intercept targets as high as 150,000 feet. The missile could be loaded with either the M-17 high explosive fragmentation warhead or W-31 variable yield nuclear warhead. The yield of the W-31 could be adjusted to 2, 20, or 40 kilotons. *Nike Hercules* could also be used as a surface to surface missile. This was particularly important in Europe, where it added another potential weapon to counter the numerically superior Warsaw Pact forces.

On June 30, 1958, *Nike Hercules* began replacing *Nike Ajax* missiles as quickly as possible. The first such exchange occurred around Chicago. By 1964, the last *Nike Ajax* missiles in the United States were removed from service. Ultimately, there were 145 *Nike Hercules* sites. Shortly after the deployment of the *Nike Hercules* began, the Army initiated a program to upgrade its capabilities. System improvements, particularly in the radar units, led to the *Improved Hercules*. In June 1960, an *Improved Hercules* intercepted a *Corporal* ballistic missile over WSMR. This was the first time a missile had been intercepted in flight.

By the time the *Nike Hercules* was deployed, Soviet bombers were not the primary threat to the United States. Intercontinental ballistic missiles (ICBMs) had become the major threat to American security. Despite the successful shoot-down of a *Corporal*, *Nike Hercules* was not capable of countering an incoming ICBM. Still, *Nike Hercules* batteries continued to guard America's skies until 1974, when the last unit in the United States was deactivated. The missile remained in service in Europe for another ten years.

Nike Ajax and *Nike Hercules* were not the only air defense missiles developed by the Army during the 1950s. In 1952, the Army began developing a medium-range surface to air missile called the Homing All the Way Killer, or *HAWK*. Raytheon received the contract for missile development. Northrop was awarded the contract for the launcher, radars, and fire-control system. A solid-fuel Aerojet M22E7 dual-thrust motor powered the early versions of the *HAWK*. The propellant grain was designed so that after an initial high-thrust boost, it continued burning at a lower thrust level to continue accelerating the missile towards the target. (The M22E7 motor was replaced with the more reliable M22E8 on later missile models.) *HAWK* had large triangular fins with control surfaces on their trailing edges. The missile carried a 119-pound high explosive warhead with both impact and proximity fuzes.

The first launch of a *HAWK* took place in July 1957. It reached an Initial Operational Capability (IOC) with the Army in August 1959, and the missile was added to the U.S. Marine Corps inventory the following year. It had an effective range of 1.25-15 miles. In 1972 a program began to upgrade the *HAWK's* capabilities. This led to the Improved *HAWK*, or *I-HAWK*. Throughout its service life, the *HAWK* and its ground equipment underwent many upgrades.

Twenty-seven countries have used, or are still using, the *HAWK*. The last American Army units to be equipped with the *HAWK* were in the South Carolina, New Mexico, Florida, and Ohio National Guards. Units in these states had all retired their *HAWK* missiles by 1997. The United States Marine Corps continued operating *HAWK* until 2002, when it was replaced with the shoulder-fired *Stinger*.

HAWK – the Homing All the Way Killer – on its mobile launcher. *Source: U.S. Army photograph.*

HAWK missile firing. *Source: U.S. Army photograph.*

14

Defending the Fleet

For the United States Navy, one of the most significant lessons from World War II was the need for an effective air defense for ships at sea. At the Battle of Midway, American Naval aviation broke the back of the Japanese Navy. This was the first naval engagement where surface ships never fired a single shot at each other. The entire battle was fought with carrier-based aircraft. Late in the war, *kamikaze* attacks inflicted frightful losses on American ships operating in the Pacific. By 1944, the situation for Japan had deteriorated to such an extent that they adopted suicide attacks against American warships as a tactic and designed special aircraft for this purpose. These suicide aircraft were actually guided missiles, with a human pilot as the guidance system. Approaching at high speeds, they were difficult to intercept or shoot down. As the war neared its end, the Navy sponsored several guided missile projects aimed at countering *kamikaze* tactics. Although none were completed in time to see service in the war, these projects lead to high speed interceptors to neutralize future threats.

The Navy Bureau of Aeronautics (BuAer) solicited a proposal from Fairchild Aircraft for an anti-aircraft guided missile in late 1944. Fairchild's engineering team responded quickly and had a design by January 1945. In March the Navy awarded a contract for 100 test missiles, which were named *Lark*, to Fairchild. Transforming the design into a flyable missile proved more difficult than anticipated, so Fairchild's progress was slow. BuAir officials were so concerned about the pace of the progress that they awarded a backup contract for another 100 *Larks* to Consolidated-Vultee Aircraft in June. There was a war on, and the Navy needed quick results to counter the *kamikaze* threat. Given the complexity of the task, neither company had a flying prototype by the time Japan surrendered.

As happened with other war-time development projects, work continued on the *Lark* after the war ended, albeit at a somewhat slower pace. Flight tests of the missile began in 1946. *Lark* was a two-stage missile, with a solid fuel booster and a liquid fuel sustainer. It had a range of ten miles. The second stage was powered by a two-chamber LR2-RM-2 engine built by Reaction Motors, Inc. The missiles produced by Fairchild were designated KAQ-1; the Consolidated-Vultee vehicles were assigned the designation

KAY-1. Both versions had cruciform wings and tailfins, and the booster assembly used a peculiar "square" fin arrangement. Fairchild equipped their missiles with wing flaps for steering, while the KAY-1 had moveable wings.

Early missiles used a relatively simple manual radio-command guidance system, where an operator on the ground steered the vehicle via radio link. Later versions tested different guidance techniques. Fairchild missiles used the manual system for the early

The Navy's first experimental surface to air guided missile was the *Lark*, which used a solid-fuel booster and liquid-fuel sustainer. *Source: U.S. Navy photograph.*

portion of their flight, then switched to semi-active radar guidance for the terminal portion of their flight. Vultee engineers relied on a radar "beam-riding" system to guide their missiles during the final portion of the flight. With this technique, ground-based radar tracks the target and the missile "rides" up the center of the radar beam. If the missile deviates from the center of the beam its guidance system corrects its flight path. The Navy conducted test firings of the *Lark* from the *USS Norton Sound.*

The Navy cancelled the *Lark* program in late 1950 in favor of the vehicles created under the *Bumblebee* antiaircraft missile program. Although the Navy cancelled the *Lark* program, Army officials used a few at WSPG as test vehicles for guidance components.

Bumblebee, which also began in 1944, was administered by the Bureau of Ordnance (BuOrd). For their missile, BuOrd went to the Applied Physics Laboratory (APL) of Johns Hopkins University in Baltimore. Johns Hopkins created the APL in 1942 to work on defense projects, particularly projects for the Navy. The Laboratory was instrumental in the development of the Variable Time (VT) Proximity Fuze. The Proximity Fuze carried a miniaturized electronics package that could detonate a shell when it passed close to its target. This was particularly useful for antiaircraft projectiles. Previously, gunners had to calculate how long it would take a projectile to reach its target to set a mechanical time fuze before firing. Any miscalculations or changes in course, altitude, or speed by the target would obviously have an adverse effect on the shell's effectiveness. (The VT fuze is also useful for field artillery fire because it can precisely control the detonation of a projectile at the optimum height over the ground for maximum effect.)

The APL project was named *Bumblebee*. Designers at the APL felt ramjets were the most promising form of propulsion for an interceptor missile. They set out to prove the concept with a series of test vehicles named *Cobra*. Testing began with the first six-inch diameter model, which was made out of a P-47 exhaust pipe, in early 1945. This first test vehicle used a dummy ramjet in order to evaluate launch and flight stability. Development progressed to larger vehicles with live ramjets, and in October 1945 a ten-inch diameter model reached a speed of 1,400 mph at an altitude of 20,000 feet. Because ramjets must reach a high speed before they can function, clusters of solid-propellant motors boosted the *Cobra* missiles through the early portions of their flights..

Within two years, the diameter of the ramjets increased to three times the size of the first test vehicle. During the 1945-1947 timeframe *Cobra* acquired another, more formal sounding name—*Burner Test Vehicle* (*BTV*). The 18-inch diameter *Cobra BTV* achieved a speed of Mach 2.4 and an altitude of 30,000 feet. Tests with this vehicle evaluated acceleration, thrust control, and the operating range of the ramjet system. (It's interesting to point out that these flights were taking place at the same time the Air Force broke Mach 1 with a piloted airplane.) The BTV gave way to an even larger missile, the *Bumblebee Experimental Prototype Missile* (*XPM*), which was 24 inches in diameter.

APL engineers planned to use a technique known as "beam riding" to guide their missile to its target. To test this technique,

APL created the *Supersonic Test Vehicle*, or *STV*—a solid-propellant missile. The *STV* proved very successful, so successful that Navy officials realized it could be converted to an antiaircraft missile before the ramjet-powered vehicle would be ready. With the beam-riding guidance system, the *STV* led to the Navy's first antiaircraft guided missile, the *Terrier*. Flight tests of the *Terrier* began in 1951. *Terrier* was a two-stage, solid-propellant missile. The Alleghany Ballistics Laboratory (ABL) built the booster for *Terrier*, which was adapted for the Army's *Nike Ajax* missile.

During 1951 the Navy constructed a unique launch site at WSPG. Dubbed the *LLS-1 USS Desert Ship*, it comprised shipboard launchers and fire control equipment installed at the Navy launch complex. *LLS* stood for "Land Locked Ship." With such a system, the Navy could fire missiles under simulated shipboard conditions and utilize the tracking and instrumentation available at WSPG. The *USS Desert Ship* is still in use.

The *XPM* flew for the first time on July 10, 1951, less than a year after General Electric wrapped up their supersonic ramjet test program under *Hermes II*. Two more test flights with the *XPM*, on 13 August and 5 October, were conducted during the remainder of the year. During that time the ramjet powered missile was named *Talos*. The first full prototype *Talos* flew in October 1952. A few months later *Talos* scored its first aerial intercept. Bendix received the contract for *Talos* production.

Talos was a two-stage missile. It had a solid-fuel booster that propelled the ramjet-powered second stage to a high enough velocity so it could operate. The Navy changed the desired performance characteristics of the *Talos* several times, so it had a protracted development period and wasn't declared operational until 1959. By that time *Terrier* had already been in service for three years. Because of its relatively large size not every ship could carry the *Talos*. The *Terrier* presented a similar problem because of its length. Therefore, Navy managers looked for a smaller, more compact missile capable of providing short-range air defense. The answer was the *Tartar*. This was essentially a *Terrier* minus its

The *USS Desert Ship* at WSPG duplicates Navy shipboard missile launchers and fire control systems on dry land. *Source: U.S. Navy photograph.*

Talos on the launcher at WSPG. *Source, U.S. Navy photograph.*

Liftoff of a *Talos*. The *Talos* used a solid-fuel booster and ramjet sustainer. *Source: U.S. Navy photograph.*

booster. It entered active service in 1962, but was not flown at White Sands until 1966.

Of the three missiles, *Talos* had the greatest range—about 50 nautical miles. It could carry either a high explosive warhead or a W30 nuclear device. *Terrier* had a range of 10 nautical miles. Like *Talos*, it could carry a nuclear warhead; in this case, the 1-kiloton yield W45 device. Being only a single-stage missile, *Tartar* was limited to a range of just 7.5 nautical miles. It was only deployed with a high explosive warhead.

Terrier and *Tartar* were not tested at WSPG; instead, they were tested at the Navy's range near Inyokern, California. In 1943, the Navy contracted with CALTECH to develop rockets. Needing

a place to test the missiles, Navy managers decided they wanted to establish an overland range reasonably close to Pasadena, California, home of CALTECH. They settled on the area around China Lake, near the small airfield at Inyokern. The Army owned the airfield and turned it over to the Navy in August 1943. About ten miles east of the airport, the Navy built the headquarters for the Naval Ordnance Test Station (NOTS). (In 1967 NOTS became the Naval Weapons Center, China Lake.) NOTS included a 900 square-mile testing range for Naval aviation ordnance.

Of the three missiles, *Talos* was the only one fired in anger. During the Vietnam War, *Talos* missiles shot down three MiG fighters. *Talos* remained in service with the Navy until 1979, when the last missiles were retired.

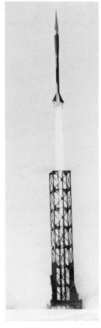

The New Mexico State University Physical Science Laboratory developed the *Pogo-Hi* rocket to release targets for guided missiles over WSPG. At the apex of its trajectory, the small rocket would release a radar reflective balloon. *The Pogo-Hi* was used during *Talos* testing. *Source: U.S. Army photograph.*

Pogo-Hi assembly. The rockets used off the shelf solid rocket motors and special nose sections that ejected a radar target balloon. *Source: U.S. Army photograph.*

Launch of a *Tartar* missile from the *USS Desert Ship*. The *Tartar* was essentially a *Terrier* without a booster. *Source: U.S. Navy photograph.*

Launch of a two-stage *Terrier* missile from the *USS Desert Ship*. The *Terrier's* booster was adapted for use with the *Nike Ajax* guided missile. *Source: U.S. Navy photograph.*

The 3 Ts – *Talos*, *Terrier*, and *Tartar* missiles at the *USS Desert Ship* in the late 1960s. *Source: U.S. Navy photograph.*

15

Tactical Missiles

In the decade following World War II, the Army developed a variety of solid-fuel missiles for use at a tactical level on the battlefield. Some of these proved very successful; others never progressed beyond the development stage. One of the areas identified in the Stilwell Report for further development was anti-tank missiles.

In April 1951, the Chief of Army Field Forces directed the Army Field Forces Board Number 4 to prepare detailed specifications with a staff study for an antitank guided missile

(ATGM). This came two months after the Ordnance Department issued a requirement for an antitank missile based on the French SS-10, which was in an advanced stage of development. The SS-10 was a "command-guided" missile. The gunner sent guidance commands to the missile via two fine wires released from spools carried inside the vehicle. One of the chief advantages of such an arrangement is that it was immune to electronic jamming or similar countermeasures. The Aerophysics Development Corporation, a subsidiary of the Curtiss-Wright Corporation, submitted a proposal for such a missile in November.

In this photo of the *Dart* experimental antitank missile, one of the housings for the guidance wires is visible at mid-body. *Source: U.S. Army photograph.*

Dart antitank missile just before launch. More than 100 were fired during the development stage, but in the end it was never deployed as an operational missile. *Source: U.S. Army photograph.*

The Army spent the next several months evaluating the proposal. Following this, Aerophysics Development received a contract for a more detailed feasibility study. The proposed missile was named the *Dart*. With a length of five feet and weighing in at just 100 pounds, this would be the smallest guided missile in the Army inventory. A dual-thrust solid-propellant motor produced by the Grand Central Rocket Company powered the *Dart*, which had a range of nearly two miles. The missile had two sets of cruciform wings and fins. The wings were mounted at the mid-body and had a span of three feet, four inches. Two bobbins that contained the guidance wires were mounted on the body near the base of one of the wings. After launch, a sodium flare in the base of the rocket helped make it more visible to the gunner. It was fired from a truck or jeep mounted launcher.

Dart became an official Army Ordnance Corps project on August 27, 1953. The first launch of a *Dart* took place a year later. Development of the *Dart* proved more difficult and more expensive than anticipated. By late 1957, more than three years after the first launch, the *Dart* was nowhere near ready for deployment. Army officials reduced the requirements for the missile and stretched the development schedule, but by that time they began to look at alternatives to the troublesome missile. Finally, in September 1958, the Army announced the cancellation of the *Dart* program. The French SS-10 would be purchased as an interim weapon for the American Army. This decision came after one hundred *Darts* had been produced.

The *Lacrosse* was another problem-plagued guided missile project, but it enjoyed a brief career as an operational weapon system. As the United States Marine Corps fought their way across Japanese-held Pacific islands in World War II, they found out how hard it was to overcome an enemy who was entrenched in fortified positions. All too often artillery and aerial bombardments did little to root out the Japanese from their fortifications. The battle for Iwo Jima was particularly hard fought. The Japanese had transformed this eight-square mile island into a fortress of interlocking strongholds with thousands of fortified caves and steel-reinforced concrete pillboxes.

Before the Marines landed, the island was subjected to 74 consecutive days of naval and aerial bombardment. When the Marine assault troops went ashore they found themselves ankle-deep in pulverized volcanic rock, but the Japanese fighting positions with their soldiers inside were largely intact. In one area just 1,000 yards long and 200 yards wide, the Marines had to smash through 800 enemy strongholds one at a time, often in hand to hand fighting. Even with the continued support of naval and aerial bombardment, the battle raged for nearly a month. By the time the fighting ended three Marine Corps Divisions had suffered 20,196 casualties, including 4,189 killed.

Shortly after World War II ended, Marine commanders identified a need for more effective artillery weapons to support troops on the ground. From this need they created specifications for a precision guided missile with a range of 1,000 to 20,000 yards that could strike a target with a circular probability error (CPE) of not more than 5 yards. They envisioned a missile that would be launched from a rearward position in the general direction of a designated target. During the terminal phase of its flight, a forward observer would take control over the missile and steer it to the target. This project was named *Lacrosse*. The name came from the sport of lacrosse, because in the game, a ball is passed downfield to a player in position to hurl it into the net.

In early 1947 the Marine Corps presented a plan to the Navy Bureau of Ordnance (BuOrd) to have the Johns Hopkins University Applied Physics Laboratory (APL) conduct a feasibility study for the missile. The *Lacrosse* project was formally established at the APL. The Applied Physics Laboratory submitted their study in mid-1948. They looked at a variety of guidance systems in their study, including homing, a form of beam riding, and a system described as "shuttlecock," where the missile was fired and guided from a helicopter. After that, the project sat largely dormant for almost a year. The BuOrd brought the Cornell Aeronautical Laboratory (CAL) into the project to study various methods for guiding the missile in June 1949, about two years after the Marines submitted their plan to BuOrd.

BuOrd tasked CAL to study and select the most promising guidance systems. They performed detailed studies of two systems: homing and command. The command guidance system used angular tracking and radio ranging to steer the missile to its target. The homing system study relied on having a beacon fired onto the target by a mortar. Further analysis showed the accuracy of the mortar fire was a limiting factor because of the problems associated with placing the beacon precisely. A lot of rounds would likely be necessary to land one within five yards of the desired target. Developing an electronic beacon that could withstand the rigors of being fired was another problem that would be prohibitively expensive to solve. The command guidance system was relatively simple by comparison. It relied upon a visual range finder and an electronics package called Sight Tracking, Electronic Equipment Ranging, or STEER. This system fed optical angular and electronic range measurements into a computer that generated course correction commands for transmission to the missile.

Lark guided missile. Unpowered versions of the second stage of this missile were dropped from aircraft to test *Lacrosse* guidance components. *Source: U.S. Army photograph.*

Unpowered *Lark* missiles that were dropped from B-26 bombers over WSPG were used to test the command guidance system for *Lacrosse*. CAL drew heavily upon the *Lark* program as their starting point for the missile design. By following such an approach, they were able to use the extensive body of design and test data available on the earlier missile.

Late in 1949, the Joint Chiefs of Staff established a new policy governing the development of guided missiles. Army Ordnance was assigned responsibility for antiaircraft and short-range surface to surface guided missiles. *Lacrosse* fell within the purview of this policy. Therefore, in March 1950 the Joint Chiefs recommended that the *Lacrosse* be transferred from BuOrd to the Department of the Army. On August 31, 1950, the Secretary of Defense formally transferred responsibility for *Lacrosse* to the Army.

The Army awarded a contract to CAL for the *Lacrosse* in February 1951. By the end of the year components were ready for testing. Early missile design studies were based upon a two-stage subsonic vehicle using a liquid fuel sustainer and solid fuel booster like the *Lark*. It soon became apparent that liquid propellants presented handling and storage problems that were not desirable in a tactical weapon system. Based on these considerations, CAL began trajectory and design studies for a single-stage configuration with solid-fuel propulsion. In January 1953 the Army created a revised set of requirements for the *Lacrosse*. These requirements included the decision to use a solid propellant motor for *Lacrosse*.

This decision was accompanied by a broadening of the *Lacrosse* mission. While it was still primarily intended to strike fortified targets, it was also assigned a mission of general support. This decision led to a requirement that the missile be able to carry an atomic warhead in addition to its one with conventional explosives. By the end of 1953 a final configuration for the missile emerged, based on two series of wind tunnel tests. *Lacrosse* was to carry a 500-pound warhead over a maximum range of 18 miles (30,000 meters). Overall length of the missile was 19 feet, and the body was 20.5 inches in diameter. It had two sets of cruciform, swept fins. The four wings, which were at the mid body, were fixed; the smaller tail fins, which were interdigitated from the wings, steered the rocket in pitch, yaw, and roll.

Because its original mission was to neutralize strong points of resistance, priority was given to developing a high-explosive shaped-charge warhead. *Lacrosse* represented a departure from traditional warhead development practices. The practice had previously been to have the Army Ordnance Department design a warhead package to fit inside a nose section designed by the research and development contractor. For *Lacrosse*, this was not

Lacrosse missile. Source: U.S. Army photograph.

Lacrosse shortly after launch. The missile was fired in the direction of the target, then directed to its impact point by a ground observer. *Source: U.S. Army photograph.*

This photograph provides a good view of the *Lacrosse* and its truck-mounted launcher. *Source: U.S. Army photograph.*

possible because the warhead made up the entire nose section and was an integral part of the missile. CAL designed and fabricated the metal parts of the warhead, including the shaped-charge liner, and shipped them to Picatinny Arsenal, where the explosives were loaded.

Cornell fabricated the first lot of eight warhead casings and shipped them to Picatinny for loading and testing at Aberdeen Proving Ground (APG) in Maryland. Two of the prototype warheads were tested at APG in early 1953. One of them penetrated seven feet of concrete, plus thirteen feet of air, plus one-half inch of steel. The second, fired at 55°, penetrated over twelve feet of concrete. In both tests, the explosions created large amounts of thick dust and about a cubic yard of rubble thrown about from spalling of the wall. In late summer, two warheads were dropped from various heights up to 40 feet onto an angle iron to test their suitability for the rigors of field use. The warheads punctured, but the explosives did not detonate. Several single shot 30-caliber bullets and a tracer round caused slight burning and shell rupture; a burst of machine gun fire did cause an explosion. Similar tests with .50-caliber bullets caused a partial explosion. Based on the results of these tests, the warhead design was deemed acceptable for field use.

Propulsion came from a single Thiokol solid propellant motor that generated a thrust of 38,000 pounds for 2.8 seconds. This was sufficient to boost the missile to a maximum speed of 1,400 feet per second. The first flight of a prototype *Lacrosse* took place on August 17, 1954, after seven years of development. CAL provided fifteen of the "Type A" versions of the missile. Martin Aircraft was selected as prime contractor for *Lacrosse* production in April 1955. The first production round was delivered in June 1956. Throughout its testing period, the *Lacrosse* proved to be a very complex weapon system with numerous reliability problems. From November 28-December 12, 1958, the Army conducted *Operation Pickle Barrel*, a series of special test firings to identify and fix problems with the missile. Based on results from this test

and other continuing problems, the Ordnance Readiness Date for the *Lacrosse* was pushed back from April to July 1959. The XM4 *Lacrosse* was finally delivered to the first field unit at Fort Sill, Oklahoma, on July 1, 1959. At that time the system was acceptable, but not fully reliable or perfected.

Although it was, in theory, the most accurate guided missile in the United States' inventory, the *Lacrosse* suffered from some serious operational weaknesses. Because it relied upon optical tracking it was of limited use during inclement weather or at night. The radio command system was susceptible to electronic countermeasures and jamming, which would make a missile uncontrollable. It also suffered from a record of poor reliability and needed extensive maintenance. In August 1959 budget limitations forced the Army to suspend efforts to correct these deficiencies. Faced with these shortcomings, the Marine Corps, which had been the original requestor for the *Lacrosse*, dropped out of the program and decided not to field the missile.

The first overseas deployment of *Lacrosse* missiles took place in March 1960, but its service life was short. Less than a year later, Army officials decided to halt *Lacrosse* procurement and to retire the missile as soon as possible. In October 1960 the missile had been subjected to a "kill or cure" field exercise to determine if the *Lacrosse* should remain in the field. Results from this exercise led to the Army's decision to halt further procurement of the *Lacrosse*. In February 1964 the *Lacrosse* was finally declared obsolete and was withdrawn from service.

The Army had far greater success with the *Sergeant* and *Honest John* missiles, both of which used solid propellants. *Sergeant* came out of work at the Jet Propulsion Laboratory (JPL), beginning with the solid-propellant Jet Assist Take Off (JATO) units created to help heavily-laden airplanes take off. The first JPL-designed JATO motors consumed an asphalt-based propellant. This propellant proved unsuitable for field artillery purposes because it possessed poor mechanical properties; temperature sensitivity; produced a lot of smoke; and too much variation in performance from batch to batch. A major breakthrough came in 1946, when JPL chemists developed a propellant that used inorganic perchlorates for the oxidizer and polysulfide rubber as the fuel. The new propellant combination could be cast inside the motor casing; was relatively insensitive to temperature variations; and showed improvements in performance per pound over the older combination. For the first time, it was possible to create large solid-fuel missiles with performance equal to the V-2.

JPL embarked on a development program named *Sergeant*, which utilized the new perchlorate-rubber polymer propellant in 1948. A series of high-acceleration flights with small rockets loaded with JPL-126 polysulfide rubber propellant proved successful, so project engineers decided to apply what they'd learned to a lager vehicle. As planned, the missile was 15 inches in diameter and about 249 inches long. The motor portion of the missile was 180 inches long. Loaded with 1,300 pounds of JPL-126, at the time it was the largest solid-propellant motor under development in the United States. The *Sergeant* was designed to fly a near-vertical trajectory with a 92-pound payload over a range of 60 miles. JPL produced a batch of 12 of these motors for static testing.

Due to JPL's commitment to the *Corporal* missile program and limited capacity of the laboratory's mixing and casting facility, in April 1950 the bulk of the motor development work was transferred to the Redstone Division of the Thiokol Chemical Corporation. JPL continued to be involved, and contributed the basic propellant formulation and the "star" configuration of the propellant grain.

One of the factors that affects the thrust produced by a solid-fuel rocket is the surface area of the propellant that is burning. In a so-called "end-burning" configuration, the propellant burns from one end to the other, like a cigarette. The surface area, and therefore the thrust, remains constant. Disadvantages of this type of motor include exposing portions of the casing to hot combustion gases for the entire burn duration. Casings for this type of motor tend to be heavy because they need to be heavily insulated. Another type of grain is known as "core burning." Propellant in this type of motor resembles a hollow cylinder. The propellant burns along the entire inner surface of the hollowed out portion. As propellant burns the surface area increases, causing thrust to increase as burning continues. Because of the increasing internal pressure as the propellant burns, casings for this type of motor also tend to be heavy. A major advance in solid-fuel motor design was due to the rubber-based propellants. The propellants could be cased around a star-shaped mandrel. As the propellant burned, the surface area remained fairly constant along with the internal pressure and thrust. The propellant also helped insulate the casing. These factors resulted in lighter casings than had been previously possible.

Of the twelve motors produced and static tested by JPL, seven suffered partial or total failures. Five months after the motor project was transferred to Thiokol a conference was held at Redstone Arsenal. As a result of the problems encountered with the static tests, Thiokol abandoned the star configuration in favor of a cylindrical core design. Despite improvements made in the physical properties of the JPL-126 propellant, scale model tests of the redesigned motors conducted in late 1950 and early 1951 were only partially successful. Seeing more promise in other projects, the Army terminated the *Sergeant* program in April 1951.

At the time the *Sergeant* project was encountering a frustrating series of problems, General Electric (GE) was having more success with the *Hermes A2* missile. Under the umbrella of *Project Hermes*, the General Electric Company began work on a tactical missile, the *Hermes A-2*, in 1949. This missile was designed to carry a 1,500-pound payload to a range of 75 miles. With a diameter of 31 inches, it was compatible with the XW-7 atomic warhead. GE considered both liquid and solid propellants for the Hermes A-2 before settling on the latter because of simplicity of operations, ease of handling in the field, and lower cost. At that time, however, the feasibility of solid motors of that size had not been proven. The Army Chief of Ordnance, in mid-1950, authorized GE to go ahead with the development of a solid-fuel *Hermes A-2*.

GE brought Thiokol into the project in May 1950 to establish the propellant formulation, grain design, and conduct static tests of the motor. JPL was retained as a consultant. Thiokol expended a great deal of effort on improving two existing polysulfide rubber/ammonium perchlorate propellants: T13 and T14. They differed slightly in the proportions of fuel to oxidizer and small amounts of other ingredients. On December 2, 1951, the first full-scale *Hermes A-2* motor was static tested. It held 7,786 pounds of T14E1 propellant. This motor was 31 inches in diameter. It had a cylindrical casing length of 118 inches; the head and nozzle ends added another 60 inches, which gave it an overall length of 15 feet. Thrust duration was 41.2 seconds, and the motor produced an average thrust of 17,172 pounds.

Although the test was a success, Thiokol engineers recognized the need for improved propellants that would enhance overall rocket performance. The latest propellant formulation was called T17E1, which was later changed to TRX-110A. This mixture contained 62% oxidizer. Twenty-one motors were successfully fired during 1952. In early 1953, four motors were successfully flown under the designation of the *RV-A-10* test vehicle. Budget limitations had already forced the Army to choose the most promising projects for development into an operational missile project, which at that time was the liquid fuel *Corporal*. The *Hermes A-2* had already been relegated to the status of a propulsion development program only, and by the end of the year it was over.

Although work on the *Hermes A-2* ended, official interest in developing a large solid-propellant field artillery missile continued. Solid propellants just offered too many advantages, including ease of handling, simplicity, and cost, over liquid-fuel missiles to be ignored. Even as the *Hermes A-2* was ending another project sprang up. The concept of developing a large solid-fuel missile emerged once again under the designation *Sergeant*. As with the early *Sergeant*, JPL was the lead agency for this missile. The first static test firing of the new *Sergeant* took place on January 7, 1954. For this test, two *Hermes A-2* casings were welded together, loaded with TRX-110A, and static fired to provide data for the designers of the new *Sergeant* missile.

Owing to its roots in the *Hermes A-2*, and designed to accommodate the XW-7 atomic warhead, the *Sergeant* was 31 inches in diameter. Once a solid-fuel motor ignites it can not be shut off like a liquid-fuel rocket, so a new means of controlling the range of the missile was needed. *Sergeant* had air brakes that increased the drag on the missile to adjust its trajectory. At first, JPL designers looked at a guidance system like the one used on the *Corporal*. That is, the missile used a combination of ground steering and inertial guidance. Such a system suffered a major weakness; the command guidance steering commands were susceptible to jamming or other countermeasures. Therefore, an all-inertial guidance system was developed for the *Sergeant*. The Sperry Gyroscope Company received the contract for the guidance system and eventually became the overall contractor for the *Sergeant* missile system.

The first rocket motor derived from the *Hermes A-2* bore the designation JPL-329. This motor was very similar to the prior design and used the same propellant, grain design, and ignition system. Once again, the propellant mixture was renamed—now it was called TP-E8080. The JPL-329 casing was 171.5 inches long and was fabricated from 4130 alloy steel. As the design for the *Sergeant* evolved, JPL engineers realized they could build a motor that was more closely optimized to the desired missile performance. Ten different designs were built and tested.

Recurring problems included combustion instability and excessive vibration, and not every design proved successful. The second motor design, the JPL-427, was one such example. As the overall missile design progressed, the engineers realized the motor could be shorter and lighter. Therefore, the second motor design was shortened by 5.5 inches. Three JPL-427 motors were static tested in November 1955. All three exhibited the instability and vibration problems, so the design was abandoned. The next motor, the JPL-438, was shortened to 141 inches. It showed similar problems to its predecessor, so it was also abandoned. The tenth motor, the JPL-500, led to the XM-100 motor, which was used for operational missiles.

The JPL-329 had met the minimum performance requirements for the missile, so it was decided to use this motor for the first few flight trials. The first *Sergeant* missile flew on January 19, 1956, with the JPL-329 motor. This test was fully successful. There were 25 flights in the Phase I, II, and III series of tests. A significant milestone was met on flight 11 on May 1, 1958, which was the

Sergeant ballistic missile. The ancestry of the solid-fuel *Sergeant* can be traced directly to the *Hermes* program. *Source: U.S. Army photograph.*

first fully guided *Sergeant*. This round impacted 2.25 miles long and 16 miles right of the target because the inertial platform "tumbled." Tests included firing missiles at minimum range, 25 miles; intermediate range, 45 miles; and a maximum range of 75 miles.

The *Sergeant* was delivered to Army field units in June 1962. The following year, the first *Sergeant* battalion was deployed in Germany. As *Sergeant* entered the inventory the *Corporal* was retired. *Sergeant* remained in service until 1977, when it was replaced by the *Lance* missile.

The same advances in atomic warhead design and solid propellant rocket motors that made *Sergeant* possible brought about another highly successful missile, the *Honest John*. In April 1950, Dr. J. B. Edson of the Research Branch, Research and Development Division, Office of the Chief of Ordnance (OCO), suggested the Army begin a study to investigate the feasibility of delivering atomic warheads with free-flight rockets. This would require a purpose-built direct support atomic weapon carrier. An examination of the problem by the Rocket Branch of the Research and Development Division indicated it would be possible for a free-flight rocket to reach a range of 15,000 yards with a warhead weighing 1,500 pounds.

The following month, the OCO directed the Redstone Arsenal to perform a design study of such a rocket, with the added stipulation that it have a circular probable error of 300 yards or less. The design team at Redstone Arsenal found that the Navy had a rocket motor that would deliver enough power to meet the Army requirements. This was the X201A1 JATO unit developed by the Alleghany Ballistics Laboratory as a booster for the *Talos* guided missile. After receiving the study results, the Chief of Ordnance asked the engineers to conduct a further consideration of a missile using the higher thrust X202C1. Funding for this study was approved in September 1950, just three months after the start of the Korean War. The X202C1 looked even more promising than the first motor considered. It was capable of delivering a 1,700-pound warhead over a range of 20,000 yards.

Meanwhile, in August 1950, the Assistant Chief of Staff, G-4, directed the Chief of Ordnance to go ahead with a limited firing program to prove the concept. (Then) Colonel Holger N. Toftoy, head of the Rocket Branch, drew up a development plan and asked the Los Angeles Ordnance District to obtain a price quote from Douglas Aircraft Company. This contract was awarded without competitive bidding or evaluation of competing proposals. Given the exigencies of the growing conflict in Korea, Toftoy realized the Army needed an interim weapon that could be deployed as rapidly as possible. There weren't that many companies with the necessary expertise to develop this weapon, and Douglas was well known to the Ordnance Department through the firm's work on other programs. Therefore, he opted for a single-source contract for the new rocket.

The scope of work outlined in the Douglas Company's proposal called for the design, fabrication, and flight test of an initial series of 15 missiles with the X201A3 JATO and a 1,000-pound warhead. These missiles were designated Model 1236E. Phase II would comprise 10 missiles, designated Model 1236F, with the X202C1 and a 1,600-pound warhead. Funding limitations forced a change to these plans. The Model 1236E missiles were cancelled, and only 5 Model 1236F rockets were built to prove the concept. At the time, there was a measure of opposition to the weapon because some senior officers in the Ordnance Department did not believe a free-flight rocket using solid-propellants could give the desired accuracy.

Dispersion was a recognized problem. At maximum range, a deflection error of only 10 mils would result in an error of 200 yards. Ten mils amounted to little more than half a degree. Range probable error had to be 300 yards or less. Various factors could affect the trajectory of the rocket, including thrust malalignment, launcher tip-off, or cross winds. Engineers considered a Model 1236G, which had a simple autopilot to control the missile during powered flight. This was dropped without a flight test, however, because one of the main considerations was that this be a simple, inexpensive missile. To minimize dispersion problems, the designers decided to use side-firing rockets to spin the missile. JPL had already used spin rockets in the *WAC Corporals* launched during the *Bumper* project. These rockets were adapted for the new missile.

The resulting missile had a distinctive shape. Specifications for the missile were dictated by the X202C1 motor. The motor itself was 23 inches in diameter; the warhead was housed in an 82-inch long ogive that was 31 inches in diameter at its base. This would accommodate a XW-7 atomic warhead, which had a yield of up to 20 kilotons. A pedestal on top of the X202C1 provided a conical adapter between the motor and nose cone. Eight spin rockets were housed in the pedestal in pairs. Once the missile cleared the launch rail, these motors ignited to impart a two revolutions per second spin on the vehicle. Four triangular fins, with a span of 104 inches, were equally spaced around the base of the motor. The fins were canted 0.5° to the right to make sure the rocket continued to spin once the spin motors burned out. Overall length of the missile was 327.5 inches, and it weighed 5,800 pounds at launch.

In October 1950, Army Ordnance ordered fifteen X202C1 motors from the Navy for static tests and the initial round of flights. The M. W. Kellogg Company in Jersey City, New Jersey, fabricated the metal parts for these motors. Particular care was given by the craftsmen at the Kellogg Company to make the parts to very close tolerances. The Alleghany Ballistics Laboratory loaded the propellants in the motors and shipped them to WSPG.

Funding continued to be a problem, so only limited laboratory testing of components could be conducted during the last four months of 1950. Still, it was enough to convince most Army Ordnance officers that the proposed large caliber rocket could successfully meet the requirements for a direct support atomic delivery system. Although the program was winning converts, there remained those who stuck to their conviction it would never work. Skeptics who remained unconvinced believed the Army was "pouring money down a rat hole." Their criticisms reached the highest levels of the Ordnance Department. At one point, the Assistant Chief of Staff for Guided Missiles insisted the entire project be scrapped. Fortunately, Colonel Toftoy managed to

present an effective counter argument and received approval for the initial series of five firings.

At the height of this controversy Toftoy dubbed the missile *Honest John*. Colonel Toftoy knew troops in the field would come up with their own nickname for a weapon if they didn't like the official one, so he sought a catchy title for the new rocket. During one of his trips to WSPG, Toftoy encountered a Texan who made statements that were hard to believe. "Why, around these parts, I'm called Honest John," was his reply when the veracity of his statements was questioned. With the missile on the verge of being cancelled because some believed a large unguided rocket could not have the accuracy to justify further effort, Toftoy felt like the Texan, so he decided to name the rocket *Honest John*.

The first flight of an *Honest John* took place on June 29, 1951, a little more than a year after the free-flight missile was proposed. *Honest John* Round #1 achieved a range of 22,495 yards with a deflection of 5 yards west of the target line. This was just 141 yards short and 53 yards west of the expected impact point. Firings occurred quickly after that, on 18 July, 25 July, 1 August, and 7 August. The last test was particularly important for the *Honest John* project; Army Secretary Frank Pace observed the firing along with a group of senior Army commanders.

Secretary Pace was so impressed with the overall simplicity of the missile system and its performance that he issued verbal instructions on the spot to place *Honest John* on a "crash program" basis. His instructions called for the firing of an additional 25 missiles by 30 September, and for dropping the Model 1236G with the autopilot. *Honest John* was given a 1A priority and the project kicked into high gear.

A contract for production of 219 sets of metal parts was awarded to Douglas Aircraft on June 16, 1952. Concerned about the ability of the Kellogg Company to produce the quantities needed the Army sought an alternate supplier. The Burnham Corporation of Irvington, New York, became a new supplier of booster cases. The Army also reactivated the Radford Arsenal in Virginia to produce

One of the early *Honest John* rockets being fired from the fixed position launcher at WSPG. *Source: U.S. Army photograph courtesy of Bill Beggs.*

Honest John on its truck-mounted launcher. *Source: U.S. Army photograph courtesy of Bill Beggs.*

This photograph of an *Honest John* shortly after launch clearly shows the spin rockets firing. *Source: U.S. Army photograph courtesy of Bill Beggs.*

the propellant grains. Hercules Powder Company of Wilmington, Delaware, operated the facility. (Hercules also operated the Alleghany Ballistics Laboratory for the Navy.)

By early 1953, a total of 159 test flights had been completed, including 79 by Type II tactical prototypes. Based on the progress to date, the Assistant Chief of Staff, G-4, for the OCO recommended that the missile be given a type classification despite the fact that service tests weren't finished. Type classification would clear the way for full scale production and deployment to field units. On February 27, 1953, the Army Field Forces refused to concur with the recommendation and insisted that type classification be withheld until service tests were finished. These tests weren't scheduled to be finished until the following year.

Minimum range for *Honest John* was 10,000 yards. In an effort to reduce this to just 5,000 yards and give field commanders greater flexibility in using the rocket, a project that became known as the *Demi John* was undertaken. *Demi John* rockets had special spoilers to increase drag on the vehicle. These were mounted near the base of the pedestal adapter between the motor and warhead. All the test rounds suffered failures of one sort or another, so the idea was abandoned.

Research and development flights were finished in January 1954, and by 1 June the first units were equipped with the M31

762-MM *Honest John* and the M289 self propelled launcher. The launcher had also been the subject of a considerable research program. *Honest John* was fired from truck-mounted rail. Such a launcher was highly mobile and could "shoot and scoot" as a way of negating counter-battery fire.

While *Honest John* was suitable for standard field artillery units, it was too large to be deployed with Airborne units. In order to provide atomic fire support to Airborne units, the Army began studying the idea of creating a smaller missile as part of a family of rockets in May 1953. On June 14, 1955, the Army formally established the *Little John* program.

Little John was just 12 inches in diameter, 14 feet long, and had a range of 11 miles. Emerson Electric Company received the contract to produce the missiles. The first flight occurred on July 27, 1956. Final development firings took place in May and June 1957, and the 101st Airborne at Fort Campbell, Kentucky, received the first Type I *Little John* rockets. The Type I version had many shortcomings—so many that it was deemed unsuitable for general field use. The rockets were left with the 101st for use in troop training while an improved Type II was developed.

The Type II *Little John* was issued to field units during the first quarter of 1961. It remained in service until 1969, when it was declared obsolete. One of the factors that affected this missile was the development of an atomic round for the 155-mm howitzer.

The 12-inch diameter *Little John* was created to provide nuclear fire support for Army Airborne units. *Source: U.S. Army photograph.*

The *Improved Honest John.* This rocket used an improved solid rocket motor and clipped fins which improved overall stability. *Source: U.S. Army photograph courtesy of Bill Beggs.*

The Air Force also tested its air-to-air missiles at WSPG. Testing of the *GAR-1 Falcon* began in 1952; the *Genie* (shown here) first flew at WSPG in 1956. Interestingly, the *Genie* was ground-launched for these early tests. *Source: U.S. Army photograph.*

The *Honest John* had a much longer service life. In the 1960s, the Army embarked on a program to create an *Improved Honest John.* These missiles had greater range and warhead capacity. Engine thrust was increased from 92,500 pounds to 150,000 pounds, and range was extended from 14 miles to 24 miles. With clipped fins that improved stability, the *Improved Honest John* looked different than its predecessor. In addition to the atomic warhead, the *Honest*

John now had high explosive and chemical warheads available. Beginning in the early 1970s, the *Lance* missile replaced *Honest John* in active Army units. By 1973, all the *Honest Johns* had been turned over to Army National Guard units. In 1982, more than three decades after the first test flights at WSPG, the *Honest John* was classified as obsolete and retired from the Army inventory. In all, nearly 8,000 had been produced.

Genie air-to-air missile ready for a test launch at WSPG. Operational versions of the *Genie* carried nuclear warheads to counter Soviet bomber formations. *Source: U.S. Army photograph.*

16

Into the Space Age

In 1954, Soviet leaders gave Sergei Korolev authorization to construct an intercontinental ballistic missile, or ICBM. Ukrainian-born Korolev headed the leading Soviet Design Bureau for rocket development. A gifted engineer and organizer, he began working with rockets as a member of the Moscow Group for the Study of Reactive Motion, or MosGIRD. In 1932 he became head of the group. Under Korolev's leadership, MosGIRD built and launched the GIRD 09 on August 17, 1933. GIRD 09 is best described as a "hybrid" rocket, since it burned a mixture of gelled gasoline and liquid oxygen. The group's next rocket, the GIRD-X, flew on November 25, 1933. Burning liquid oxygen and ethyl alcohol, this was the first all-liquid fuel rocket in the Soviet Union.

Denounced by a professional rival in 1938, Korolev was imprisoned during Stalin's Purges and ended up in a hard-labor camp. His fortunes improved during World War II, when he was transferred to a special work camp where he designed rocket powered aircraft. After the German surrender, although he was still technically under arrest, Korolev was assigned to reopen the V-2 production line at Mittelwerk. This was not an easy task; for example, at first no technical drawings for the missile could be found because the Americans had already captured the technical archives at Peenemünde. After considerable searching the Soviets found a set of blueprints in an archive in Czechoslovakia.

The American Army occupied Mittelwerk first and had already shipped 640 tons of hardware to WSPG. Because the area of Central Germany where Mittelwerk was located was scheduled to be turned over to the Soviets, the Americans limited their recovery efforts to missile components. (No complete missiles were found on the production line.) When Korolev arrived he found very little rocket hardware, but the production tooling and heavy machinery was still there. Carefully and methodically, Korolev's team rebuilt the assembly line so it could produce V-2s once again. Once the production line was running, Korolev supervised having it moved to the Soviet Union.

Korolev initially launched copies of the V-2 from a range in the pre-Volga Steppes. The copies flew well enough, but Korolev soon began improving the design. After this technology was mastered,

he progressed beyond the German missile and created larger, more capable rockets. As his rockets grew in size and complexity during the early 1950s, Korolev gave considerable thought to constructing an ICBM. He and his team studied various configurations, finally settling on a "rocket packet" that used a cluster of identical rockets that could be jettisoned during the ascent as their propellants were used up arranged around a central core. The ICBM was the seventh long-range rocket built by Korolev, so it became known as the R-7. Korolev designed the R-7 to lob a 12,000-pound warhead 5,400 miles. Those who worked on the missile referred to it by the Russian word for seven, *Semyorka*.

Korolev was ready to test the *Semyorka* by the spring of 1957. On 15 May the first R-7 lifted off. A miscalculation in the design of the flame pit beneath the engines deflected the fiery exhaust upward, engulfing the missile. At first observers gasped, fearing the rocket had caught fire, but then breathed a sigh of relief when they saw it rise from the inferno. Steadily gaining speed, the R-7 climbed out of sight. The launch had been a success, but during ascent one of the boosters malfunctioned and destroyed the vehicle. The problem was later ascribed to a broken fuel line that started a fire in the booster.

The next R-7 also failed, and another rocket was removed from the launch pad due to a continuing series of malfunctions. Korolev's critics openly questioned his design, and he found himself in a very difficult position. Despite the criticism he remained convinced the design was sound. The next launch, on 21 August, proved him right. The rocket reentered over Kamchatka, just as planned. With this success, the Communist Party Central Committee approved a request from Korolev to launch an earth-orbiting satellite.

Both the United States and Soviet Union had announced plans to launch satellites during the International Geophysical Year, which ran from 1957-58. The Soviets published a description of their satellite, even listing its frequencies and how to pick up the signals. Most western observers did not take the Soviet announcement seriously, smug in their assumption that the Communists did not possess the technology for such a feat. When the 100th anniversary of Russian space pioneer Konstantine Tsiolkovsky's birth passed in September without a satellite the Soviet pronouncement was dismissed as so much hype and bombast.

Unknown to the West, Korolev labored day and night with the satellite project. Originally he wanted to launch a very heavy geophysical laboratory, but that phase of the project started to lag. One of his engineers, Mikhail Tikhonravov, suggested they build a much smaller payload, called PS-1, for *Prosteishyi Sputnik*. Korolev agreed, and the satellite was quickly built.

PS-1 was a smooth, highly polished, 22.8-inch diameter sphere with four 9-foot antennae, and contained a battery powered radio transmitter. It was pressurized with nitrogen. Fans inside the sphere circulated the gas for thermal control. While small by today's standards, *Sputnik's* 184-pound weight was much heavier than the American IGY satellite, *Vanguard*.

Korolev fretted over American progress; he wanted his *Semyorka* to propel the first artificial satellite into orbit. The launch was set for 6 October, the same day as the announced presentation of a paper in honor of the IGY titled "Satellite in Orbit" in Washington, D.C. Korolev feared the Americans would launch a surprise satellite to coincide with the presentation. Despite assurances by the KGB that the Americans were not planning a launch, Korolev moved the launch date up two days just to make sure.

On 4 October Konstantine Gringauz climbed to the top of the gantry and checked the satellite in the R-7's nose. Reaching inside the shroud that protected the sphere, he checked the transmitter one last time, then sealed the cover. He was the last person to touch *Sputnik*. The day proved very frustrating, and there were numerous delays. Finally, a little past 10:00 PM Moscow time, the *Semyorka* that carried *PS-1* roared to life. As the rocket disappeared from sight the launch team began to cheer. Korolev quickly silenced them, saying there should be no shouts or celebrations until they knew the probe was in orbit. Everyone quietly proceeded into the canteen and waited. Only an hour and a half later, when ground stations picked up the beeping radio signal, did cheers erupt. *Sputnik* was in orbit! Korolev had been first!

Sputnik broadcast a series of beeps or pulses every 0.3 seconds. Professional and amateur radio operators could receive the signal. By analyzing the signal, Soviet scientists learned about the ionosphere and the temperatures inside *Sputnik*. The density of the upper atmosphere could be deduced by observing the decay of *Sputnik's* orbit. Powered by chemical batteries, *Sputnik* broadcast for 22 days.

Soviet Premier Nikita Khrushchev reportedly took the news casually at first. He only appreciated the importance of the achievement when he saw reactions in the world's newspapers. Most of Korolev's senior staff took well-earned holidays immediately after the launch. Many of them had been working non-stop for the past eight years! Their vacations only lasted a few days, however, for Korolev summoned them back to work before some could even unpack. Korolev met with Khrushchev after he'd had a chance to see what a major impact *Sputnik* had on the rest of the world. The Premier told Korolev to prepare another space spectacular in time for the next anniversary of the Communist

Revolution. That gave Korolev less than a month to prepare and launch a second satellite.

When Korolev's associates returned, he told them they would launch a dog aboard the next *Sputnik*. At first the task seemed impossible but, largely through Korolev's force of character, exhortations, and tireless leadership, the satellite was ready in time. *Sputnik-2* was assembled so quickly that no detailed blueprints were prepared, only sketches.

On November 3, 1957, "Laika" became the first animal to orbit the Earth. *Sputnik-2* weighed 1,120 pounds and circled the earth every 103 minutes. While Laika sailed overhead in a sealed cabin, scientists on the ground monitored her respiration, blood pressure, and temperature. Television images showed her moving around and eating from a special food dispenser. Laika made several rocket flights before going into orbit, but this would definitely be her last launch. Lacking the means to return her from orbit, the Soviets launched Laika on a one-way journey into space. During orbital insertion, a section of insulation tore away from the capsule so it overheated. Temperatures inside *Sputnik* soared above 100° Fahrenheit. This proved deadly for Laika, and she died from the heat after only a few hours. At the time, the Soviets reported she had been painlessly put to sleep.

The *Redstone* missile, which formed the basis for America's first space launch vehicle, the *Jupiter-C*. On January 31, 1958, a *Jupiter-C* launched the first American satellite, *Explorer-1*, into orbit. *Source: U.S. Army photograph.*

Major General Waldo E. Laidlaw, who commanded White Sands Proving Ground when it became White Sands Missile Range in 1958. *Source: U.S. Army photograph.*

America reacted with understandable concern over the *Sputnik* launches. Not only had the Soviets caught the West by surprise, but the launches demonstrated the technological prowess of the Soviet Union. Beyond a shadow of a doubt, the Soviets possessed missiles capable of launching nuclear warheads against the United States of America. There were calls for an American response to what became known as the "missile gap." Calls for a revamping of American missile programs began to be heard.

Actually, the Army had already begun to reorganize its missile activities. On February 1, 1956, the Army Ballistic Missile Agency came into being. Headquartered at Redstone Arsenal in Alabama, the core of the ABMA came from the Guided Missile Development Division of the Arsenal's Ordnance Missile Laboratory. ABMA inherited some 1,600 personnel, including the German scientists who came to America with Dr. Wernher von Braun. Initially the ABMA was responsible for the *Redstone* missile project.

After the second *Sputnik*, von Braun was given permission to launch a satellite for America. He used a launch vehicle called the *Jupiter-C*. This four-stage booster comprised a modified *Redstone* for the first stage topped by three solid-fuel stages. The Jet Propulsion Laboratory (JPL) provided the solid-fuel stages, which were scaled-down *Sergeant* rocket motors. On January 31, 1958, the ABMA/JPL team launched *Explorer I*, the first American satellite.

The Army created the Army Ordnance Missile Command (AOMC) on March 31, 1958. Elements assigned to the AOMC included the ABMA, Redstone Arsenal, JPL, and WSPG. A new organization, the Army Rocket and Guided Missile Agency (ARGMA), became part of AOMC on April 1, 1958. The ARGMA assumed the technical projects previously assigned to the Redstone Arsenal. As part of the reorganization, WSPG became the White Sands Missile Range (WSMR) on May 1, 1958.

Major General Waldo E. Laidlaw was Commanding General of WSPG during its transition to WSMR. A native of Cincinnati, Ohio, he began his military career in 1920 with the 147th Infantry

of the Ohio National Guard while he was still a student at Hughes High School. Upon high school graduation Laidlaw entered the United States Military Academy at West Point. When he graduated from West Point in 1926 he was commissioned a Second Lieutenant in the Infantry.

In 1931, after serving with the 10th and 31st Infantry Divisions, Lieutenant Laidlaw transferred to the Ordnance Corps. He received special schooling at the Massachusetts Institute of Technology, earned a Bachelor of Science degree in mechanical engineering, and was promoted to First Lieutenant. From 1931 until 1937 Lieutenant Laidlaw was stationed at Picatinny Arsenal in New Jersey, where his duties involved the development and manufacture of ammunition. During this assignment he was promoted to Captain.

Captain Laidlaw then served with the 1st Cavalry Division at Fort Bliss, Texas, from 1937 to 1939. His duties during this period mainly concerned troop training and organization. From June 1939 to July 1942 he was first Assistant Chief and then Chief of Military Organizations and Publications Division, Office of the Chief of Ordnance. He was promoted to Major in February 1941, and then to Lieutenant Colonel in February 1942.

Colonel Laidlaw was Ordnance Officer of the Overseas Supply Division of the New York Port of Embarkation from July 1942 to July 1945, where he directed the shipment of all ordnance materiel to the European and Mediterranean Theaters. He was promoted to Colonel in October 1942. In July 1945, with the war in Europe over, Colonel Laidlaw relocated to the San Francisco Port of Embarkation, where he performed similar duties in connection with the war in the Far East. He was then transferred to the European Command at Bad Nauheim, Germany, in December 1945, where he served as Assistant Chief of Staff for Logistics. He returned to the United States in July 1947.

From September 1947 to June 1951 Colonel Laidlaw served as Chief of the Ordnance Section, Fourth Army Headquarters, Fort Sam Houston, Texas. He then spent a year at The Ordnance School, Aberdeen Proving Ground, Maryland, first as Assistant Commandant and then as Commandant. During this time he was promoted to Brigadier General, and also served as Deputy Maneuver Director of LOGEX-52, the Army's annual logistical exercise held at Camp Pickett, Virginia.

In July 1952 General Laidlaw was assigned as Deputy Commanding General of the Ordnance Ammunition Center at Joilet, Illinois. He assumed the command two months later, and remained there for nearly two years. In June 1954 he was transferred to the Caribbean Command, where he served as Chief of Staff to the Commanding General of all Army forces in the Caribbean, and as Assistant Division Commander, 23rd Infantry Division. Laidlaw was promoted to Major General on December 21, 1955.

General Laidlaw succeeded General Bell as Commanding General of WSPG on February 1, 1956. General Laidlaw retired from active service on June 30, 1960, after 40 years military service. Thus, he has the distinction of being the last commander of WSPG and the first commander of WSMR.

Rocket and guided missile activities at WSMR increased in the post-*Sputnik* era. The American response to the Soviet satellites included the creation of a new civilian space agency, the National Aeronautics and Space Administration (NASA). This agency absorbed the existing National Advisory Committee for Aeronautics (NACA); the Naval Research Laboratory *Vanguard* program; large engine projects from the Air Force; lunar programs from the Army and Air Force; and the Jet Propulsion Laboratory (in December 1958). NASA officially came into being on October 1, 1958. Later, those elements of the ABMA working on large boosters under Wernher von Braun also became part of NASA.

WSMR assumed an even bigger role after the creation of NASA. Not only was the range used by the military services, but also by the new civilian space agency. The range was a great place to conduct space science using sounding rockets. Within five years, NASA decided they needed a permanent presence at WSMR. To accommodate this, NASA created the White Sands Test Facility (WSTF) in 1963. Situated on the west side of the Organ Mountains, the WSTF gives NASA a locale for testing and evaluating potentially hazardous materials, components, and systems. Whole propulsion systems have been tested there, including the ascent and descent engines for the Apollo Lunar Module. In the mid-1960s, NASA tested the Apollo Launch Escape System with the *Little Joe II* rocket, which was fired from a specially built pad near the Navy launch site. Today, the assembly building that was first erected for the *Little Joe II* is used to assemble and inspect sounding rockets. The ground station for the Tracking and Data Relay Satellite System that NASA uses to remain in contact with the International Space Station and scores of satellites that orbit overhead is located at WSMR. The range includes Northrup Strip, which was renamed the White Sands Space Harbor after the Space Shuttle Orbiter *Columbia* landed there in 1982 at the conclusion of its third flight.

At the same time, WSMR has remained true to its original mission of providing a testing center for America's military services. Every missile currently in the Army, Navy, Air Force, and Marine Corps inventories has been tested at WSMR. Today, WSMR has a workforce of nearly 10,000 people, and the pace of rocket and missile tests conducted there shows no sign of slowing down. More than sixty years after becoming "the birthplace of America's rocket and space activity," WSMR remains a critical national asset that supports national defense and scientific research in the 21st Century.

Appendix 1:
American V-2 Firings

The information in the following tables is not arranged in chronological order but by the assigned V-2 number. Some rockets received numbers but were never fired. The following organizations/agencies have been identified as sponsoring V-2 flights or experiment packages:

APL = Applied Physics Lab (John Hopkins University)
ARDC = Air Research and Development Command
GE = General Electric Company
NIH = National Institute of Health
NRL = Naval Research Lab
PU = Palmer Physics Lab (Princeton University)
SCEL = Signal Corps Engineering Lab (University of Michigan)

V-2 #	Date	Time (Local)	Altitude (Miles)	Agency	Experiments
1	March 15, 1946		n.a.		Static firing-no payload
2	April 16, 1946	1447	3.4	GE	Cosmic radiation (APL)
3	May 10, 1946	1415	70	GE	Cosmic radiation (APL)
4	May 29, 1946	1410	69.7	GE	Cosmic radiation (APL)
5	June 13, 1946	1640	73	GE	Solar radiation, ionosphere (NRL)
6	June 28, 1946	1203	67	NRL	Cosmic radiation, solar radiation, pressure, temperature
7	Jul7 9, 1946	1230	83.5	GE	Cosmic radiation, ionosphere (NRL)
8	July 19, 1946	1211	3	GE	Ionosphere (NRL)
9	July 30, 1946	1240	100.4	APL	Cosmic radiation, ionosphere (NRL), biological (Harvard)
10	August 15, 1946	1100	4	PU	Cosmic radiation
11	August 22, 1946	1015	0	ARDC	Pressure, density, ionosphere, sky brightness
12	October 10, 1946	1102	108	NRL	Cosmic & solar radiation, pressure, temperature, biological
13	October 24, 1946	1218	65	APL	Cosmic & solar radiation, winds, photography
14	November 7, 1946	1331	0.2	PU	Cosmic radiation
15	November 21, 1946	1000	63	ARDC	Pressure, temperature, ionosphere, sky brightness
16	December 5, 1946	1308	95	NRL	Cosmic & solar radiation, pressure, temperature, photography
17	December 17, 1946	2218	114	APL	Cosmic radiation, meteorites, biological (NIH)
18	January 10, 1947	1413	72.2	NRL	Cosmic radiation
19	January 23, 1947	1722	31	GE	No experiments
20	February 20, 1947	1116	68	ARDC	Pressure, ionosphere, sky brightness, biological, photography
21	March 7, 1947	1123	101	NRL	Cosmic radiation, pressure, temperature, photography, biological
22	April 1, 1947	1310	80.3	APL	Cosmic & solar radiation, photography
23	April 8, 1947	1713	63.5	APL	Cosmic & solar radiation, photography
24	April 17, 1947	1422	88.5	GE	Pressure, temperature (SCEL)
26	May 5, 1947	1604	84	NRL	Cosmic & solar radiation, temperature, ionosphere, photography
0	May 29, 1947		49.3	GE	*Hermes II* Missile 0
29	July 10, 1947	1218	10	NRL	Cosmic radiation, pressure, temperature, ionosphere, biological (Harvard)
30	July 29, 1947	0555	99.9	APL	Cosmic & solar radiation, photography
	September 6, 1947		6		Launch from USS *Midway*
27	October 9, 1947	1215	97	GE	Solar radiation (NRL), pressure, composition (SCEL)

V-2 #28. Source: U.S. Army photograph courtesy of Bill Beggs.

GE Spec.	November 20, 1947	1647	16.6	GE	No payload
28	December 8, 1947	1442	65	ARDC	Pressure, temperature, solar radiation, sky brightness, ionosphere, photography
34	January 22, 1948	1312	99	NRL	Cosmic radiation, pressure, temperature, ionosphere
36	February 6, 1948	1015	69	GE	No payload
39	March 19, 1948	1610	3.4	GE	Magnetic field, composition, winds, temperature (SCEL)
25	April 2, 1948	0640	89.5	SCEL	Density, pressure, temperature, composition, cosmic & solar radiation (NRL)
38	April 19, 1948	1254	34.8	NRL	Cosmic & solar radiation, pressure, temperature
Bu-1	May 15, 1948	V-2 – 69.1 WAC – 79.1		GE	*Project Bumper*
35	May 27, 1948	0716	86.8	APL	Cosmic & solar radiation, photography, composition (SCEL)
37	June 11, 1948	0322	38.7	ARDC	Pressure, temperature, composition, ionosphere, sky brightness, solar radiation, biological
40	July 26, 1948	1103	54	APL	Cosmic radiation, photography, pressure, temperature
43	August 5, 1948	0507	103	NRL	Cosmic & solar radiation, temperature, pressure, ionosphere, photography
Bu-2	August 10, 1948	V-2 – 8.28 WAC – 8.1		GE	*Project Bumper*
33	September 2, 1948	1800	93.6	SCEL	Density, pressure, temperature, composition
Bu-3	September 30, 1948	V-2 – 93.4 WAC – ---		GE	*Project Bumper*
Bu-4	November 1, 1948	V-2 – 3 WAC – ---		GE	*Project Bumper*
44	November 18, 1948	1534	90.3	GE	Biological (Harvard), solar radiation (NRL), composition (SCEL)
42	December 9, 1948	0908	67.4	SCEL	Winds, pressure, temperature, solar radiation (NRL)
1	January 13, 1949			GE	*Hermes II* Missile 1
45	January 28, 1949	1020	37.2	NRL	Cosmic & solar radiation, pressure, temperature, photography
48	February 17, 1949	1000	62.5	APL	Cosmic & solar radiation, photography (NRL), composition (SCEL), biological
Bu-5	February 24, 1949	V-2 – 63 WAC – 248		GE	*Project Bumper*
41	March 21, 1949	2343	83	ARDC	Ionosphere, sky brightness, solar radiation, composition, photography
50	April 11, 1949	1505	54.2	SCEL	Temperature, composition, solar radiation (NRL), biological
Bu-6	April 21, 1949	V-2 – 3 WAC – ---		GE	*Project Bumper*
46	May 5, 1949	0815	5.5	GE	Solar radiation (NRL)
47	June 14, 1949	1535	83	ARDC	Cosmic & solar radiation, temperature, pressure, ionosphere, photography, biological
32	September 16, 1949	1619	2.6	ARDC	Composition, ionosphere, meteorites, solar & cosmic radiation, sky brightness, biological
49	September 29, 1949	0958	93.7	NRL	Cosmic & solar radiation, meteorites, pressure
2	October 6, 1949			GE	*Hermes II* Missile 2
56	November 18, 1949	0803	77	SCEL	Winds, composition, temperature, cosmic radiation (APL), solar radiation (NRL)
31	December 8, 1949	1214	81	ARDC	Composition, ionosphere, meteorites, solar radiation, sky brightness, biological
53	February 17, 1950	1101	92.4	NRL	Cosmic & solar radiation, pressure, temperature
Bu-8	July 24, 1950			GE	*Project Bumper*, first launch at Cape Canaveral, FL
Bu-7	July 29, 1950			GE	*Project Bumper*, launch at Cape Canaveral, FL
51	August 31, 1950	1009	84.8	ARDC	Ionosphere, meteorites, sky brightness, density, biological
61	October 26, 1950	1602	5	NRL	No payload
2-A	November 9, 1950			GE	*Hermes II* Missile 2-A
54	January 18, 1951	1314	1.0	NRL	Cosmic & solar radiation
57	March 8, 1951	2016	1.9	ARDC	Composition, air glow, sky brightness, ionosphere
55	June 14, 1951		0	NRL	Solar & cosmic radiation
52	June 28, 1951	1443	3.6	ARDC	Solar radiation, air glow, sky brightness
60	October 29, 1951	1404	87.6	SCEL	Pressure, temp
TF-1	August 22, 1951	1200	132.6		No payload
59 (TF-2)	May 20, 1952	0906	64.3	SCEL	Composition, photography
TF-3	August 22, 1952	0033	48.5	NRL	Composition, pressure, magnetic field, solar radiation, cosmic radiation (NIH), sky brightness (ARDC)
TF-5	September 19, 1952	0849	16.8	SCEL	Temperature, composition, cosmic radiation (NIH)
58	- - - - -	- - - - - - - - - -		- - - - -	This rocket never fired
TF-4	- - - - -	- - - - - - - - - -		- - - - -	This rocket never fired

Appendix 2:
WAC Corporal Launches
1945-1947

This table includes booster-only launches for the Army/Jet Propulsion Laboratory *WAC Corporal* program. It does not contain the *Project Bumper* flights, which used a V-2 to boost a *WAC Corporal*.

Flight	Date	Results
A	September 26, 1945	Booster test
B	September 26, 1945	Booster test
C	September 26, 1945	Booster test
D	September 27, 1945	Booster test
1	September 27, 1945	Booster test w/250-pound load
2	September 28, 1945	Booster test w/dummy *WAC*
3	October 1, 1945	*WAC* carried 1/3 propellant load; reached 28,000 feet
4	October 2, 1945	*WAC* carried 1/3 propellant load; reached 28,000 feet
5	October 11, 1945	Fully fueled; reached 235,000 feet
6	October 12, 1945	No radar track; reached 235,000 feet
7	October 16, 1945	Premature nose release; only reached 90,000 feet
8	October 19, 1945	Premature nose release but reached 235,000 feet
9	October 25, 1945	Leak before launch; no record of performance
10	October 25, 1945	Night launch; nose release failed
11	May 7, 1946	Booster test
13	May 20, 1946	Booster test of parachute recovery system
14	May 23, 1946	Booster test of parachute recovery system
15	May 23, 1946	Booster test of parachute recovery system
16	May 24, 1946	Booster test of parachute recovery system
17	May 24, 1946	Booster test of parachute recovery system
18	May 26, 1946	Booster test of parachute recovery system
19	May 26, 1946	Booster test of parachute recovery system
20	May 29, 1946	Booster test of parachute recovery system
21	December 2, 1946	Booster test of parachute recovery system

NOTE: Beginning with this series, flights were recorded by missile number rather than by flight number.

Missile	Date	Results
11	December 3, 1946	Last *WAC A*; lost fins; short burn time; only reached 94,000 feet; unstable flight
12	December 6, 1946	First *WAC B*; lost 1 fin; unstable; only reached 92,000 feet; successfully recovered
13	December 12, 1946	Reached 105,000 feet; fins remained intact; recovered but damaged slightly on landing
14	December 12, 1946	Telemetry unit lowered on parachute; reached 160,000 feet
15	December 13, 1946	Reached 175,000 feet; parachute tangled and did not open
Booster	February 17, 1947	Test of Mk I Mod I booster. Carried 680 pounds of lead ballast
16	February 18, 1947	Reached 144,000 feet, but velocity lower than expected
17	February 24, 1947	Reached 240,000 feet; chute did not open; not recovered
18	March 3, 1947	Reached 206,000 feet; recovered nearly intact. Used Mk 1 Mod 1 booster.
19	June 12, 1947	Reached 198,000 feet; parachute deployed but broke loose; not recovered

Aerial view of the Army launch area in January 1947. The V-2 pad with movable gantry and *WAC Corporal* launch tower were both located about 600 feet north of the blockhouse. *Source: U.S. Army photograph courtesy of Bill Beggs.*

Appendix 3:
Viking Launches

Number	Date	Altitude (Miles)	Remarks
1	May 3, 1949	50	Engine shut down prematurely
2	September 6, 1949	32	Engine shut down prematurely
3	February 9, 1950	50	Engine shut down by ground command
4	May 11, 1950	105	Launched from *USS Norton Sound*
5	November 21, 1950	108	Lower than expected thrust
6	December 11, 1950	40	Night launch; fin failure
7	August 7, 1951	136	Last flight of RTV-N-12 design
8	June 6, 1952	4 (?)	Rocket broke loose during static test
9	December 15, 1952	135	First successful RTV-N-12a flight
10	Jun3 30, 1953	0	Engine explosion, did not lift off
10	May 7, 1954	136	Flight of rebuilt rocket
11	May 24, 1954	158	Altitude record
12	February 4, 1955	144	
TV-0	December 8, 1956		Vanguard test vehicle
TV-1	May 1, 1957		Vanguard 2-stage test vehicle

Viking 7, the last one of the RTV-N-12 rockets. *Source: U.S. Navy photograph courtesy of Bill Beggs.*

Viking 12. Source: U.S. Navy photograph courtesy of Bill Beggs.

Bibliography

Baumann, R. C., and Winkler, L. *Rocket Research Report No. XVIII – Photography from the Viking 11 Rocket at Altitudes Ranging up to 158 Miles.* NRL Report 4489. Washington, D. C.: Naval Research Laboratory, February 1, 1955.

Baumann, R. C., and Winkler, L. *Rocket Research Report No. XXI – Photography from the Viking 12 Rocket at Altitudes Ranging up to 143.5 Miles.* NRL Report 4489. Washington, D. C.: Naval Research Laboratory, April 22, 1959.

Bergstralh, Thor A. *Rocket Research Report No. VIII – The Rocket Impact Point Computer.* NRL Report 3851. Washington, D. C.: Naval Research Laboratory, October 26, 1951.

Best, Nolan R. *Rocket Research Report No. XV – A Counter-Type Precision Phase Source.* NRL Report 4418. Washington, D. C.: Naval Research Laboratory, September 8, 1954.

Bragg, James W. *Development of the Corporal: The Embryo of the Army Missile Program.* Historical Monograph No. 4. Huntsville, Alabama: Army Ballistic Missile Agency, April 1961.

Braun, Wernher von. "Major U. S. Programs," *The History of Rocket Technology.* Edited by Eugene M. Emme, Detroit: Wayne State University Press, 1964.

Braun, Wernher von, Ordway, Frederick I., and Dooling, David. *Space Travel: A History.* New York: Harper and Row Publishers, 1985 (4th edition of a book previously published under the title *History of Rocketry and Space Travel.*)

Brown, Eunice H., Robertson, James A., and Kroehnke, John W., et. al. *White Sands History: Range Beginnings and Early Missile Testing.* White Sands, New Mexico: White Sands Missile Range Public Affairs Office, no date. (Reprint of a 1959 report of the first decade of the White Sands Missile Range.)

Cagle, Mary T. *Development, Production, & Development of the Nike Ajax Guided Missile System 1945 - 1959.* Huntsville, Alabama: Army Rocket and Guided Missile Agency, 1957.

Cagle, Mary T. *History of the Basic (M31) Honest John Rocket System 1950 - 1964.* Huntsville, Alabama: Redstone Arsenal, 1964.

Cagle, Mary T. *History of the Lacrosse Guided Missile System 1947 - 1962.* Huntsville, Alabama: Redstone Arsenal, 1962.

Cagle, Mary T. *Loki Antiaircraft Free-Flight Rocket, December 1947 – November 1955.* Huntsville, Alabama: Redstone Arsenal, 1957.

Chapman, J. L. *Atlas, The Story of a Missile.* New York: Harper and Brothers, 1960.

Consolidated Vultee Aircraft Corporation. *MX-774 Ground to Ground Missile.* Summary Report ZR-6002-002. San Diego, 1 December 1949.

"Convair MX-774," *Space Frontiers.* Volume 1, No. 4, September – October 1985.

Cox, Robert B. "ASP," *Sounding Rockets.* Edited by Homer E. Newell, Jr. New York: McGraw-Hill Book Company, 1959.

Cunningham, Chester B., Bissell, E. E., et. al. *Rocket Research Report No.III – Vibration in the Viking No. 3 Rocket.* NRL Report 3695. Washington, D. C.: Naval Research Laboratory, July 10, 1950.

Department of the Army. *Army Ordnance Department Guided Missiles Program.* 1 January 1948.

Durant, Frederick C., III. "Robert H. Goddard and the Smithsonian Institution," *First Steps Towards Space.* Washington, D. C.: Smithsonian Institution Press, 1974.

Emme, Eugene M. *Aeronautics and Astronautics, An American Chronology of Science and Technology in the Exploration of Space 1915 – 1960.* Washington, D. C.: U.S. Government Printing Office, 1961.

Fraser, L. W., and Siegler, E. H. *High Altitude Research Using the V-2 Rocket, March 1946 – April 1947.* Bumble Series Report #81, Silver Spring, Maryland: The Johns Hopkins University Applied Physics Laboratory, July 1948.

Garstens, M. A., Newell, H. E., and Siry, J. W. *Upper Atmosphere Research Report Number 1.* Naval Research Laboratory Report No. R-2955, Washington, D. C.: Office of Naval Research, October 1, 1946.

Gatland, Kenneth. *Missiles and Rockets.* New York: MacMillan Publishing Company, 1975.

Glenn L. Martin Company. *RTV-N-12 Viking Rockets 1 to 7 Design Summary.* Baltimore: Glenn L. Martin Company, January 1954.

Glenn L. Martin Company. *RTV-N-12A Viking Rockets 8 to 10 Design Summary.* Baltimore: Glenn L. Martin Company, August 1955.

Glenn L. Martin Company. *What is the Viking?* Baltimore: Glenn L. Martin Company, 1955.

Goddard, Robert H. *A Method of Reaching Extreme Altitudes.* Smithsonian Miscellaneous Collections Volume 71, Number 2, Publication 2540. Washington, D. C.: Smithsonian Institution, 1919.

Goddard, Robert H. *Liquid-Propellant Rocket Development.* Smithsonian Miscellaneous Collections Volume 95, Number 3, Publication 3381. Washington, D. C.: Smithsonian Institution, 1936.

"The Goddard Rocket Research," *Roswell Museum Bulletin.* Volume II, Number 8, Winter 1953 – 54.

Hanrahan, James S., and Bushnell, David. *Space Biology.* New York: Basic Books, Inc., 1960.

Henry, James P., et. al. "Animal Studies of the Subgravity State During Rocket Flight," *Journal of Aviation Medicine.* V. 23, No. 10, October 1952.

Hintze, Guenther. *Special Report Missile I.* Fort Bliss, Texas: Department of the Army Ordnance Research & Development Division Suboffice (Rocket), June, 1949.

Historical Division, Air Force Missile Development Center. *History of Research in Space Biology and Biodynamics at the Air Force Missile Development Center, Holloman Air Force Base, New Mexico, 1946 – 1958.* Holloman Air Force Base, New Mexico: 1958.

Hüzel, Dieter. *Peenemünde to Canaveral.* Englewood Heights, New Jersey: Prentice-Hall, Inc., 1962.

Kennedy, Gregory P. *Germany's V-2 Rocket.* Atglen, Pennsylvania: Schiffer Publishing, 2006.

Kennedy, Gregory P. *Vengeance Weapon 2: The V-2 Guided Missile.* Washington, D. C.: Smithsonian Institution Press, 1983.

Kurzman, Dan. *Day of the Bomb.* New York: McGraw-Hill, 1996.

Lasby, Clarence G. *Project Paperclip.* New York: Ateneum, 1971.

Lehman, Milton. *This High Man.* New York: Farrar, Straus and Company, 1963.

Ley, Willy. *Rockets, Missiles, and Men in Space*. New York: The Viking Press, 1968.

Magazine & Book Section, Public Information, Navy Department. "Navy Fires V-2 Rocket From Deck of USS Midway." Washington, D. C., Navy Department, September 8, 1947.

Malina, Frank. "The Jet Propulsion Laboratory," *The Coming of the Space Age*. Edited by Arthur C. Clarke. New York: Meredith Press, 1967.

Mallan, Lloyd. *Men, Rockets and Space Rats*. New York: Julian Messner, Inc., 1955.

Masterson, John E. "Loki-WASP," *Sounding Rockets*. Edited by Homer E. Newell, Jr. New York: McGraw-Hill Book Company, 1959.

Meeter, George F. *The Holloman Story*. Albuquerque: University of New Mexico Press, 1967.

Mengel, John T., and Uglow, Kenneth M., Jr. *Rocket Research Report No. XI – A Phase-Comparison Guidance System for Viking*. NRL Report 3982. Washington, D. C.: Naval Research Laboratory, May 5, 1952.

Mengel, John T., Best, Nolan R., and Easton, Roger L. *Rocket Research Report No. XIII – A Single-Axis Phase-Comparison Angle-Tracking Unit*. NRL Report 4393. Washington, D. C.: Naval Research Laboratory, September 2, 1954.

Newell, H. E., and Siry, J. W., *Upper Atmosphere Research Report Number II*. Naval Research Laboratory Report No. R-3030, Washington, D. C.: Office of Naval Research, December 30, 1946.

New York Times, "V-2 Assembly Plant is Found in Mountain," April 14, 1945.

Niles, Allen W., and Easton, Roger L. *Rocket Research Report No. XVII – Propellant Level Sensors for Viking*. NRL Report 4454. Washington, D. C.: Naval Research Laboratory, December 17, 1954.

Oberkommando des Heeres (High Command of the Army). *Das Gerät A-4, Baureihe B*, (The Device A-4, Model B). January 2, 1945 (translated by the General Electric Company, Schenectady, New York.)

Oleson, Merval W., and Cunningham, Chester B. *Rocket Research Report No. XVI – Vibration in the Viking 9 Rocket*. NRL Report 4440. Washington, D. C.: Naval Research Laboratory, November 19, 1954.

Ordway, Frederick I., and Sharpe, Mitchell R. *The Rocket Team*. New York: Thomas Y. Crowell Publishers, 1979.

Provan, John, and Davies, R. E. G. *Berlin Airlift*. McClean, Virginia: Paladwr Press, 1998.

"Rocket Experts Plan New Tests After Setting 135-Mile Record," *The Washington Star*, August 8, 1951.

Rosen, Milton W. *The Viking Rocket Story*. New York: Harper and Brothers, 1955.

Rosen, Milton W., and Bridger, James M. *Rocket Research Report No. I – The Viking No. 1 Firings*. NRL Report 3583. Washington, D. C.: Naval Research Laboratory, March 28. 1950.

Rosen, Milton W., and Bridger, James M. *Rocket Research Report No. II – The Viking No. 2 Firings*. NRL Report 3641. Washington, D. C.: Naval Research Laboratory, March 28, 1950.

Rosen, Milton W., and Bridger, James M. *Rocket Research Report No. IV – The Viking Shipboard Firings*. NRL Report 3751. Washington, D. C.: Naval Research Laboratory, October 26, 1950.

Rosen, Milton W., and Bridger, James M. *Rocket Research Report No. V – The Viking No. 1 Firings*. NRL Report 3583. Washington, D. C.: Naval Research Laboratory, December 19, 1949.

Rosen, Milton W., and Bridger, James M. *Rocket Research Report No. XIX – The Viking 10 Firings*. NRL Report 4513. Washington, D. C.: Naval Research Laboratory, May 5, 1955.

Rosen, Milton W., Bridger, James M., and Jones, Alton E. *Rocket Research Report No. IX – The Viking 6 Firings*. NRL Report 3854. Washington, D. C.: Naval Research Laboratory, September 21, 1951.

Rosen, Milton W., Bridger, James M., and Jones, Alton E. *Rocket Research Report No. X – The Viking 7 Firings*. NRL Report 3946. Washington, D. C.: Naval Research Laboratory, March 25, 1952.

Rosen, Milton W., Bridger, James M., and Jones, Alton E. *Rocket Research Report No. XII – The Viking 8 Firing*. NRL Report 3854. Washington, D. C.: Naval Research Laboratory, September 21, 1951.

Rosen, Milton W., Bridger, James M., and Snodgrass, Richard B. *Rocket Research Report No. XIV – The Viking 9 Firings*. NRL Report 4407. Washington, D. C.: Naval Research Laboratory, October 8, 1954.

Rosen, Milton W., Bridger, James M, and Spitz, Hillel. *Rocket Research Report No. VII – The Viking No. 5 Firings*. NRL Report 4169. Washington, D. C.: Naval Research Laboratory, July 9. 1953.

Rosen, Milton W., and Seddon, J. Carl. *Rocket Research Report No. VI – Conversion of Viking Into a Guided Missile*. NRL Report 3829. Washington, D. C.: Naval Research Laboratory, April 1, 1951.

Rosen, Milton W., and Bridger, James M. *Rocket Research Report No. I – The Viking No. 1 Firings*. NRL Report 3583. Washington, D. C.: Naval Research Laboratory, December 19, 1949.

Sandberg, W. A., and Barry, W. B. *Design and Fabrication of the WAC Corporal Missile, Booster, Launcher, and Handling Facilities*. JPL-GALCIT Report No. 4-21. Pasadena, California: Jet Propulsion Laboratory, February 19, 1946.

Santiago, Dawn Moore, ed. *New Mexico Space Journal, Number 1*. Alamogordo, New Mexico: New Mexico Museum of Space History, June 2001.

Schlesinger, Arthur M., Jr., ed. *The Almanac of American History*. New York: Barnes & Noble Books, 1993.

Schultz, H. A. *Technical Data on the Development of the A-4 (V-2)*. Huntsville, Alabama: The George C. Marshall Space Flight Center, 1965.

"Second Viking Rocket Will Soon be Ready to Explore Conditions in Air Above Stratosphere," *The Martin Star*. August 1949.

Simons, David G. *Use of V-2 Rockets to Convey Primates to Upper Atmosphere*. Air Force Technical Report 5821, Dayton, Ohio: Air Force Materiel Command, May 1959.

Snodgrass, R. B. *Rocket Research Report No. XX – Flight Measurements of Aerodynamic Heating and Boundary-Layer Transition on the Viking 10 Nose Cone*. NRL Report 4531. Washington, D. C.: Naval Research Laboratory, June 16, 1955.

Stine, G. Harry. "The ASP Rocketsonde," *Model Rocketry*. Volume 1, number 6, May 1969.

Thomas, Shirley. *Men of Space, Volume 1*. Philadelphia: Chilton Book Company, 1960.

Townsend, John W., Pressly, Eleanor C., Slavin, Robert M., and Kraff, Louis. "The Aerobee-Hi Rocket," *Sounding Rockets*. Edited by Homer E. Newell, Jr. New York: McGraw-Hill Book Company, 1959.

United States Army Ordnance Corps and the General Electric Company. *Hermes Guided Missile Research and Development Project 1944 – 1954*. Technical Liaison Branch, Chief of Army Ordnance, September 25, 1959.

United States War Department. *Handbook on Guided Missiles of Germany and Japan*. Washington, D. C.: 1946.

Van Allen, James A., Townsend, John W., and Pressly, Eleanor C. "The Aerobee Rocket," *Sounding Rockets*. Edited by Homer E. Newell, Jr. New York: McGraw-Hill Book Company, 1959.

"Viking Launched; 2nd Being Readied," *The Martin Star*. June 1949.

White, L. D, *Final Report, Project Hermes V-2 Missile Program*. Schenectady, New York: General Electric, Report No. R52A0510, September 1952.

Winter, Frank H. *Prelude to the Space Age*. Washington, D. C.: Smithsonian Press, 1983.

Zimney, Charles M. "The ASP, A Single-stage Solid Propellant Sounding Rocket," *Jet Propulsion*. March 1957.

Internet Resources:

White Sands Missile Range Public Affairs

http://www.wsmr.army.mil/pao/pao.html

White Sands Missile Range Museum

http://www.wsmr-history.org

Redstone Arsenal History Office

http://www.redstone.army.mil/history/

Index